The (ers

MICHAEL TIPPETT

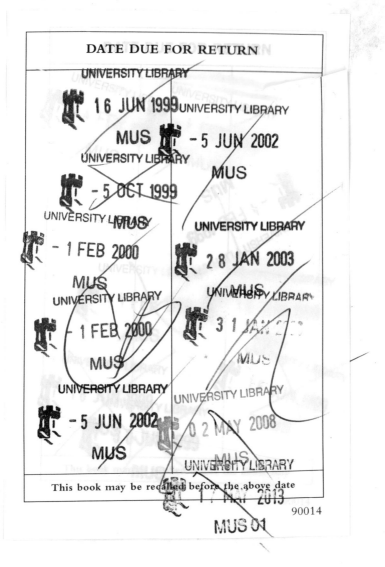

The Contemporary Composers

Series Editor: Nicholas Snowman

MICHAEL TIPPETT
Meirion Bowen

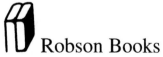 Robson Books

First published in Great Britain in 1983 by Robson Books
Ltd. This edition published in 1997 by Robson Books Ltd.
Bolsover House, 5-6 Clipstone Street, London W1P 8LE.

British Library Cataloguing in Publication Data
A catalogue record for this title is available from the
British Library

ISBN 1 86105 099 2   T

Typeset by FSH, Ltd., London
Printed in Great Britain by Creative Print & Design Ltd.,
Ebbw Vale

1001374890

Contents

to John Leedham and Jane Flint

... You ask the secret.
It has just one name:
again

Miroslav Holub, Ode to Joy

Editor's Preface

It is no secret that our epoch favours a museological rather than a prospective approach to musical activity. Such a situation is, of course, the reflection of a cultural climate, but it is also the result of problems particular to the evolution of musical language during this century.

Whatever the fundamental causes, the effects are clear. The repertoire of 'classical' music has been extended backwards in time and enlarged with the inclusion of.many important works as well as a great number of lesser ones. At the same time the 'standard' works of the eighteenth and nineteenth centuries have become more than ever entrenched in a musical world very largely conditioned by market considerations and thus inimical to contemporary endeavour. One cannot blame record company employees, concert promoters and artists' agents for being more interested in quick turnover than in the culture of their time. The results are inevitable: re-recordings of the same symphonies and operas multiply; performances of the same 'early' music, claiming to be less inauthentic than their rivals, abound; and conductors' careers are made with an ever-diminishing bunch of scores.

Where does this leave the music written yesterday and today? The answer is not encouraging. As far as western Europe and the United States are concerned, contemporary works inhabit a number of well defined ghettos.

In West Germany it is the radio stations that commission and perform new scores and, naturally enough, their concern is to satisfy their specialist listeners rather than to cultivate a wider public. Except for a certain number of important but brief 'shop window' festivals, contemporary music is hardly a living affair.

In the United States composers find sanctuary in the universities – comfort and security but little contact with the general musical public outside the walls. And in times of economic regression, enterprising and excellent modern music ensembles encounter increasing financial difficulties, whilst symphony orchestras, reliant for their existence on the whims of the rich and generally conservative, play safer than ever.

In the UK, outside the BBC and one or two imaginative enterprises like Glasgow's Musica Nova, the situation is depressing – on the one hand, inadequate state funds spread too thinly, on the other, excellent but hungry orchestras competing for the same marketable fodder. Britain, in spite of at least two recent determined attempts, cannot even boast a modest but representative contemporary music festival worthy of international attention.

France, with its rigorous but narrow education system giving little place to the non-literary arts, has suddenly in these last few years woken up to the charms of music and begun to invest more and more heavily in this new passion. Though it will take years before this musically rootless country can boast the proliferation of performing talent of its neighbours, native respect for the 'intellect' ensures that the music of today is discussed, played and subsidized relatively correctly. Yet in spite of all the activity, contemporary music outside Paris attracts small audiences; the work of 'decentralization' so dear to Gallic politicians is more arduous here than in other countries.

This is not the place for a thorough survey of the status of contemporary music in the world in general. However, it seems clear that even a brief glance at a few different countries reveals the existence of an uneasy relationship between the contemporary public and its music. Certainly, a few independently minded and cultivated musicians seek by their artistic policies to persuade the musical public to accept the endeavours of the present as well as the rich and varied musical traditions and structures of the past.

This new series of books, each introducing a different living composer, seeks to supplement the work of the pathfinders. The scope of the series does not reflect any particular musical 'party line' or aesthetic; its aims are to be representative of what exists, and to supply the listener who stumbles across a new piece at a Prom or on record with the essential facts about its composer – his life, background and work.

Nicholas Snowman
London
June 1981

Editor's Preface to the Second Edition

The Contemporary Composers series was first launched some fifteen years ago. In that time exceptional changes have taken place in the world of classical music. The traditional concert with its established repertoire based mainly in the eighteenth and nineteenth centuries is now showing signs of vulnerability, whereas contemporary music is flourishing in a way that would have been difficult to imagine in the early 1980s.

Until relatively recently music-lovers had.to come to concerts to hear unfamiliar repertoire. With the arrival of CDs, and in particular budget price reissues of superlative and celebrated recordings, acquainting oneself with, for example, a lesser known Dvořák symphony has become a far easier task than it was when there was no alternative but to catch a live performance. Now the public quite rightly wishes to experience major events rather than run of the mill evenings of classical or, indeed, any other music. The future must surely lie in the presentation of fewer but more stimulating concerts.

These past fifteen years have also seen the arrival in prominent positions of conductors with a greater sense of adventure and idealism than most of their predecessors. The two most potent symbols of status quo and tradition in classical music, the Berlin Philharmonic and the Vienna Philharmonic, have both undergone profound transformation. Not only are these orchestras now conducted by a range of musicians representing a new breadth of interpretative styles, but the players themselves have responded remarkably to change as well as bringing fresh young talent into their own ranks.

These changes are particularly marked in the United Kingdom where symphony orchestras have moved from simply replaying the established canon of works to a broader repertoire including pieces from the post-Second World War and contemporary eras. Before, such repertoire had been left largely to the BBC. Now distinguished festivals devoted to contemporary work exist in Huddersfield and the Vale of Glamorgan, whilst arts centres and concert halls up and down the country demonstrate that the contemporary is ever more integrated with the traditional.

These developments are matched in the record industry. Though the attractiveness of reasonably priced reissues has rendered the endless re-recording of standard works uneconomical, this situation has encouraged companies to investigate the distant past as well as the present far more imaginatively than before. Of course, financial constraints are increasingly to be felt world-wide, but it is most encouraging to sense the new vigour in the promotion of contemporary work internationally.

When these books were first launched, not only was the situation for contemporary music less healthy than today but some of the composers we featured, for example, Birtwistle, Ligeti and Maxwell Davies, whilst known to a specialist international audience, were not the familiar names they have now become. Hopefully, this series will continue to play a modest but precise role in increasing the enjoyment of the music it celebrates.

Nicholas Snowman
London 1997

Acknowledgements

I am most grateful to Jeremy Robson at Robson Books and to the General Editor of the Contemporary Composers series, Nicholas Snowman, for the opportunity to make a completely revised edition of this book. My gratitude extends also to the editor Kate Mills, for her patience and expertise in seeing it through to publication. The main inspiration for this edition derives, it almost goes without saying, from Sir Michael Tippett himself. His prodigious creativity in the period since the book was first published made a new version of it absolutely essential: and the privileges of helping him bring so many major new works to fruition and wide performance have been innumerable and unique. Perhaps the best I can say by way of acknowledgement is that when writing this book, every time I thought I would 'polish off' (as Tippett might say) a whole sequence of works, I have been stopped in my tracks, ensnared afresh by the inventive power, originality and sheer beauty of each one of them in turn.

I am especially grateful to David Clarke for the loan of his *Language, Form and Structure in the Music of Michael Tippett*, which set in train far more ideas and possibilities than I could ever accommodate in this introductory volume. Exchanges of information and ideas with Ian Kemp, Tippett's most scholarly biographer to date, concerning countless minutiae to do with the composer's life and work, as well as many larger issues, began well before the first edition of this book appeared and are likely to continue indefinitely. Here, I should specifically thank him for reading through the manuscript, for commenting on its style, substance and logic and for correcting incidental errors of fact.

Also, since the first edition, the establishment of a Tippett office has helped immensely in the compilation of information and other archival material on the composer: indirectly, therefore, I must acknowledge a decade and a half of work undertaken by the Tippett office personnel – most notably by Christopher

Senior, Nicholas Wright and Peter Owens.

Sally Groves and her colleagues at Schott & Co. Ltd have striven to ensure that all of Tippett's compositions are now available, often re-printed afresh in better, more accurate editions. I should thus not only like to thank Schott & Co. Ltd for permission to reproduce the musical examples included here, but to acknowledge their attempts to represent as favourably as possible a composer not unknown for his quirks of notation and performing requirements.

I am grateful to Ursula Vaughan Williams for permission to quote from a letter to Tippett from her late husband and to Hugh Cobbe at the British Library for helping to date it and decipher its rather wayward episodes. (RWV, according to his wife, 'usually had a cat on his writing knee and wrote at a gallop!') I am also grateful to the estate of the late Edward J. Dent for permission to include sections from a letter dating from 1955. I have to acknowledge permission from Pimlico Books for quotations from Tippett's *Those Twentieth Century Blues*; Oxford University Press for permission to quote the composer's writings as published in their volume *Tippett on Music*; and Thames and Hudson for permission to quote from *Oskar Kokoschka: Letters 1905–1976*.

Mr Emre Amraci drew my attention to the connection between Tippett and Ahmet Ahnan Saygun and provided me with photocopies of the letters from Tippett to Saygun, held at the Saygun archives at Bilkent University in Ankara. I am also grateful to Mr Amraci for enabling me to include a short quotation – which he translated from the original Turkish – from Saygun's diary, which is also held at Bilkent University.

Lastly, I was delighted to receive from Timothy Reynish a photocopy of the programme for a concert in Oxted in 1928, which his mother-in-law Sylvia Spencer had attended and which featured the première (in part) of an early Tippett piano sonata.

The original dedication to Jonn Leedham acknowledged a close personal and intellectual friendship of just over a decade. In my re-dedication here, I am delighted to include his brilliant wife, Professor Jane Flint who, for many years, has shared many of our artistic enthusiasms, not least the music of Tippett.

MB

Introduction

When this book first appeared in 1981, Michael Tippett was in the midst of composing his biggest concert-hall work, *The Mask of Time*. Many, including the present writer, were deceived into thinking it might be his last major composition. The composer was then in his mid-seventies and there was no hint of any new works of significance to come. It seemed entirely plausible that thereafter he would rest on his laurels. Indeed, he himself put it about that he would simply engage in compositional diversions, writing short pieces of chamber music and other miniatures.

Not so. In 1984 he completed an imposing five-movement Fourth Piano Sonata. Thereafter, confounding the example of most earlier octogenarian composers, withstanding a major operation for colonic cancer, continuing to conduct and attend performances of his music worldwide, Tippett spent the next decade writing a fifth opera, *New Year*, a setting of Yeats's *Byzantium* and a Fifth String Quartet. All were large-scale pieces, forging ahead into new territory, rather than depending nostalgically on past ideas and procedures.

In 1993, however, after completing his orchestral work, *The Rose Lake*, Tippett made a firm decision to write nothing more: and although he came out of retirement briefly with 'Caliban's Song', a contribution to the 1995 Purcell tercentenary celebrations, the likelihood of any further major pieces can now be categorically ruled out. Old age and physical disabilities have finally caught up with him. Tippett has remained mentally alert and forward-looking, but the self-imposed responsibility to invent afresh every time he tackled a new project eventually produced such a degree of stress that his very survival was threatened. So he stopped.

Against this background, the second edition of this book has to take on a different character. Tippett's achievement may now be considered as a whole, without the prospect of further innovative works that might alter its overall slant or emphasis. The account of his life given here, more extended than my original one, can be supplemented in greater detail by reading the composer's own autobiography, *Those Twentieth Century Blues* (1984) – another product of his fruitful eighties. A definitive collection of his writings, *Tippett on Music* (1995), also offers a parallel source, uncovering the full breadth of his intellectual and artistic ideas. Tippett's music is also more generally available. Scores of all his mature compositions are now published. Recordings abound, as Tippett's music has percolated down to new generations of performers: in particular, a series of discs devoted to Tippett, and already covering all his major orchestral and chamber works, has been released – and remains in progress – on the Chandos label. At the time of writing, the only major work of his of which there is no commercial recording is his opera *New Year.*

When this book first appeared, Tippett could still be called 'the most loved, but least analysed of composers'.* Here again, there has been a considerable change. Analytic studies of Tippett's music, often starting as academic dissertations, are now more forthcoming. And whereas many of these exemplify the time-honoured process of academia catching up with artistic innovation and are often nit-picking and inconclusive, there have been notable publications, such as Arnold Whittall's comparative study, *Britten and Tippett,* and David Clarke's *Language, Form and Structure in the Music of Michael Tippett,* which tackles the composer's pluralism with an apt diversity of analytic tools, from set theory to semiotics. Every recent book and article on Tippett that has appeared must inevitably draw upon the extensive research on the composer's life and background, and the detailed examination of his works in Ian Kemp's large-scale study, *Tippett: The Composer and His Music,* published in 1984. This one is no exception.

Lastly, one other factor that is bound to make the second

---

* Andrew Clements, in *Music and Musicians,* January 1980, p. 14

edition of this book somewhat different in emphasis is the author's own association with the composer – as manager, artistic assistant and intimate friend for nearly thirty-five years. Some readers may well think this rules out altogether the likelihood of objectivity in the assessment of Tippett's achievements. On the other hand, Tippett has always preferred critical candour and a healthy irreverence to hero-worship. An essential element in our relationship has been a continuing debate on the pros and cons of creative choices and decisions. There have also been a few special benefits.

One such for myself has been the opportunity to watch a number of pieces evolve from some initially inchoate state into properly formulated conceptions. Sometimes I was able to participate by providing raw materials, ideas for developing them and possible solutions to tricky technical problems. I was not, of course, alone or unique in any of this: Tippett has always tested out his notions speculatively on professional friends of his – such as his amanuensis of many years' standing, Michael Tillett. A more percipient and tidy-minded associate would have kept a record of the twice-daily (at least) telephone calls, extended discussions at home and on holiday, that might – when laid end to end – have charted the growth of new musical projects. Tippett would have been appalled, however, by any such archival entombment of his communications during his own lifetime, just as he is baffled by analytic dissection of his compositions.

Another benefit has been my constant exposure to the performance of Tippett's music. If the current edition of this book is distinguishable from its predecessor in one particular respect, it is in the way it draws upon a fund of experience of changing interpretation and modes of execution. This is important: for Tippett it is self-evident, but nevertheless of major significance, that what the composer does is incomplete without the contributions made by the performers.

Tippett has never been the sort of composer who cocoons his music, protecting it from the tampering busybodies who think they know better. While anticipating some effort to comprehend and respect his compositional intentions, Tippett exults in the new perspectives which changing interpretations can bring to his music. If this introduction to his work turns out thus to be helpful to performers as well as music lovers, then it will have contributed something towards ensuring its survival into the future.

The bulk of Tippett's major works for the opera house and concert hall are discussed here in Chapters 6 and 7. Preceding them are two chapters that focus on two particular strands in Tippett's musical make-up – his abiding fascination with song (Chapter 4) and his attempts (from *A Child of Our Time* onwards) at using music as a form of polemic or protest (Chapter 5). The later chapters deal with two summatory works – *The Vision of St Augustine* and *The Mask of Time* (Chapter 8) – and the final crystallization of his artistic personality in *Songs for Dov* and the works of his late eighties (Chapter 9). My collaboration with the composer on various arrangements of his pieces is covered in an appendix. Finally, I have revised and updated completely the list of Tippett's works and the discography, along with the selected bibliography that follows.

Meirion Bowen
London
May, 1997

1
Innocence and Experience

The first extraordinary fact about Michael Tippett is his remarkably long lifespan. It embraces almost the whole of the twentieth century. When he was born in London, on 2 January 1905, Mahler, Grieg, Albeniz, Rimsky-Korsakov, Bruch and Balakirev, while not far off the ends of their lives, were nevertheless still active. Since then, Tippett has managed to outlive not only most other composers born the same year as himself, such as Constant Lambert, Alan Rawsthorne, William Alwyn, Matyas Seiber and Giacinto Scelsi, but near contemporaries like Elisabeth Lutyens, Shostakovich, Henk Badings, Britten and Lutoslawski. At the start of Tippett's life, the car, air travel, film, radio and recordings were all in their infancy. By contrast, in his late years, he has often flown on Concorde and now has an Internet address.

A second extraordinary fact about Tippett is his consistent and total dedication to composition, once he had reached creative maturity. That meant a continuous output of mostly major, often innovatory works from his early thirties to his late eighties, rivalled amongst living contemporaries only, perhaps, by Elliott Carter. All this was achieved despite the fact that Tippett was a classic late developer. Unlike Britten, for instance, he was never a prodigy and had little opportunity to acquire an appropriate training and wide experience of the repertoire until he left school. After he left the Royal College of Music, it was at least seven more years – including a period of further tuition – before he found his feet and began to produce works that bore his own discernible imprint.

None of Tippett's immediate family was musical. His father, Henry William Tippett (1858–1944) was a lawyer, who retired early having made some successful financial investments: these included the Lyceum Theatre in London and a hotel near Cannes in the south of France. His mother, Isabel Clementine Binny Kemp (1880–1969) trained as a nurse. Although they were from the well-to-do middle class, both parents espoused non-Establishment views and causes. Tippett's father was a Manchester liberal and rationalist. His mother was a novelist, Labour party member and suffragette (for which she went to prison), with a strong sense of social obligation. They coped rather more easily with their elder son, Peter (1904–1992), who was to distinguish himself, first in the Navy, then as a naval historian, than with young Michael, whose musical ambitions left them bemused. Neither they nor their second son had any clearly formed notions as to what a musical career might entail, let alone what a budding composer should do to fulfil his creative longings.

The year Michael Tippett was born, the family moved from Eastcote in Middlesex to a house in the village of Wetherden, Suffolk. Away from the London concert scene, Tippett remained innocent of serious professional music-making throughout his childhood. His mother sang drawing-room ballads by Roger Quilter and others; he himself enjoyed being a member of the local church choir, taking part in the hymns and anthems. Popular tunes stuck in his mind: one was 'Everybody's doing it', which he heard sung by one of the two village girls who came to do the housework; in addition there were the songs sung by young men marching off to the First World War – and their full significance he only realized later. Unlike composers today, he had no alternative access to musical experience through radio or recordings.

When Tippett was nine, his parents sent him to a preparatory school in Dorset, where his independence as a thinker soon manifested itself with an essay on the impossibility of the existence of God. After that, he proceeded to Fettes boarding school near Edinburgh. His stay there was nasty, brutish and short. He found the bullying and the emphasis on cold baths in winter quite intolerable. Homosexuality was also rife and when he himself became involved with another boy and disclosed his loss of virginity to his parents, they removed him from the school, encouraging the elderly headmaster at the same time, in his plans for retirement.

Tippett then went to Stamford Grammar School in Lincolnshire.This was more congenial. He excelled in science subjects and history. His English teacher, Waldo Acomb, stimulated his interest in Samuel Butler and when he later came to London, introduced him to Butler's biographer and lifelong friend, Henry Festing Jones. Tippett argued his way out of organized religion and the cadet corps and thumbed his nose at the headmaster by passing a matriculation exam in Italian independently of the school. Throughout the whole of this period, his parents, because of the financial difficulties brought on by the First World War, had gone to live at the hotel they owned in Cannes, eventually selling it to the manager who had run it for them while they were in England. For nearly two decades they lived in a succession of inexpensive hotel suites in France, Italy and Corsica. Tippett often spent his vacations with them, travelling out at first with his brother, then on his own. Having learnt French from his father in early childhood, he now spoke it fluently. Ever more self-confident, intellectually, he felt insecure and deprived through being without a family and a fixed, welcoming home: all this left a permanent scar.

During his Stamford days, Tippett's musical appetite received further stimulation, but was never properly satisfied. Music – together with other 'inessential' subjects, such as horse-riding – was, for reasons of so-called patriotism, excluded during wartime from the school curriculum. Tippett received piano lessons from a local teacher, Mrs Tinkler, and came to know some of the Beethoven piano sonatas. When he was fourteen, he was taken to an orchestral concert in Leicester, conducted by Malcolm Sargent. Enthralled, in particular, by Ravel's suite, *Mother*

Goose, he set his mind on becoming a composer. Thereafter, nothing would stand in his path.

Meanwhile, Tippett's atheism was now threatening to turn into an epidemic at the school, and at the request of the headmaster, his parents removed him to lodgings in Stamford, which were immediately placed out of bounds to other boys. Tippett began to teach himself to compose. His starting-point was Charles Stanford's *Musical Composition*, which he ordered from a local bookshop. One sentence early on in the book left an indelible impression: 'The first principle to be laid out is ... *to study counterpoint first, and through counterpoint to master harmony.*'[1] Instinctively, Tippett knew this method was right for him and so sought mastery first and foremost as a contrapuntal composer. A chance encounter with a trained musician on a train opened his parents' eyes to the existence of the Royal College of Music. On condition that Tippett would aim to become a Doctor of Music, they agreed to pay their son's fees for a period of study there. After an interview with the Principal, Sir Hugh Allen, Tippett was accepted, despite his lack of skills and ignorance of music in general. He began to attend the RCM in the summer of 1928.

This was Tippett's first encounter with the world of professional music. He studied briefly with Charles Wood, who impressed him by explaining some of the formal subtleties of Beethoven's music, by which he was already ensnared, having heard all but one of the nine symphonies conducted by Henry Wood at the 1923 Prom concerts. When Charles Wood died, Tippett chose not to continue his studies with Vaughan Williams – who had attracted pupils like Imogen Holst, Gordon Jacob and Elizabeth Maconchy – as he felt it might only turn him into a slavish VW imitator. Instead, he enrolled with an arch-pedant, Dr C. H. Kitson. Mutual agony ensued as Kitson's harmony-based teaching clashed with Tippett's contrapuntal inclinations. Over the next five years, his venerable tutor was not alone in expressing disbelief at the notion of Tippett entering upon a musical career. Nevertheless, Tippett persevered. He acquired a general musical education by going to a wide variety of concerts. Curious to know what sixteenth-century music sounded like, he attended services at Westminster Cathedral, copying out in advance from RCM library scores the masses and motets by Palestrina and others which were to be performed. He went a lot to the theatre, discovering Chekhov, Ibsen, Strindberg and, above all, Shaw. He continued to read voraciously. Mainly for musical purposes, but also because he wanted to read Goethe, he taught himself German.

At the RCM, he studied the piano with Aubin Raymar, but practised less than he should have done. Already, the piano was for him only a tool that enabled him to compose. He also studied conducting with Malcolm Sargent, who was patronizing though down-to-earth and practical: he ensured that Tippett was at least equipped to rehearse and perform with amateurs. Kindest of all Tippett's teachers was Adrian Boult, then in charge of the First (or Senior) Orchestra at the RCM. Boult allowed Tippett to sit beside him on the rostrum at rehearsals every Friday afternoon for four years. This helped him develop an inside knowledge of what an orchestra sounded like, how it functioned. 'Boult's darling', as he was called, also thus became familiar with many standard classics. The RCM under Allen was a lively place and during his stay there Tippett acted as a repetiteur in a stage production of Wagner's *Parsifal* and sang in some unusual new compositions, such as Vaughan Williams's *Sir John in Love* and Holst's *Hymn of Jesus*. At his first attempt, he failed his final examinations, but eventually graduated with a Bachelor of Music degree in 1928.

Composition was now his top priority and in order to make it so, he confined his other musical work to a minimum, content to live at almost subsistence level. For a while he stayed in London. But then he was invited to conduct a concert and operatic society promoted by the Oxted and Limpsfield Players, and he combined this with a madrigal group (mainly to explore the sixteenth-century repertoire for his own purposes). Through the local friendships that developed there, he managed to rent a small cottage – a rarely used sanatorium at Hazelwood Preparatory School – and moved in during 1929. He did some French teaching at the school and played the organ for services, for which he received about £80 a year, as well as plenty of time off to compose. In 1932, he moved into one half of a double cottage on a local farm in Limpsfield, which gave him the peace and isolation he most desired in order to work. Six years later, his father lent him enough money to buy the entire cottage and some land around it. Tippett then obtained a loan which he used to have a bungalow built nearby. Renting out the cottage, he made the bungalow his home for the next thirteen years.

Life was spartan. Tippett collected wood and built his own fires; he ate lunch at a nearby farm, but otherwise cooked for himself, using recipes from a review copy he had been given of *Minnie, Lady Hindlip's Cook Book*, but never advancing far beyond porridge, marmalade and dishes made with eggs and cheese. When not composing or teaching, he undertook some enterprising productions with the local society, including a double bill of *Everyman* and Vaughan Williams's *The Shepherds of the Delectable Mountains*, Stanford's *The Travelling Companion* and Tippett's own version of the eighteenth-century ballad opera, *The Village Opera*. From school days, the stage had always excited him. He had sung in the chorus in Stamford Operatic Society's production of Planquette's *Les Cloches de Corneville* (conducted by Malcolm Sargent), played the King's Fool in Edward German's *Merrie England* and during the 1926 General Strike appeared at Covent Garden as one of the 'strike-breaking' extras substituting for Grenadier Guardsmen in walk-on parts in Wagner's *Die Meistersinger*. All this enabled him to observe the practicalities of stage-production, nurturing also his understanding of the techniques of operatic music and the differences between the setting of words to music in opera and oratorio.

Conducting two complete performances of Handel's *Messiah*, which was rarely presented unabridged in those days, brought further illumination. Tippett decided to study first the libretto, as

Handel would have, just to see how, subsequently, his great predecessor had set about structuring his musical setting. At the performances, Tippett provided the audience with copies of the libretto and gave an introductory talk before each part. Later, when he came to write his own oratorio, *A Child of Our Time*, he used *Messiah* as a model.

Tippett's own early compositions occasionally found their way into Oxted concerts. On 15 December 1928, for instance, the pianist Cyril Smith – whom he had known at the RCM – played three movements of his Sonata in C minor.[2] Smith later rejected the (published) Piano Sonata No. 1 (as did Clifford Curzon), though his wife, Phyllis Sellick, was prepared to take it on. On 5 April 1930, the first concert of Tippett own's music took place – an entire programme of first performances directed by a former fellow-student, David Moule-Evans, in the Barn Theatre at Oxted. It included Tippett's Concerto in D, for flute, oboes, horns and strings; Three Songs; 'Jockey to the Fair' for piano; a String Quartet in F: and Psalm in C, for chorus and orchestra, a setting of 'The Gateway' by Christopher Fry. (Tippett himself designed the programme and absent-mindedly omitted his own name.)

A review of the concert in *The Times*[3] two days later said that Tippett's music had 'a personal distinction and sincerity which is absent from the work of the Central European composers of today': a comment revealing not so much discernment as parochialism of the kind that prevented the young Benjamin Britten at this time from going abroad to study with Alban Berg. A *Daily Telegraph* review also expressed enthusiasm, but suggested that 'Michael Tippett will probably prefer to put all behind him and go on to fresh ideas.'[4] Tippett did precisely that. The concert had revealed to him distinct limitations in his technique. He therefore withdrew the works that had been included and arranged, through the Royal College of Music, to undertake further studies with R. O. Morris. Tippett had been taught by Morris earlier, when he deputized for the terminally ill Charles Wood at the RCM. On one occasion, Morris had refuted in detail his headstrong student's cursory dismissal of Mozart and thereby won his admiration. Morris was a noted expert on sixteenth-century polyphony and (when not occupied in devising crossword puzzles for *The Times*) wrote polyphonic pieces of his own. Tippett now willingly succumbed to his rigorous discipline for four terms, studying fugue in the style of Bach. Only after this training did he return to original composition. His own subsequent mastery as a contrapuntist and general appreciation of the need for formal and stylistic consistency can undoubtedly be attributed to Morris's guidance.

If the mid-1920s and early 30s saw many advances in Tippett's musical training, concurrently there were significant developments in his intellectual, political, social and personal life. These naturally overlapped. Tippett's extra-musical interests – reading, attending the theatre and concerts – were nurtured by Aubrey Russ, whom he had met during his first visits to the Proms. Russ was older than him, an employee in his father's legal firm, a theatre enthusiast and a bass in the Oxted Choir. He was gay, but this played no significant part in his friendship with Tippett. Russ enabled Tippett to see for the first time plays by Ibsen and Toller, along with uncensored Restoration drama at Sunday night theatre clubs. He lent him books (like Frazer's *The Golden Bough*) and records (such as the Lener Quartet's recordings of Beethoven's string quartets). Thus were Tippett's intellectual leanings given a substantial boost.

Through Russ, Tippett came to meet David Ayerst, then a history graduate at Oxford and like himself, a great admirer of Samuel Butler. Ayerst – later a journalist and leader writer for the then *Manchester Guardian*, becoming one of its trustees and biographers, as well as a noted educationist – was to remain one of Tippett's closest friends, right up to his death in 1992. Their friendship crystallized in the 1930s when they were jointly involved in left-wing political activity.

Socially, Tippett found solace in local families, most notably the Shaxsons – Eric (who had a fine tenor voice) and Dorothy (who sang alto in the choir): their four sons he taught at

Hazelwood School. Tippett began a lasting friendship also with the Hungarian mathematician, Paul Dienes, and his second wife, Sari, who, as communists, had fled from the counter-revolution in Hungary. Dienes became Professor of Mathematics at Birkbeck College, London: he introduced Tippett to Bartók's quartets and the writings of anarchists like Kropotkin and Bakunin.

During his youth, Tippett became aware of his own homosexual inclinations and accepted them as an instinctive, perfectly natural way of expressing himself. He was undeterred by the legal prohibitions in his own country that forbade homosexual activity even in private. Blessed with good looks, charm and charisma, he was propositioned by many women and dealt with the situation as best he could, without wanting to hurt any of them – though many often felt wounded by rejection, so attached had they become to him. In the sexually repressive climate of the times, misogyny was common amongst homosexuals, but this was never part of Tippett's character. Nor did he become, either then or later (after the law on homosexuality was reformed by the Wilson Government in the late 1960s), a militant, proselytizing gay, though he supported campaigns for further reform.

What disturbed Tippett most was that after his own family had disintegrated, his sexuality separated him further from 'normal' family life: 'being unable to enter into a biological relationship with a woman,' he later wrote, 'it seemed that I was excluded from an understanding of half the human race.'[5] He could not turn to his parents, even when they came back to England in the 1930s: for while politically liberal and altruistic by nature, they were as disapproving of his homosexuality as they were of his attempts to make a career in music. While Tippett enjoyed the physical side of gay sex, he was hurt by the fact that his inclinations made him a kind of outsider, if not a complete social outcast.

Three people entered his life at this point. One was Evelyn Maude, wife of the Permanent Secretary to the Ministry of Health, Sir John Maude, also an amateur cellist in the Oxted

Players. She fell deeply in love with Tippett, but drew back from any attempt at a physical relationship. A lady of great personal integrity, she became a tremendous source of strength to him: indeed, Tippett has compared their relationship with that between Goethe and Frau von Stein, which Schiller described as 'pure and blameless'; likewise Evelyn Maude was more an elder sister than a potential wife. She remained for many years a regular confidante, for Tippett valued greatly her mature, sensitive response to his many difficulties. When later he received a prison sentence, Tippett chose Evelyn Maude as the one person with whom would be allowed to correspond regularly.[6]

Then there was Francesca Allinson, a musician who worked as a choral conductor and pursued research on folksong: her other interests included puppetry, and she wrote a memoir of her own childhood.[7] Tippett met her in London through his cousin Phyllis Kemp. A convinced Marxist and specialist in Slavonic languages, Phyllis was also consumed with passion for him. She became deeply jealous of the attachment that now grew between him and Francesca who, according to David Ayerst, was 'the gayest and daintiest of women'.[8] Tippett and Francesca (who also had a lesbian side) more than once contemplated adopting children, but this came to nothing. Their sexless love-affair remained intense and intimate. Together, they enjoyed a memorable walking holiday in Bavaria, Prague and Dresden. She helped him financially and supported him in countless other ways. He tried to help her complete and publish her folksong research, without success. Physically frail and psychologically hypersensitive, she took her own life just before the end of the Second World War. Her death was probably the biggest personal blow Tippett ever suffered: Ayerst, many years later, reminded him that it was 'a boundary stone which still marks a period in your life.'[9]

Lastly, through David Ayerst Tippett had met Wilfred Franks, a London-born painter and crafstman, who had studied at the Bauhaus in Weimar and had wandered all over Germany and Italy. Tippett has described their encounter as 'the deepest, most shattering experience of falling in love: and I am quite certain that it was a major factor underlying the discovery of my own individual musical "voice" – something that couldn't be analysed purely in technical terms: all that love flowed out in the slow movement of my First String Quartet, an unbroken span of lyrical music in which all four instruments sing ardently from start to finish.'[10] Tippett soon joined Franks on hiking holidays in the north of England, learning from him how to survive when remote from everyday amenities. They also went with Ayerst on holiday to Spain, just after it had been declared a republic.

Tippett met Ayerst and Franks at a time when he was becoming increasingly aware of how music-making and theatre could be of assistance to the poor and deprived sections of the community. Already, as a student, he had woken up to harsh realities of the First World War. During 1930, he visited a *Kinderheim* (children's home) in Bavaria started by a young couple – cousins of Francesca Allinson – to help some of the waifs abandoned in the streets of Berlin, when the Allies had continued their blockade of Germany after the First World War. The children at the *Kinderheim* had no parents and no nationality, but formed a family of their own with their foster parents. The blockade itself was eventually broken by the efforts of the Swiss and the Swedes in setting up the Save the Children Fund. But the experience of being with these innocent victims made an indelible impression upon Tippett – indeed, it sowed the seeds not only for *A Child of Our Time*, but for his opera *New Year*, written nearly sixty years later.

In the late 1920s and early 30s Tippett also became aware of the social injustices caused by the Depression and mass unemployment in his own country. Hiking up into the north of England with Wilf Franks, he saw 'for the first time, with horrified eyes, the undernourished children. When I returned to the well-fed South, I was ashamed.' Tippett became 'quite certain that ... somewhere music could have a direct relation also to the compassion that was so deep in my heart.'[11] He began to link his

music-making directly with political activity. He gave up
teaching at Hazelwood School, started conducting amateur choirs
– the Royal Arsenal Cooperative Society Choir and two others
sponsored by the RACS at Abbey Wood and New Malden – and
acted as choral adjudicator for the London Labour Choral Union
competitions. Initially, his choirs performed songs of a political
nature, though later they embarked upon light opera. When they
performed for the poor of London's East End, Tippett arranged
that each choir member should bring *two* meals, so that they
could feed the audience as well as themselves. Through David
Ayerst, he went in 1933 to work at the experimental farms at
Boosbeck and Cleveland in Yorkshire, which had been sponsored
by a local landowner, Major Pennyman, and a trade union, in an
attempt to alleviate the misery of unemployment amongst
ironstone miners (rising at the time to over 90 per cent in
Cleveland).[12] The farm offered cheap local produce and
opportunities to work. Furniture-making, music and drama were
included. At the first work-camp in 1932, led by Rolf Gardiner
and Alan Collingridge (a friend of Ayerst), students from the
German *Wandervogel* movement participated; but their organizer
Georg Goetsch was not available for the second work-camp and
Tippett (after attending a course at Goetsch's Musikheim in
Frankfurt an der Oder) replaced him.

Initially, he joined in the farming work, but then decided he
could better contribute by putting together a special version of
The Beggar's Opera, in which as many local people as possible
could take part. Wilf Franks, who had a reputation as a pub
singer, was offered the part of Macheath, but turned it down as he
couldn't read music; he took the role of Filch instead and
Macheath was assigned to a local insurance agent. A coal-miner's
daughter sang Polly Peachum and Lucy Lockett was played by
Francesca Allinson. The performance in the church hall next to
the Boosbeck Miners' Institute was a distinct success and it was
decided that Tippett would compose a totally new work for
performance in East Cleveland, *Robin Hood*. Having first lived in

Cleveland with students in a tent, Tippett now joined Franks in new lodgings at a sweetshop. The task of writing the libretto was shared between Major Pennyman's wife, Ruth, and David Ayerst (who helped give it some political bite): they were billed jointly as 'David Michael Pennyless'. There were six solo parts: a soprano, alto, two tenors, baritone and bass, plus a trio for three bridesmaids. The orchestra consisted of an oboe, horn, violin, cello and piano. *Robin Hood* included some 20 musical numbers, mostly arrangements of folksongs and of the Helston Furry Dance, a brass band test-piece popular in the region. While it offered few harbingers of Tippett's mature style, it contained much that he was able to re-work later in his *Suite for the Birthday of Prince Charles* (1948). *Robin Hood* was subsequently revived in 1937 for a series of performances in London by the RACS, but Tippett has never felt inclined to have it published or updated for modern use.

Through Alan Collingridge, Tippett now began to conduct the South London Orchestra, formed largely from players whose work in cinemas had disappeared with the arrival of 'talkies'; these players joined forces with out-of-work theatre musicians and students and gave concerts in colleges, theatres, school halls, parks and churches and at their rehearsal base in Morley College, in Lambeth, south London. Tippett was paid by the London County Council and the players shared the income they received from concerts. They performed mainly popular classics, but there were sometimes novelties such as Stravinsky's recently premièred Violin Concerto, which Tippett, as a composer, wanted to get to know.

Through Francesca Allinson, Tippett had struck up a close friendship with the composer Alan Bush, who was five years older than him and conductor of the London Labour Choral Union. Bush was an adventurous composer who subsequently became the figurehead in England for politically slanted music-making. Tippett acted as his assistant at *A Pageant of Labour*, a six-part epic for choir and orchestra commemorating the centenary of the Tolpuddle Martyrs, at the Crystal Palace in 1934, and conducted one of the seven performances. Tippett also sang tenor in Bush's LLCU Choir at the International Workers' Music Olympiad Competition in Strasbourg and joined the executive committee of the newly formed Workers' Music Association. Bush remained an orthodox Marxist right up until his death in 1995. Tippett preferred Trotsky's internationalism to Stalinism's 'Socialism in one country'; likewise, Trotksy's concept of a permanent revolution led by the proletariat was far more acceptable to him than Stalin's 'democratic centralism'. Thus, when Tippett joined the Communist Party in 1935, he tried to subvert it from within and turn it towards Trotskyism, but this plan failed and he left within a few weeks. Annoyed at his refusal to accept orthodox Marxism, as well as being piqued at his rejection of her sexual advances, his cousin Phyllis broke off relations with him: they only met again in the late 1940s, when she was married and living in East Germany.

Another musician-friend from the North, Jeff Mark, drew Tippett's attention to C. B. Douglas's theory of 'social credit' (which had greatly influenced Ezra Pound): this provided him with one of the sources for his agit-prop play, *War Ramp*, exposing the way wars are built on a 'ramp' of credit which ordinary people have ultimately to finance.[13] *War Ramp* was performed at various Labour Party rallies in 1935. Rather wooden as a dramatic text, Tippett's play proved a turning-point in his own thinking: for the logic of its argument culminated in the advocacy of revolution by violent means – and from this he recoiled.

Trotskyism also seemed powerless to answer the barbarities of Nazism or Stalinism (as Tippett discovered when reading Ulia de Beausobre's exposé of the torture camps in *The Woman Who Could Not Die*).[14] Tippett was thus drawn to pacificism: and in 1935 he became one of the 100,000 or so people who responded to the letter sent to the press by the First World War pacifist, Rev. Dick Sheppard, inviting anyone who was opposed to war to send him a postcard with the pledge, 'I renounce war and never again, directly or indirectly, will I support or sanction another.' From this emerged the Peace Pledge Union, of which Tippett was to become a prominent, active member – eventually its president.

Aside from all his political involvements, Tippett was beginning to make real headway as a composer. His String Quartet in A was featured in a programme of chamber music by the Brosa Quartet at the Mercury Theatre, London, in December 1935. Although he later revised the piece – substituting a new first movement for the original first *two* movements – he felt that it was here that his own personal voice was being heard for the first time: eventually it became his earliest published work. He was not so happy with other works from this period and suppressed them. They included a Symphony in B flat (whose first movement was rehearsed and performed by the London Symphony Orchestra under the composer's baton, at a Royal College of Music Patron's Fund concert in 1935); a setting of Blake's 'Song of Liberty'; a Hanns Eisler-ish piece for chorus and piano, 'Miners', to a text by Francesca Allinson's lesbian actress friend, Judy Wogan; and a children's opera (with a text by Christopher Fry), *Robert of Sicily*, whose staging deliberately emulated the methods used in a Max Reinhardt production, *The Miracle*, which Tippett and Fry had seen in Cologne in 1929.

After the First String Quartet, however, came a series of compositions all of which were to attain performance and publication, such as the Piano Sonata No. 1 and the Concerto for Double String Orchestra.

In the meantime, a curious conjunction of inward and outer turmoil precipitated him towards the composition of his first major work, the oratorio *A Child of Our Time*. His relations with Wilf Franks, who was ill at ease with homosexuality, ended when the latter announced his impending marriage; only in 1985 did they re-establish contact and resume a happy friendship. The break-up with Wilf, coupled with the difficulties in his affair with Francesca, brought about an acute emotional crisis. The resolution of all this resulted from his lately found interest in

Jungian analysis. Evelyn Maude had earlier given him Jung's *Psychology of the Unconscious* and he became so fascinated that thereafter he read every volume of Jung he could obtain. David Ayerst had also introduced him to a Jungian analyst, John Layard, who, at an initial meeting, analysed one of his dreams for him. Unable to afford continuing treatment, but understanding the basic procedures involved, Tippett thereafter undertook self-analysis. Thus, after the break-up with Wilf Franks, for something like nine months Tippett wrote down all his dreams and attempted analyses of them.[15]

The often chaotic contents of Tippett's dreams reached a climax three nights before the war broke out, in one which he called the 'classic dream of a forced death: I was going to be strangled by four men. I accepted it – I said, "Let what must, happen" – and realized afterwards that I had turned a corner. A kind of rebirth was now happening. I stopped writing down my dreams. Three days later, on 3 September 1939, the war began: simultaneously, I started writing the music for *A Child of Our Time* ... In the final dream, death is confronted ... the quarrel inside myself, instead of interfering with my creativity, now enhanced it – I had greater control of my powers as a composer ... the process of "individuation", as Jung called it, produced an acceptance that I would not be married. I was thus ejected out into the world as a loner.'[16]

The solution to Tippett's psychological crisis thus favoured the primacy of composition in his life, but left him without any guidance or objectives regarding the fulfilment of his sexual and emotional needs. Thereafter, his obdurate and obsessive devotion to composition was to result in many great achievements. On the other hand, in his personal life he walked wounded, remaining both vulnerable and guilt-ridden, aware that his creativity sometimes caused him unwittingly to ride roughshod over human relationships.

Meanwhile, Tippett felt increasingly compelled by outside events to try and crystallize plans for a major work that would express his solidarity with the oppressed and the deprived. He contemplated writing an opera based on the 1916 Easter Rebellion in Ireland. This had potential for Easter symbolism inspiring an avowal of hope for a new springtime. Soon, though, he realized that the work gestating inside him was contemplative in character, obviating the need for stage action.

In 1938, the shooting of a German diplomat in Paris by a young Polish Jew, Herschel Grynspan, made desperate by the Nazi persecution of his family and of his race in general, led to one of the most terrible pogroms of Jews in central Europe – the infamous 'Crystal Night' of 9 November. It was widely reported in the press, notably in *Picture Post*.[17] Tippett shared in the public horror that it aroused. He felt inwardly that he must respond with a composition which, as it turned out, was to be his first major statement as an artist, and the work by which he is still best known: *A Child of Our Time*.

A few years earlier, he had become friendly with the poet T. S. Eliot and this contact developed into the biggest professional influence in his entire career. Tippett later often described Eliot as his 'spiritual father', valuing greatly their discussions on aesthetics and particularly on the relationship between words and music. Tippett now asked Eliot if he would write the libretto for his projected oratorio. Eliot agreed to consider it on condition that the composer prepared a 'scenario' for him, showing the shape and character of each episode or musical 'number', sketching in his own ideas about the text. This Tippett did, modelling the work overall on Handel's *Messiah* and Bach's Passions. He thus laid out the basis for a three-part oratorio, using standard baroque methods such as recitative for the narration and arias and ensembles that culminated in Negro spirituals – the best modern counterpart he could find to the Lutheran chorales of Bach's time. Producing ideas for the text involved him in an arduous process of selection from a great accretion of images – from Blake, Wilfred Owen, Jung and other sources. He also wanted to make the piece as clear and direct as possible.

After studying the scenario carefully for a few weeks, Eliot advised Tippett to complete the writing of the text himself, as he felt that any words that he, a poet, might provide could compete for attention with Tippett's music. Tippett accepted this advice and ever after wrote his own libretti. When Paul Dienes drew his attention to a recently published translation of a novella by the anti-Nazi writer, Odon von Horvath, *Ein Kind unserer Zeit – A Child of Our Time*[18] – he knew that he had found the right title. For while many fellow radicals of the period were rushing off to Spain to participate in the Civil War, and were attacking governments and economic institutions, Tippett wanted to focus on the outcasts and scapegoats in societies in general. *A Child of Our Time* is thus prophetic of the horrors and social consequences of war, but not tied to the specific events that had sparked it off. Its ultimate Jungian message was really the collective application of what Tippett had recently experienced in his own personal life: 'I would know my shadow and my light, so shall I at last be made whole.' The subsequent history of performances of the oratorio worldwide has seen its contents re-interpreted in relation to many different situations in which people have been made scapegoats and persecuted – from the victims of the Hiroshima bomb, the unwanted children in the streets and poor ghettos of São Paulo to the oppressed sufferers of AIDS.[19]

Tippett took two years to complete the work, but it was not performed until 1944. Meanwhile, his reputation as a composer was growing steadily, even though hardly any of his pieces had received professional performances and the BBC, ISCM Festival and the publishers Boosey & Hawkes had all turned down works such as his Concerto for Double String Orchestra. The first published article about his music, by Scott Goddard, appeared in 1939.[20] In the 1944 *Hinrischsen Year Book*, Robin Hull – who had looked at a number of Tippett's works in manuscript – declared that they 'are all steeped in the magic of that "soaring" quality which is true ecstasy in music': he foresaw 'a great event in the future will be some superlative performance of what may prove to be Tippett's most important work so far, namely, *A Child of Our Time*'.[21] A privately made recording of his First Piano Sonata, played by Phyllis Sellick,[22] had also made something of an impact. Released in August 1941, it was reviewed by Wilfrid Mellers in *Scrutiny*,[23] and in the *New Statesman and Nation* by Edward Sackville-West;[24] and two years later, in the *Observer*, William Glock discussed it alongside his Second String Quartet, beginning, 'A new composer has emerged in English music' and focusing especially on the use of rhythm in these two works.'[25]

In May 1939 Tippett had attended a concert performance of Hindemith's *Mathis der Maler*, conducted by Boult at the Queen's Hall, London. During the interval, he was introduced to Willy Strecker, the director of Schott's music publishing firm in Mainz. Strecker asked to see a representative selection of his work and Tippett obliged. Just after the outbreak of war, he received a reply which stated that Schott would publish his Piano Sonata No. 1 and Concerto for Double String Orchestra. In the event, the publication of Tippett's work was undertaken by Schott's London branch. The success of the Sellick recording meant that the first piece of his to appear in print (in 1942) was the First Piano Sonata – then still called *Fantasy Sonata*. It was followed by his *Fantasia on a Theme of Handel* (written between 1939 and 1941), and in 1944, *A Child of Our Time*.

When the war started, adult education was suspended. The South London Orchestra and Tippett's RACS choirs were disbanded: so Tippett returned briefly to Hazelwood School to teach classics. But then in 1940, he was invited by the Principal of Morley College, Eva Hubback, whom he had met through Wilf Franks's father, to take over as Director of Music there from Arnold Foster who, as master of music at Westminster School, had been evacuated with his pupils (though Tippett's most illustrious predecessor in in the post was Gustav Holst). When a landmine hit and badly damaged the building, classes were moved to a nearby school. Neverthless, during the next eleven years, Tippett gave Morley College musically a new lease of life.[26]

The Morley choir grew from ten singers, after the bombing, to between 40 and 50, and Tippett attracted on to the staff a number of musical refugees from central Europe. These included the composer Matyas Seiber, the musicologist Walter Bergmann, the conductor Walter Goehr and three teenage string players who were later to join forces with a fourth (English) player to form the Amadeus Quartet. Tippett discovered the countertenor Alfred Deller in Canterbury Cathedral and brought him to Morley to sing the important solos in Purcell's Odes, thereby attracting much attention. He organized and took part in a variety of performances – from the first complete rendition in modern times of Monteverdi's *Vespers* (1610) to Stravinsky's *Les Noces* and Frank Martin's *Le vin herbe*. At a time when London musical life was distinctly impoverished, the events at Morley College attracted a wide following. Tippett described his efforts thus:

In the 1942–43 session, we decided to experiment with a series of monthly concerts in the small Holst Memorial Music Room at the College. The programmes for this series varied from a recital of the works of Orlando Gibbons by the College Choir and outside professional instrumentalists, to the first London performance of Stravinsky's *Dumbarton Oaks* concerto, with Walter Goehr conducting.

These concerts have become the central feature of our work. They are in part educational, designed primarily for members of the College, but the general public is welcomed in so far as we have space to receive it, and can attend by becoming members of the Concert Club. There is a fixed price for concert tickets, and a fixed, but small, honorarium for professional artists who take part, irrespective of their notoriety, their age, or the length of the item they contribute.

The concerts would not be possible at all but for the willing cooperation of so many musicians, professional and amateur alike, and the only direct subvention so far to the inevitable financial loss has come from the outside earnings of the choir. For by 1943 the policy of concentrating on a really first class *a cappella* choir had succeeded so well that we found ourselves able to undertake, for instance, concerts at short notice for the French National Committee at the Wigmore Hall, and for the National Gallery Committee; and by the end of the session the choir had a repertoire which included Monteverdi madrigals in Italian, Bach cantatas in German, Ravel and Debussy in French and Purcell in English.'[27]

Visiting London in 1946 at the invitation of the British Council, the Turkish composer Ahmet Adnan Saygun was introduced to Arthur Bliss, whom he found 'a reserved and a kind man' and Tippett, who was friendly and lively, but 'did not seem to care much about protocol'. Saygun went to hear Morley College Choir rehearse that evening. He later wrote in his diary: 'Tippett handed me a bass part and asked me to join in. We rehearsed Purcell's "Ode to St Cecilia" and Britten's "Rejoice in the Lamb". All these people were amateurs, who were singing beautifully, though I think I would have been a little more cautious with them myself.'[28]

The choir's reputation led eventually to some BBC broadcasts: and one project – Tallis's 40-part motet, *Spem in Alium* – which took two years to rehearse properly – resulted in their making the first ever recording of the work.[29] A few years later, Walter Legge wanted a chorus-master for his newly formed Philharmonia Chorus. He turned first to Tippett – who rejected the offer, as it would have been too great a distraction from composition.

The war and Tippett's allegiance to the pacifist cause presented further distractions. Called up into the army, Tippett applied to register as a conscientious objector. His statement in support of his application succinctly summed up his opposition to war from late teenage years onwards:

People of my age entered to a war-torn and war-weary world. My first political act was to attend an International Congress of Youth at Brussels in 1922 called by Jeunesse Suisse Romande to discuss methods of raising money to send child victims of the Great War to sanatoria in the Swiss mountains. I was 17 years old. It is not now possible for me to be at war with what amounts to those same children or to take part in a state of war which will result in the same victimization. When I was 18, I saw the war film, *The Four Horsemen of the Apocalypse*, which ended with photographs of the vast Flanders graveyards. I and the student friends with me made a sort of vow, or promise, afterwards to see that such a thing could never happen again. That promise was quite real to me then and still is so now, though I do not now see the matter optimistically. At no time has my opposition to war been a merely personal matter. There is some sense of a dedication to the memory of those who did horrible things last time in the belief that they fought a war to end war. Not to stand against a repetition is to make a mockery of their sacrifice. Our present-day pacifism holds that the present horrors and evil results of modern total war are far greater than the evils which the wars hope to eradicate. The Great War was a war to end war and it left the world afterwards one vast mad arsenal. The present war threatens to engulf the whole world in what Dean Inge calls cooperative suicide about a European dispute. War has its own logic of madness but the pacifist is in some degree dispassionate. I think we feel the virtue of peace as an enduring state which must be struggled for even in war itself. Values, especially the good ones, cannot be scrapped one day and replaced the next.

Some people feel they have a necessity, a duty to serve those values in times when they are in general danger. There is no confusion between professional life as a musician and my political life as a pacifist. There is certainly confusion between the world of imagining music and the world of cooperative suicide. In the Napoleonic wars there were many great artists alive in Europe – Beethoven, Schubert, Schiller, Goethe, Shelley, Keats, Wordsworth, Byron, Blake. None of them except Goethe was conscripted into that madness. Total war, in wishing to conscript every man and woman alive, forces the struggle for liberty back on to the individual, whether it is Ossietzky in Germany, or Nehru in India. I imagine that only by the endurance of individuals who refuse (non-co-operation) can the madness of the war be in any degree shortened.'[30]

The tribunal which he attended in 1942 gave him conditional registration – he had either to do full-time work with Air Raid Precautions, the Fire Service, or work on the land. Another alternative was some kind of cultural activity and he was offered various jobs – Music Organizer for ENSA in Northern Ireland, librarian for the RAF orchestra and choir-training with the National Fire Service. Tippett rejected all these alternatives. By continuing to compose, teach and direct musical performances he felt he was serving a cause no less moral than that which he might uphold by fighting for the Allies. Many of his friends and colleagues had advised him to 'bend with the wind', but he would brook no compromise. Vaughan Williams, in particular, disagreed with him and wrote to him (on 17 December 1941):

I will not argue with you about your pacifist scruples which I respect though I think they are all wrong. But I *do* join issue with you in the idea that it is anyone's business at a time like this to sit apart from the world to create music until he is sure that he has done all he can to preserve the world from destruction and helped to create a world where creative art will be a *possibility*.

If your house was on fire you would not ignore it & go on creating till you had helped put it out and saved the inmates – if for no other reason because if your music paper was burnt you would not be able to go on composing.

There is a great danger now of our spiritual music paper being burnt & we must save it *now* so that creative art may flourish later.

This does not apply, of course, to using one's craft for definite useful purposes (e.g. arranging Xmas carols for the troops in Iceland which I did the other day).

I certainly cannot feel that peace of mind which is necessary for composing until I have done all the little jobs which I believe will help us out of our present terrible dilemma (too few, alas, for me with my advanced years and circumstances) ... Another point – you are not the only composer in this predicament – what about Rubbra & Finzi & Bush who have all temporarily given up their creative work & gone in to various kinds of 'war-work'. If you are to be exempted so as to carry on your composition, why not they? However wrong & dreadful we think war (and we all do) – here it is & we can't blink it – & surely we could all do a little bit to try & bring it to an end.[31]

Nevertheless, when Tippett was summoned to appear at Oxted Crown Court, on 21 June 1943, for refusing to comply with the conditions laid down by the tribunal, Vaughan Williams joined Eva Hubback and David Ayerst (by now an army colonel) in speaking in his defence – but to no avail. He was sentenced to three months' imprisonment and was taken off to Wormwood Scrubs in a police van, chained to a young soldier who had killed someone with his army vehicle and had received a borstal sentence. Tippett's immediate neighbours in prison were a rapist and a murderer. He sewed mailbags, not very efficiently, studied Bach's *Art of Fugue* and tried to assist with the small prison orchestra.

Already a thin man, Tippett became even thinner on prison diet. Nevertheless, as he put it later, he felt he had 'come home'. There were other conscientious objectors far less well known than himself (they included Fred May, formerly leader of the South London Orchestra)[32] and in serving a sentence alongside them, he felt he was making a definite gesture of support. His mother later declared it her 'proudest moment when her son went to prison for his principles, as she herself had done years before. After his release – one month early, for good behaviour – he attended a small celebration and a performance of his Second String Quartet, then went for a short holiday in Cornwall with some Morley College associates – composer Antony Hopkins and his future wife, Alison Purves, and John Amis – narrowly escaping a further term of imprisonment when a coastguard apprehended them all bathing in the nude.

Tippett's letters from prison to Evelyn Maude[33] speak of the symphony that was gestating inside him. And indeed, despite his incarceration and the continuing difficulties produced by wartime, including the partial destruction of his cottage at Oxted, his musical career was advancing almost inexorably. Not long before going to prison, Tippett had formed a close friendship with Benjamin Britten and Peter Pears, who had lately returned from the USA. They appeared at Morley College concerts and sometimes stayed with him at Oxted. In 1943, Tippett wrote for them a cantata, 'Boyhood's End' – a piece that reflected their common interest in Purcell.

Aware of his impecunious state, Britten arranged for a small portion of his commission fee for the festival cantata, 'Rejoice in the Lamb', to be paid to Tippett so that he could write a fanfare to introduce the Northampton concert where it was due to receive its première. Britten also asked to see the score of *A Child of Our Time*, was immensely enthusiastic about it and urged Tippett to arrange a first performance. This came about, eventually, on 19 March 1944, at the Adelphi Theatre in London. Pears was one of the four soloists and Walter Goehr conducted. *The Times* reviewed it, favourably. Glock, in the *Observer*, called it 'the most moving and important work written by an English musician for many years.'[34]

Two years later, Tippett himself conducted a performance at the Royal Albert Hall, in aid of Polish refugee children. For the programme of this concert, Oskar Kokoschka and Augustus John both contributed drawings. Subsequently, in 1948, Kokoschka wrote a letter to the Viktor Matejka, the head of Vienna's department of education:

'You must issue an invitation, at once, in the name of the Burgomaster and the City of Vienna to Michael Tippett, Morley College Concerts Society, 61 Westminster Bridge Road SE1, to perform his 'Oratorio' in Vienna, on his way to Budapest, where he is is to conduct it in March. He is the best conductor and teacher, a fine composer, and caused a stir with the very successful concerts he gave there during the war ... I should dearly love to see Austria acquire him for good, to make the country's musical life mean something in the world again, as in Schubert's day, when every family, in the city and the country alike, nurtured a musical tradition. All we have today is blether about 'City of Song'. He ought to be appointed as a kind of national musical adviser, with a particular duty to remind the people of their musical heritage.[35]

Meanwhile, Tippett's oratorio had made its way to the Continent through the efforts of Howard Hartog, who was working for Hamburg Radio (then in Allied hands) and who was later to join the staff at Schott's in London. The work made a profound impact in Arnhem, Brussels and Hamburg and has since become Tippett's most widely performed composition.

Britten and Tippett were now clearly the focal figures in post-war continuation of the 'second Renaissance' of English music, begun by Elgar, Holst and Vaughan Williams. One thing the two of them shared was a disdain for the notion of the gentleman amateur composer that persisted in England well into the middle of twentieth century – the type that combined a parochial outlook with an inadequate, slipshod technique. Together, the two composers can, in retrospect, be seen to have inaugurated a new epoch in which the composer behaves and expects to be treated as a professional.

However, they associated far less with each other after the première of the latter's opera *Peter Grimes*, in 1945. Its success brought Britten such fame that he began to distance himself from former friends and colleagues, excluding some of them from his milieu abruptly and cruelly. At the same time, his meteoric rise to fame aroused in some of his contemporaries – such as William Walton, Elisabeth Lutyens and Alan Rawsthorne – a considerable degree of insecurity. Tippett was unaffected in this way. When Walton went to great lengths to depict Britten as the figurehead of a conspiracy by a homosexual clique to become the dominant force in British music, Tippett called his bluff. Walton treated him quite benevolently, in fact: being no tyro, Tippett was of course not such a threat and they stayed friends, even though neither had much time for the other's music.[36] Likewise, despite going their separate ways, Britten and Tippett remained respectful of each other's attainments and maintained a deep, warm-hearted relationship right up until Britten's death in 1976.

2
Trials and Tribulations

After the war, Tippett continued living at Oxted, frugally as ever. He began to limit his activities at Morley College, and his other commitments, as he wanted more time for composition. Unremitting work had now begun to affect his health. When he contracted severe hepatitis and had to take a break, Britten and Pears invited him to convalesce at their house in Aldeburgh. Lately, he had started giving talks on BBC Radio, notably on the World Service. This activity blossomed with the creation of the new Third Programme, providing him with a modest secondary income. Thus, in 1951, he decided to resign from Morley College – though not before he had conducted the choir in a performance of Tallis's *Spem in alium* as part of the Festival of Britain.

By this time, Tippett had written his First Symphony; Sargent conducted the première in Liverpool in 1945 and Walter Goehr introduced it to London the following year. Also, in 1946, the Zorian Quartet gave the first performance of Tippett's Third String Quartet. But his main obsession now was the opera he wanted to write – *The Midsummer Marriage*. This he began in 1946, at first collaborating on the libretto with a young writer called Douglas Newton: Tippett had met him originally at Doolittle Farm, near East Grinstead (an enterprise Francesca Allinson had started, to enable conscientious objectors to find work as an alternative to military service). Their joint effort was shortlived, however, and Tippett continued thereafter entirely on his own. For the next six years the opera dominated his existence. He had not been commissioned to write it, nor did he have any idea as to whether it would ever reach the operatic stage. He composed it simply out of sheer inner necessity. It became an act of faith, involving tremendous self-discipline. Often he was exhausted. Once he fell so ill, he thought he had cancer and wrote to Willy Strecker at Schott Mainz in despair. Strecker responded with words of encouragement that persuaded him never again to consider giving up on a composition. The only distractions from *The Midsummer Marriage* were his *Suite for the Birthday of Prince Charles* – a BBC commission in 1948 – and his song-cycle, *The Heart's Assurance*, a long-considered memorial to Francesca Allinson, the première of which, in 1951, was entrusted to Pears and Britten.

In this period, Tippett had become involved in intermittent relationships with a gifted young musician, John Minchinton, and with a painter, Karl Hawker. Minchinton was recommended to him by Britten and Pears, and – still a teenager – turned up at his house in Oxted one night in 1942. Although Minchinton never lived with Tippett and eventually married, he was in and out of Tippett's life for more than ten years, undertaking tasks like the proof-reading of the full score of *The Midsummer Marriage*. Minchinton studied with Karajan and later conducted many enterprising concerts, including the London première of Stravinsky's late ballet, *Agon*, in 1958, which influenced Tippett greatly when he came to write his second opera, *King Priam*.

Tippett had met Hawker somewhat earlier: Aubrey Russ had brought him to Oxted and he stayed the night after Russ had left. Their contact developed further when Hawker, a conscientious objector during the war, worked at Francesca Allinson's farm. But then Hawker married and had children, and with this altera-tion in his circumstances, he and Tippett saw nothing of each other until after the break-up of the marriage several years later.

Having decided to leave Morley College in 1951, Tippett agreed to join his mother in a large, leaky, tumbledown manor, Tidebrook, in Wadhurst, Sussex. She was in a position, after the death of Tippett's father in 1944, to contribute most of the cost of purchasing it. Karl Hawker also came to live there. Tippett invited the cockney family of a young conscientious objector he had assisted at a tribunal some years earlier to move in with them and look after the domestic tasks – cooking, cleaning and so on. They all ate together in the kitchen and thus, more by accident than by design, Tippett seemed to have found the kind of extended working-class family atmosphere of which he had always dreamt.

There was nevertheless ample discord, especially between the lifestyles of the composer and his mother. She kept all the windows open in winter. He wanted them closed against the cold, and built roaring fires. She kept her part of the garden in fastidious order. He allowed his to run wild. She had long been a vegetarian. He liked a varied diet. She was much influenced by the ideas of Rudolf Steiner and took to faith-healing. Now in her seventies, she also began painting, imbuing all her efforts with religious symbolism. Disconcertingly, also, she maintained a belief in laxatives, alarming her son by sometimes mixing them into the main course for dinner when they had guests.

Karl Hawker, meanwhile, found that living with so overwhelming and creatively self-centred figure as Tippett inhibited his own activities as a painter. He went for short periods to London, taking refuge in part-time teaching there. Unsure as to whether or not he really was gay, he went to John Layard for analysis. At Tidebrook, he also lived separately in an upper room. Tippett's mother found his neurotic behaviour hard to take. She also made clear her disapproval of the homosexual relationship between him and her son. Matters were not helped when the cockney family started to make insinuating remarks to the effect that they knew what was going on and might take advantage (in those days, blackmail was always one of the risks of homosexuality); so Tippett asked them to leave.

Into this curious country commune came numerous visitors of some artistic or intellectual repute, such as Walton and his wife, Aaron Copland, the young Luigi Nono and Edward Sackville-West. Paul Dienes, his wife having left him and gone to America, was now seriously ill with heart trouble: at Tippett's invitation, he came to Tidebrook and spent the last six months of his life there. At the same time, Tippett was himself becoming a ubiquitous figure in metropolitan artistic circles. During the war he had been introduced by Edward Sackville-West to Edith Sitwell and had set to music her poem 'The Weeping Babe', for a BBC radio programme. After the war, he sometimes joined her entourage, mingling with Osbert Sitwell, Stephen Spender and others.

More of a kindred spirit was the Russian émigré, Anna Kallin. She produced a number of Tippett's talks for the BBC Third Programme, most notably a series planned as an extended tribute to Schoenberg, who had died in in 1951. Tippett's prominence as a broadcaster in the 1950s led to his being invited by the editor of the *Observer*, Michael Astor, to contribute a regular weekly column: he turned down the offer, for the usual reason that it would have distracted him from composition. He did, however, in 1952 write for the paper a series of five articles entitled 'The Birth of an Opera',[1] discussing the conception and formulation of *The Midsummer Marriage*, and he contributed articles very occasionally thereafter.

To a limited extent, Tippett also began to move in musical circles abroad. He attended the first performance of *A Child of Our Time* in Brussels and went to Hungary to conduct it there in 1948. The following year he returned to Budapest as a member of the jury for a string quartet composition, and in 1950, after attending the Vienna première of *A Child of Our Time*, he continued on to Warsaw to be one of the judges for violin pieces written for the Wieniawski competition.

But his most significant contact abroad was with the Swiss conductor Paul Sacher.[2] At his suggestion, Tippett turned the four Ritual Dances from Acts II and III of *The Midsummer Marriage* into a concert suite, which Sacher conducted in Basle in February, 1953 – two years before the opera itself received its première. Sacher commissioned another piece from him for the Basle Chamber Orchestra and was perhaps disappointed when Tippett turned up with the lightweight *Divertimento on Sellinger's Round*, the second of whose five movements had already been written and performed the previous year, as Tippett's contribution to a 'collective' set of variations on *Sellinger's Round* for the Aldeburgh Festival. Through Sacher he received invitations to conduct in Switzerland, directing there not only *A Child of Our Time*, but Purcell's *Dido and Aeneas*, sung in Italian.

While Tippett was gradually achieving recognition at home and abroad, his compositions were vulnerable to charges of intellectual pretentiousness and excessive technical demands as regards performance. In the 1950s, such charges were legion. Ernest Ansermet, conducting the BBC Symphony Orchestra in 1952 in a performance of Symphony No. 1, wrote to say the slow movement was just 'paper music', with no harmonic relations between its ground bass and variations.

As Tippett was finishing *The Midsummer Marriage*, he received a commission to write a piece to celebrate the tercentary in 1953 of the birth of Corelli, with a guaranteed second performance at the Promenade Concerts in London the same year. The outcome was his *Fantasia Concertante on a Theme of Corelli*. Sargent was due to conduct the first performance, but withdrew because he thought the work overburdened with notes. Sargent told Howard Hartog that he was determined 'to get the intellectuals out of music' and, when Tippett took over the première himself, made slighting remarks at a press conference about composers conducting their own works. Thus a cloud of scepticism hung over the work for more than a decade, despite its advocacy by Hans Schmidt-Isserstedt (who had made a great impact in 1949, conducting the Hamburg Radio Orchestra in the Concerto for Double String Orchestra). But from the mid-sixties onwards the *Corelli Fantasia* became one of Tippett's most popular, widely performed and most recorded works.

Denigration of Tippett reached a climax with the first production of *The Midsummer Marriage* at Covent Garden in January 1955. Many fell in love with the music, though only a limited number were able to grasp its dramatic significance. The press had a field day. Beforehand they made much of the inability of the singers to understand the plot, even attributing to them expressions of disbelief which they had not uttered. The obscurity of the opera was satirized. 'Not since Salvador Dali tried to introduce a flying hippopotamus into the cast of Strauss's *Salome*,' wrote James Thomas in the *News Chronicle*, 'has the Royal Opera House had such a baffled cast on its hands as the one which will launch Michael Tippett's *The Midsummer Marriage* into the world tomorrow night.'[3]

Condemnatory reviews abounded, mostly focusing on the libretto: the composer later observed that since it was in English, most of the critics thought they could have written something better, or at the very least ignored the fact that it was written to be sung rather than read as literature. Ernest Newman in the *Sunday Times* actually admitted that he had written his review before hearing a note of the music and pronounced himself 'unable to make head or tail of Michael Tippett's opera'.[4] But he admitted subsequently that 'there is so much first-rate music in it that it is painful to contemplate the possibility of it not becoming a success.'[5] *The Times*'s critic wrote (anonymously) that Tippett had 'overloaded his allegory ... The force behind the conception of the opera had been too much for his control.' Martin Cooper in the *Daily Telegraph* called the libretto 'an extraordinary jumble of verbal images and stage mumbo-jumbo',[6] while Cecil Smith in the *Daily Express* declared it to be 'one of the worst in the 350 year old history of opera'.[7] (The same writer later wrote, however, in *Musical America*, that '[The music] reveals Tippett as a composer of first stature ... The work as a whole grows cumulatively and possesses the quality of apparent inevitablity that one discovers only in the work of a top-grade creative musician ... however harshly some people may scoff at Tippett's libretto, his opera has established him in a single stroke as a composer of no less stature than Britten and Walton.')[8] The opera was regarded more sympathetically by Peter Heyworth,[9] in the *Observer* and William Glock in *The Score*.[10] An appreciative and perceptive letter (dated 24 February 1955) also reached the composer from the musicologist, opera historian and translator

Edward J. Dent, who went to all the performances:

> ...The musical world seems, as far as I hear from the conversa-
> tion, to have made up its mind that your opera is a great work,
> though most of them are bewildered by the plot ...
>
> The general symbolism of the opera is pretty straight-
> forward to anyone who knows *The Magic Flute* and it is
> interesting to me to see that *you* in 1955 can take it for
> granted that everybody does – whereas in 1900 or earlier it
> would have been incomprehensible: the *Zauberflöte* in those
> days was *Il Flauto Magico* and the silliest nonsense ever
> put together. The obscurity of your opera is due to the mix-
> up of several different symbolisms, though you may
> maintain that they are all the same in ultimate reality. The
> general background seems to be modern English and English
> country; how you get a *Greek* temple there is incompre-
> hensible. Roman, yes, or Stonehenge, even Phoenician in
> Cornwall, but Greek in England? Never mind; we'll call it
> 'antique'. And I can accept the staircase to the stars and the
> chromium grating to the cellar, but who is 'Joan' who is
> once mentioned? Sutherland [who sang Jenifer in the
> original cast], Cross [the soprano Joan Cross, who sang in
> many Britten premières] ... Someone suggested that she was
> Mlle d'Arc[11] – if so, we have also Catholic symbolism, and
> in Act III Egyptian (Mme Sosostris) and Hindu, and possibly
> Anglican at the end with what sounds like a suggestion of
> a V.W. hymn-tune hinting at *Pilgrim's Progress*.

Dent thought the opera too long: 'In Act I the sticky places are at
the start (Mozart nearly always made that mistake) and after
Mark and Jenifer meet in their new clothes ... You will perhaps
remake Act III and I hope make a better job of it than Verdi did
with his rehashed older operas. But I expect you will find it more
agreeable to write an entirely new opera on an entirely different
sort of subject.'

There was a general consensus, then and for many years afterwards, that *The Midsummer Marriage* was too long. From the outset, the composer sanctioned cuts in the dance music of Act II and almost all productions have made cuts – approved or not – in either Act I or Act III, or both. Only when the opera was presented absolutely uncut for the first time, at Covent Garden in 1996, was this opinion reversed to some degree, even if doubts remain regarding certain episodes in Act III.

Tippett later felt that in his libretto he specified the staging requirements in too much detail: since then he has given only general indications to the producer and designer, entrusting the rest to their expertise. The production team for the first production was not ideal. Taking the view (on Eliot's advice) that contemporary opera should relate to the contemporary theatre, Tippett had asked for Peter Brook. But the then General Administrator at Covent Garden, David Webster, procrastinated and after many delays and failures of communication, it was belatedly assigned to a house-producer, Christopher West, who then had insufficient time to do it justice: hence the general view that Act III had been static and unsatisfactory. The designer, Barbara Hepworth, supplied a neo-classic temple which was impressive but impractical to light. She imagined that the holes through which the lovers disappeared would be visible, but the chorus in front interfered with this. Her abstract trees for Act II and the immobile temple itself took up badly needed stage space. English opera audiences in the 1950s were far more reluctant than now to accept a high degree of symbolic content. They anticipated some new version of Puccini-an *verismo*, so Walton's *Troilus and Cressida*, first seen the previous year, was far more to their taste.

Although there was a revival of the production in 1957, with some new cast members, the opera was still regarded as unwieldy and 'too preoccupied with the expression of transcendental imponderables ... The work scarcely belongs in the theatre.' Nearly forty years later, after it had been staged by other companies in the UK, Europe, America and Australia, and received a TV presentation on Channel 4, a review of the twelfth production (Covent Garden's third) of *The Midsummer Marriage* could still be headlined 'Staging the unstageable.'[12]

When, in 1963, William Glock, newly appointed Controller of Music at the BBC, organized a studio performance conducted by Norman Del Mar, using some of the singers from the original cast (such as Richard Lewis as Mark) and some newcomers (including the young Janet Baker as Sosostris), attitudes towards *The Midsummer Marriage* began to change. Colin Davis heard it and proposed to Covent Garden that there should be a new production. This took place in 1968: and if the staging by Ande Anderson failed to tap the imaginative richness of the piece, it gained for it a new following and Davis's conducting of it was a revelation. After a revival of the production, Davis and the Covent Garden forces were able to make a recording for Philips which was a best-seller not only in the UK, but in America, selling 3,750 copies there in the first week it became available. On 25 September 1984, the status of the opera was secured at least nationally when a British postage stamp was issued, commemorating the British Council: it had on it a picture of a young man playing the violin against the background of a page from the score of *The Midsummer Marriage*.

In the remainder of the 1950s, further troubles lay ahead for the composer. Tippett's Piano Concerto, commissioned by the City of Birmingham Symphony Orchestra, was declared unplayable by the appointed soloist, Julius Katchen. Fortunately, Louis Kentner was free to replace him, playing it from memory at the première in 1956. Tippett's Second Symphony had a more dramatic launch, the performance breaking down during the first movement and having to be re-started. The conductor, Sir Adrian Boult, told the audience it was entirely his own fault. An official letter to *The Times* a few weeks later[13] implied that the composer was to blame. What really put the performance at risk and made it generally more insecure than might otherwise have been the case was the attitude of the leader of the BBC Symphony Orchestra, Paul Beard. He insisted on having the string parts re-barred in a conventional way, so that rhythmic patterns were not grouped across the bar-lines in the way the composer had written them. Beard made things harder for the players. Tippett consulted Barbirolli, who was hoping to conduct it with the Hallé Orchestra, and he, a string-player, discerned no basic problem in the original notation. Tippett's Piano Concerto and Second Symphony later won acceptance, when a younger generation of soloists, conductors and orchestras resolved to observe the composer's directions and meet his technical challenges.

For all this to happen to a composer already in his mid-fifties and, to some extent, a known figure, might have deterred him from embarking on further major projects – indeed, it might even have been a crushing blow. But Tippett bore it all with cool, imperturbable good humour. He said later that if he survived it was only because he had 'the right mixture of patience and arrogance'. Amidst all the hubbub he was in fact moving towards some radical changes in his musical thinking. Foreshadowed in the Second Symphony, these now came to the fore with his second opera, *King Priam*.

Dent had shrewdly observed that Tippett might prefer to go on and write a new opera, rather than revising his first one. Exactly so. After *The Midsummer Marriage*, Tippett started sketching a masque-like composition, which he called *The Windrose*. When offered a commission from the Koussevitzky Foundation, Tippett thought it might be possible to turn it into a choral piece. But the lure of the theatre was too strong and it soon took definite shape as an opera. Consultations with two distinguished theatre-directors, Peter Brook (who pleaded with him to take his subject-matter from an existing story rather than inventing one afresh himself) and Gunther Rennert (who urged him to distil the story-line down to such a basic form, that it could virtually be written on a postcard), then a meeting with the writer on classical history Gertrude Levy[14] led him to extract his situations and characters from Homer: hence *King Priam*.

The première of *King Priam*, again by the Royal Opera was a high profile affair, as it took place in the Coventry Theatre in the context of a special festival, in June 1962, that celebrated the opening of the new Coventry Cathedral, which had been bombed during the war. (The following night saw the première there also of Britten's *War Requiem*.) This time Tippett had the kind of producer and designer he wanted – Sam Wanamaker and Sean Kenny, both of them experienced in the worlds of film and theatre. At David Webster's instigation, they actually trained the Covent Garden lighting staff in more advanced techniques, and the results benefited the presentation of the new opera considerably. There was some unpleasant back-stage intrigue involving the conductor John Pritchard, who made a number of cuts and re-scorings without consulting with the composer, let alone obtaining his approval. But the brilliance and splendour of the production, allied to superb singing and orchestral playing, gave the opera a magnificent send-off.

If many professed mystification at the plot of *The Midsummer Marriage*, there was no excuse with *King Priam*, for its story-line, based on Homer, was crystal clear and recapitulated many times. Criticism now focused on its hard-hitting, abrasive musical idiom, which entailed breaking up the pit orchestra into a multiplicity of ensembles and soloists, and a predominantly declamatory rather than lyrical vocal style. Not everyone seemed to appreciate the relevance of Tippett's mosaic-like musical forms to his Brechtian handling of the presentation. But at least there was no more questioning of the composer's basic competence and craftsmanship. Later, *King Priam* came to be understood as marking a significant sea-change in Tippett's development as a composer.

3
Brave New Worlds

Tippett's stature as a composer was now attracting official recognition. He was awarded a CBE in 1959; a knighthood was to follow in 1966, after which academic and public awards arrived with increasing frequency, though not the financial prizes that would have given him absolute security and independence. He nevertheless continued after *King Priam* with projects, such as the choral composition, *The Vision of St Augustine*, that were unlikely to earn him a fortune but which satisfied his artistic aspirations. Right the way through into his late eighties, he resisted invitations to produce concertos and other works that were tailor-made for specific artists, preferring to create music out of a deeply felt inner obligation. Moreover, he never agreed to deadlines for new works which he was not absolutely sure of meeting. In all cases, the individual artists, orchestras, ensembles and opera companies received scores from him well in advance, so that they had ample time to study the music and absorb it fully. Rarely, after the mid-1940s did he revise or re-write works, other than in smallish details that facilitated performance. Noting Eliot's comment that, for himself as a poet, 'the words come last', Tippett only began writing down the notes when he had a clear concept of the structure and character of the piece in question. He invariably composed straight into full score: and he always started at the beginning of the piece, continuing until he reached the end – then he stopped. Taken overall, this kind of compositional procedure is fairly unusual.

In some respects, Tippett's lifestyle did change. After a decade in the isolation of the Wadhurst manor, he decided to move to a small country town: thus, in 1960, he took over from Bryan Fisher, David Ayerst's brother-in-law, the rental of a beautiful Georgian house owned by the Methuen family, in Corsham,

Wiltshire. He began living there with Karl Hawker in 1960. His mother meanwhile moved to a cottage in Maldon in Essex, where she could be close to her elder son and receive proper care during her declining years. The back of the Corsham house had a lawn which they levelled out so that it could be used for croquet, at which both of them were quite accomplished. Beyond lay Corsham Park, originally designed by Capability Brown; thus, after a morning's composition and lunch, Tippett regularly went out there for a long walk across the fields – a routine he followed regularly right into his mid-eighties.

Nearby also was the Bath Academy of Art, where Henry Boys, a friend of William Glock's and a notable writer on contemporary music, was teaching. Tippett became involved there, officially as a music adviser and external examiner, unofficially establishing close friendships with some of the staff and students, who often came round for dinner, television and games of mah-jong, or joined him on visits to the theatre. Other visitors included old friends like the Ayersts, the Arts Council's Literature Director, Eric Walter White and his wife, and the composer Priaulx Rainier; and newcomers such as the rising stars of the postwar English avant-garde, Peter Maxwell Davies, Alexander Goehr and Harrison Birtwistle. The latter trio organized two summer schools focused on contemporary music at Wardour Castle, in 1965 and 1966. Tippett once joined in a memorable seminar there at which all four of them discussed the operas they were currently engaged in writing.

Occasionally, Tippett went to London, continuing as a member of the music committee of the British Council and serving also on the advisory panel to the BBC. He still found time also for such extra-musical concerns as the Peace Pledge Union, to which he had been elected President in 1957.

In 1965, Tippett's sixtieth birthday was celebrated modestly with a Morley College concert of chamber music and songs – including the last performance Pears and Britten were to give of *Boyhood's End* – and some BBC broadcasts. At an Arts Council party, he was presented with a special copy of *King Lear* with illustrations by Kokoschka; it was signed by all those who had contributed to the cost. Faber & Faber also published a valuable symposium on Tippett, edited by Ian Kemp,[1] which was the first book to examine all his music to date in some detail.

More significantly, that summer, Tippett went for the first time to America, as guest composer at the music festival in Aspen, Colorado. The invitation came through Alfred Deller, who persuaded the manager of the festival, Jim Cain, to present *A Child of Our Time* there. The visit proved to be something of a watershed in Tippett's life and work. He immediately fell in love with the canyons, mesas and deserts of Arizona. Later, he became equally excited about the big cities. The landscapes and polyglot culture of America thereafter filled his dreams and stimulated his imagination. He steeped himself in American literature and history. Moreover, in the candour and openness of young Americans he found an antidote to English class distinction and sexual hypocrisy. America became for him a 'newfoundland of the spirit' that released him both creatively and humanly. Lorca, going to live in New York in the 1930s, had a similar experience, coming to terms with his gay orientation and discovering a new poetic language.[2]

Tippett was currently at work on his third opera, *The Knot Garden*. Almost certainly, this would have turned out differently had he not visited America. Its stylized interplay of characters might well have remained at the level of Bloomsbury-ish charades. Tippett now provided them with a well-defined context in modern urban culture: moreover, the opera became a far more explicit examination of sexuality, openly featuring gay and bisexual characters. The vernacular element in Tippett's musical style – stimulated particularly in the 1930s by his interest in jazz and blues, but dormant since the Negro spirituals of *A Child of Our Time* – also came back now into the foreground. The electric guitar and jazz-style percussion were both prominent in his scoring for *The Knot Garden* – even more so in his subsequent operas, *The Ice Break* and *New Year*.

Tippett had recently become closely associated with the Leicestershire Schools Symphony Orchestra, as guest conductor and artistic adviser.[3] He wrote one work for them, *The Shires Suite* (1965–70) – a kind of résumé of most of the idioms he had explored to date, even embodying quotations from *The Knot Garden*, then in progress. Tippett's concert programmes with the orchestra often focused on American music – e.g. Copland's *Quiet City* and Charles Ives's *Three Places in New England* – and Ives, in particular, was to influence not only *The Shires Suite*, but more substantial compositions like his Symphony No. 3.

When Tippett went to America, he found that his music was already known there, largely through recordings, broadcast especially on classical music radio stations on university campuses. He immediately made many friends and contacts who were keen for him to return. Copland introduced Tippett to a New York agent, Herbert Barrett, who along with his sculptress wife, Betty, was to become one of his closest friends in the States. In 1968, Barrett secured for him his first conducting engagement in the States, replacing Stravinsky (who was ill) in some concerts with the St Louis Symphony Orchestra: he conducted them in an English programme including his own Symphony No. 2. Further such engagements followed.

In the course of the next few decades, Tippett's own music became widely performed across America. The main launch-pad was Boston. From 1972 onwards, when Colin Davis began to appear regularly as principal guest conductor with the Boston Symphony Orchestra, he introduced most of Tippett's major compositions one by one. The first large-scale celebration of his music in the USA came, in fact, in 1974, as a result of the coincidence of the US première of Tippett's Third Symphony, conducted by Davis in Boston, followed by a performance conducted by the composer in Chicago, along with a production of *The Knot Garden* at Northwestern University, Illinois. Buoyed by the success of their *Midsummer Marriage* album, Philips used the opportunity to do a lot of publicity which raised Tippett's profile in the States considerably. Since then there have been major festivals of his work in most of the major US cities.

Another outcome of Tippett's success was that many of his major compositions thereafter were American commissions: the first was his Symphony No.4, written for the Chicago Symphony Orchestra; others (such as his fifth opera, *New Year*, and his final orchestral composition, *The Rose Lake*) were international co-commissions including an American organization. Not only now was there a considerable following for Tippett amongst young American musicians and music lovers (such as the four students who turned up in Chicago in 1974 wearing T-shirts bearing the slogan 'Turn on to Tippett'), but his music was finding its way into the general repertoire of orchestras and concert-giving organizations.

Back in the UK, Tippett was becoming acknowledged as a force to be reckoned with in the operatic domain. But he continued to write like an avant-garde playwright, rather than as a conventional opera composer satisfying a conservative audience with predictable routines. Unnervingly for some, each new piece explored new dramaturgical territory. In both *The Knot Garden* and *The Ice Break* – each premièred at Covent Garden – Tippett deployed techniques from cinema and television, doing away with cumbersome scenic transitions and cross-cutting forwards and backwards in time. The music that articulated such manipulations of time, place and action, was free-ranging and embodied a wide gamut of stylistic references and quotations.

A comparable freedom in the texts brought a chorus of critic-ism from those who found Tippett's use of slang distasteful and his fondness for quotation gimmicky. Many were also bewildered by the replacement of a story-line in *The Knot Garden* in normal chronological sequence with plays within plays. In fact, the cryptic compression of Tippett's libretto enabled it admirably to fulfil its function as a series of 'gestures for music' – in this case, often very fast-moving music. Steeped, above all, in back-references to

Shakespeare's *The Tempest*, *The Knot Garden* sports one of the most successful, indeed virtuoso pieces of libretto-writing to be found in any contemporary opera.

Once more, Tippett was lucky in securing an apt production team for this opera, thus ensuring a successful launch at Covent Garden. Using miles of rope, which imaginative lighting and film could transform into a garden or labyrinth, the designer Tim O'Brien contrived the most magical stage-pictures for the constant metamorphoses within the action: and Peter Hall was in his element directing the game-playing of the seven characters. *The Knot Garden* is essentially an intimate opera whose impact could have been less potent in a large theatre like Covent Garden had not Hall built a ramp out across the orchestra pit so that the characters could come forward and communicate closely with the audience.

After its Covent Garden première in 1970 and revival in 1972, and the first US production two years later, the opera had, however, to wait until 1984 to be staged again: and then it was taken on tour by Opera Factory London Sinfonietta using a reduced version of the score prepared by the present writer. This version seemed to give the work a new lease of life, for there have since been eight further productions – three in London (two of them by Royal Academy and Royal College of Music students) one in Gelsenkirchen, one in Melbourne, Australia, one in Paris (in French translation) and two in America (again by students in Cincinatti and Boston, respectively).

Living near Bath, Tippett was an obvious choice to take over as artistic director of the festival there which, under Yehudi Menuhin, had come near to financial ruin. He helped put it back on its feet, broadened its scope and potential audience appeal – notably by including a folk-festival element with Led Zeppelin that attracted young people in their hordes – and dispelling its atmosphere of elitism and social exclusivity. At his own insistence, he retained the position for only five years (1969–74).

In the 1940s and 50s Tippett had been a champion of the BBC

Third Programme[4] and gave many radio talks, some of which were published in 1959 in a collection entitled *Moving into Aquarius*.[5] Now, in the 1960s and 70s he was increasingly drawn into television, making a number of appearances in arts programmes (notably in Huw Wheldon's pioneering *Monitor* series), as well as becoming a keen follower of all kinds of TV entertainment – detective series, soap operas, quiz games, Westerns etc. He was himself the subject of some major documentaries. By far the most memorable were the two directed for the BBC by Mischa Scorer – *Poets in a Barren Age* (1971) and *Songs of Experience* (1991).

In 1977, to coincide with the Covent Garden première of his fourth opera, *The Ice Break*, Colin Davis brought together a group of Tippett's friends to organize a retrospective exhibition, *A Man of Our Time*, documenting the composer's life and achievements. Subsequently, Schott arranged for a travelling version of the exhibition to be devised and in this form – constantly updated to include new material – it has been seen all over the world. This exhibition, together with a sudden proliferation of recordings of Tippett's music – an amazing turn-around after the dearth of recordings throughout the fifties and sixties – helped disseminate awareness of the composer and his achievements and consolidate his reputation.

Difficulties arose over the production of Tippett's next opera, *The Ice Break*, at Covent Garden in 1977, as Peter Hall – originally scheduled to direct – had to withdraw after he accepted an invitation to run the National Theatre. At first, Harold Prince (whose New York production of *Pacific Overtures* Tippett much admired) was invited to replace him, but in the end it was once more Sam Wanamaker who took over. Up against time, Wanamaker added dancers to the singing chorus and brought in the choreographer Walter Raines. Ralph Koltai's production very nearly featured holography but, because of workshop errors, the technological ingredient was limited to laser beams. The first performances attracted full houses and respectful criticism, much of which was reversed a couple of years later when the production was revived. After another production in Kiel, Germany, the following year, and an idiosyncratic staging under Sarah Caldwell's direction in Boston (1979), where it was the best-seller of the season, *The Ice Break* then disappeared into limbo.

In retrospect, the composer has felt that he may have over-estimated the speed with which the chorus could be moved around, given the absence of any connecting music between scenes. Critical opinion, as usual focusing on the libretto and denigrating its use of contemporary slang, has tended to dismiss the work as a faded documentary about sixties race riots and flower power. To do so, of course, is to neglect the *non*-journalistic element in the work.

The shrewdest observation was made by the producer Peter Sellars, a great enthusiast for Tippett's operas, who prepared for Opera North a production of *King Priam*, which was scheduled for 1985 but then dropped in favour of *The Midsummer Marriage*. Sellars remarked, *à propos The Ice Break* and *The Knot Garden*, that he would prefer to direct these in future decades when they would have 'dated' sufficiently. Certainly, as happened with *King Priam* in the 1980s, a recording a decade later of *The Ice Break* – once more with the London Sinfonietta, conducted by David Atherton – prompted a revaluation of the opera, revealing new perspectives that might one day prompt a new stage realization.

From the mid-1960s onwards, Tippett had become a prominent public figure, a face known not just from appearances in the concert-hall and opera house, but on television and record-sleeves. He had difficulty balancing the demands made upon him against the privacy and isolation necessary for him to compose. Increasingly, in reaction to excessive public exposure and uncritical adulation and ovations, he suffered a psychosomatic stomach sickness that was often acute and caused him to cancel engagements at short notice. Apart from a heart fibrillation which began in the mid-1970s and which is controlled by drugs, his health nevertheless remained good and his energy astonishing until he reached his early eighties. His biggest problem lay with his eyesight. This was never particularly good, but by 1970, macular dystrophy – a disease of the retina, inherited matrilineally and pronounced incurable – was diagnosed. It became immensely difficult for him to write down notes accurately and read with precision. Now he had to compose onto very large-size manuscript paper, using special magnifying glasses for reading; he also cut down on public speaking and conducting engagements.

Towards the end of the 1960s, the imminent construction of a multi-storey car park at the back of Tippett's Corsham home and the need for greater privacy, led him to think about moving house again. When his mother died in 1969, Tippett was left just enough money for him to be able to purchase a modern Colt-style frame-house, built by its one previous owner in an enclave in the middle of farmland near Calne, in Wiltshire. Known as Nocketts, it had breathtaking views across rolling countryside, and every photographer, TV interviewer or documentary-maker who visited thereafter took full advantage. Nocketts also boasted an indoor swimming pool, which Tippett continued to use right up into his mid-eighties until a fire caused by a defective heating thermostat caused it to burn down.

Tippett and Hawker moved to Nocketts in 1970, but by this time their relationship had greatly deteriorated and although Hawker continued to some extent as Tippett's secretary and travelling companion, they tended to live independent lives under the same roof and take their holidays separately. Hawker's hostility towards a number of the composer's friends deterred them from visiting. To a limited degree, Tippett took refuge in conducting engagements abroad. In the end, he contrived a legal separation and financial settlement and Hawker left to live in London; in 1984, however, he committed suicide.

From the mid-1970s onwards, Tippett's social life blossomed. The Ayersts were now not only regular visitors, but companions on at least one holiday each year. Anna Kallin, elderly and *toute grande dame*, visited once a year and was treated to the best

Russian caviar. Alan Bush and his wife Nancy also paid an annual visit to debate Marxism. Tippett enjoyed too the company of the Oxford-based scholar, Frederick J. Sternfeld and his wife Sophie, deriving great stimulation from their discussions about Goethe, Shakespeare, early opera and the artistic milieu in general. Creative work still required a life of isolation, so much of his socialising was done by telephone and regular calls were thus made to the Ayersts, the Sternfelds and Michael Tillett (his musical amanuensis since Morley College days – also an amusing, warm-hearted character who cheered him up when he was exhausted by the day's work). For some years, Tippett's relationship with his brother and the rest of his relatives had remained somewhat distant. Now, he managed to mend the fences, somewhat, and once or twice a year exchanged visits. Tippett also visited his cousin Phyllis a few times in East Berlin in the years immediately preceding her death (in 1989) and resumed something of the ardour of their youthful friendship, despite her total allegiance to Marxism.

Tippett now acquired many new friends from a much younger generation. Amongst them were the latest batch of artists who were championing his music – for example, the Lindsay Quartet; the conductor, Andrew Parrott; the pianist Paul Crossley and his friend Michael Vyner (who, as artistic director of the London Sinfonietta, was responsible for many tours of Tippett's music, birthday concerts and, in 1986, an entire Britten/Tippett Festival). Young composers beat a path to his doorstep. With some of them – Steve Martland, Mark-Anthony Turnage, Rupert Bawden and David Haines, for instance – he established close friendships. Many of the new names in his entourage were from other disciplines – such as the distinguished immunologist Tony Davies and his physiotherapist wife Agneta; and a young architect, Graham Modlen, who regularly took him on adventure holidays.

Tippett's travels yielded a host of new friends: Canadians, such as the writer Timothy Findley, and Jeff Anderson, director of several radio and television programmes involving the composer; Australians, such as the composer Nigel Butterley and the multi-talented musician Philip Griffin who made for Tippett the dazzling psychedelic trousers that he wore at the 1991 Prom performance of *Byzantium*: and Americans of all ages and sexes.

While Tippett never made a secret of his homosexual inclinations, he never allowed Nocketts to become a gay ghetto. Always he preferred an open, tolerant social environment. For some people, Nocketts nevertheless occasionally resembled the psychological knot garden of his eponymous opera, wherein one encountered a changing kaleidoscope of marital tensions and sexual proclivities, the host finding it difficult to resist playing Mangus: however, cheerfulness and frivolity broke into all this considerably more than it did in the opera.

In the mid-1970s, after Karl Hawker had left, the present writer took over as the composer's main assistant, coordinating both his personal and professional activities and acting as travel companion. The arrangement was reinforced by the establishment, late in 1979, of an actual Tippett office, firstly with Christopher Senior, then two years later, Nicholas Wright, in charge. From June 1982 onwards, the main celebrations and performances of Tippett's music, his public appearances, travels, recordings and publications were – and continue to be – chronicled in a twice-yearly newsletter, *Tippett in Focus*, circulated free of charge to the main musical organizations, as well as to thousands of fans worldwide. With the office taking care of all correspondence and negotiations, and acting as a buffer between himself and the press, Tippett was able to give undiluted attention to major works, the first of them his largest concert-hall work, *The Mask of Time*. Commissioned by the Boston Symphony Orchestra, its world première in 1984 (conducted by Colin Davis) and European première at the Proms the same year (conducted by Andrew Davis) – later relayed on BBC TV – brought the composer more acclaim than almost any piece he had written so far.

International travel was now an integral part of Tippett's lifestyle. In 1975, he attended a performance of *A Child of Our Time*
in Zambia, which involved a mixture (roughly 50–50) of ex-patriate
Europeans, local Zambian choirs and members of the State Police
Band. In 1978 he took his first extended break from composition
in fifty years, undertaking a world tour that took in holidays in Bali
and Java (where the sound of gamelan orchestras began to colour
his ideas for a forthcoming Triple Concerto), followed by
professional engagments in Australia (including the première there
of *A Child of Our Time* at the Perth Festival and *The Midsummer
Marriage* at the Adelaide Festival), a holiday in Hawaii, ending
with him conducting *A Child of Our Time* in Los Angeles and
attending a performance of 'Ritual Dances' in New York.

He undertook another world tour in 1984. This time his music
was featured in the Hong Kong Festival, in Japan, Shanghai and
the Philippines, then in Sydney, Brisbane, Melbourne and Canberra;
a vacation in Tahiti preceded his arrival in Boston for the première
of *The Mask of Time*. In 1985, he went to Brazil for a month,
attending concerts of his music in Rio de Janeiro, and the first
Brazilian performance of *A Child of Our Time* in São Paulo, and
conducting his Piano Concerto there, but also spending time on a
vacation that took him to the Amazon jungle, to Salvador and
Brasilia.

Travel certainly fuelled Tippett's imagination. There is little
doubt, for instance, that his visits to the Far West of America – to
the canyon country and Monument Valley – and to the Mayan and
Aztec pyramids in Mexico provided him with concrete
manifestations of those cosmic concepts that formed the backcloth
to *The Mask of Time*. Winter holidays in Jamaica, Antigua, Tobago
and other Caribbean islands brought him close to the West Indian
culture that offered fresh vernacular material for his fifth opera,
New Year. Right into his eighties and early nineties, Tippett retained
a passion for holidays in exotic places, relishing both the risks and
the stimulation of such places as Eastern Turkey, Thailand and Sri
Lanka. The last trip that was directly fruitful in compositional terms

was one he undertook with Graham Modlen to Senegal, late in 1990. By accident, there, they arrived at midday at a small lake known locally as Le Lac Rose. Just as they arrived, its waters were, under the impact of the sun, turning from whitish green to whitish pink. 'The sight of it,' Tippett later wrote, 'triggered a profound disturbance within me; the sort of disturbance which told me that the new orchestral work had begun.'[6] For *The Rose Lake*, the composition that developed out of this experience, Tippett has received every conceivable accolade, except (so far) an award for services to Senegalese tourism.

Tippett's own accounts of his travels – from his early schooldays to his expeditions late in life to far-flung places – are one of the chief attractions of his autobiography, *Those Twentieth Century Blues*, which appeared in 1991. As with many of Tippett's major compositions, the book was loved and hated in about equal measure. For the most part, writers with no conceivable axes to grind – personal, artistic or whatever – and especially those writing for the popular or provincial press, welcomed it. The diatribes ranged from the usual attacks on the Tippett's taste for colourful clothes and sneakers to one all-out onslaught, by the Cambridge University-based composer Robin Holloway, ruthlessly demolishing everything Tippett had written since 1960.[7]

Central to the book was its inclusion of a large selection of Tippett's dreams – his earliest nightmare concerning the threats posed by a Biting Lady lurking outside the house; his most recent, conjuring up a blissful new home-life surrounded by happy young people; and the long sequence of dreams he wrote down and analysed just before the outbreak of the Second World War. Peter Heyworth, who had begun his career for the *Observer* with a profile of the composer, shortly before his death submitted a review of Tippett's autobiography in which he remarked that '[the dreams'] relevance to his creative life became increasingly evident. In particular, the series of works that were to establish his reputation during and after the war and to culminate in *The Midsummer Marriage* ... hove into view. The therapy had worked...'[8]

After *The Mask of Time* was completed, late in 1982, few expected Tippett to go on producing further major works. For a year or so, in fact, he confined himself to smaller-scale pieces, such as *The Blue Guitar*, commissioned by Julian Bream, and a piece for brass band, *Festal Brass with Blues*. With a major world tour ahead of him in early 1984 and eightieth birthday celebrations coming up the following year, it would, in any case, have been difficult for him to concentrate on a project of great dimensions. But his extended, five-movement Piano Sonata No. 4 hinted that there were more big pieces to come: and its première performances by Paul Crossley, first in Los Angeles, then in London, certainly ensured that the eightieth birthday concerts and festivals were more than just another retrospective.

Significantly, it was America, rather than Britain, that launched the celebrations of both his eightieth and eighty-fifth birthdays. Two of the original T-shirted Tippett fans from Texas, Steve Aechternacht and Victor Marshall, were by now in key administrative positions at the Houston and Dallas Symphony Orchestras, respectively. They collaborated, thus, in planning two successive weeks of concerts at the start of 1995, in which Tippett shared the rostrum with Sergiu Comissiona and James Rives-Jones, respectively, in concerts of his music. He was also fêted on his actual birthday at an official Houston lunch, excerpts from which were broadcast live on local radio, and his honorary Texan status was sealed with the presentation of a superb stetson. Five years later, he appeared in Pittsburgh for eighty-fifth birthday performances of *The Mask of Time*, at the start of a three-month-long tour, most of which was spent in Australia.

In the wake of all this, it was hardly surprising that when Tippett made it known in 1985 that he was contemplating a new opera, there was considerable interest on both sides of the Atlantic. After much negotiation, a tripartite deal was concluded which enabled Houston Opera to give the première in 1989, Glyndebourne to bring the same production to its festival the following summer, then tour it around the UK, after which the BBC could undertake a television production. Virgin also agreed to make a recording and video, but withdrew from the latter around the time of the Houston première. They then withdrew from the sound recording, which was linked to the BBC production, giving less than seven weeks' notice. Cancellation of the project was averted only because of determined advocacy by Dennis Marks and Alan Yentob at BBC TV, who felt that the considerable expense was justified, given that the BBC had never before undertaken a television presentation of a Tippett opera and that if postponed, the project might never see the light of day again.

Meanwhile, in the middle of composing the opera, in 1987, Tippett underwent a major operation for colonic cancer. He recovered miraculously quickly and after a period of recuperation and a short vacation in the Canaries, returned not only to composition but conducting – spending two weeks at an extended Tippett/Debussy festival in Manchester, later going to Stockholm to conduct his Fourth Symphony. The opera was completed on time, a year ahead of its première.

Owing to difficulties in accommodating all the players required in the pit at the smaller of Houston's two theatres, the scoring had to be scaled down, which was not to the advantage of *New Year*. The full orchestration was only heard for the first time when the opera came to Glyndebourne. Peter Hall, who was to direct, arrived late for rehearsals at Houston, because of his involvement in an award-winning Tennessee Williams production in New York. Much of the rehearsal work early on was thus undertaken by the choreographer, Bill T. Jones; and he did much to ensure that the two choruses – one singing and one dancing – were finely merged. *New Year* was a complex opera to put together. It included electro-acoustic effects (such as space-ship music, a speaking computer, a chattering fountain and a groaning lake) which had to be integrated into the general canvas of sonority. Much was achieved in this initial production – and certain cast members, such as Krister St Hill as the delinquent, rapping Donny and Richetta Manager as Regan, iron maiden of the future, made a riveting impact. Audience reaction to this new exploratory opera was, however, tepid. Local criticism, also centred on peripheral aspects of the production, such as the use of cartoon-style captions, rather than subtitles, to lead the audience through the opera, including such jokey irreverences as 'New Year's Eve – y'all have a nice night' – which were considered by some an affront to Texan dignity; (English critics at Glyndebourne responded with equal sniffiness to captions such as 'The picnic's over'). Tippett's new exploratory opera, with its fresh-sounding invention and an almost flawless dramatic craftsmanship made more impact when the work reached Glyndebourne. For most people attending it there, this, the achievement of a composer now in his mid-eighties, seemed quite incredible.

In truth, Tippett was beginning at this time to experience the frailties of old age. If composition was still a labour of love, it was now increasingly a labour – most of his greatest difficulties being caused by deteriorating eyesight. Tippett felt it unlikely also that he could continue forever inventing afresh and saw little point in doing the opposite, i.e. repeating himself. Further compositions were in gestation. Tippett's deep fascination with Yeats reached its apogee in a setting of the poem 'Byzantium' – his second commission from the Chicago Symphony Orchestra. His abiding love for the string quartet and for Beethoven's late quartets inspired yet another work, his fifth for the medium. This was, in fact, his first English commission for many years, the Lindsay Quartet proudly claiming it for their annual chamber music festival in Sheffield. When Colin Davis asked the composer if he might write a new piece for the Tippett ninetieth-birthday festival he was planning with the London Symphony Orchestra at the Barbican Centre, the composer took his time to consider what he might do – as ever not wanting to write a superficial *pièce d'occasion* or rehash of some earlier ideas. Ezra Pound's adage, 'Make it new', remained uppermost in his mind. The experience at Le Lac Rose in Senegal made it seem a possibility. Listening to Solti rehearse the Chicago Symphony

Orchestra in *Byzantium*, the following year, he was so entranced all over again by the inherent brilliance and potential of orchestral sonority that his imagination once more took flight.

Nevertheless, he agonized over the composition of *The Rose Lake*, often collapsing with a mixture of exhaustion and depression, unable to continue. For his doctor, housekeepers and friends, it was a taxing time, boosting his morale and spirits to the end of the piece. The death of David Ayerst in 1992 was, amidst all this, a grievous blow: for Tippett regarded him and his wife Larema (who survived him) as his 'oldest dearest of friends' (as he put it in his dedication of *New Year* to them) and he was to miss him greatly. To make things worse, Tippett's eyesight now made it virtually impossible to see accurately which notes he was writing down. After a while, he gave up trying and brought in Michael Tillett to assist: only the first third or so of the manuscript of *The Rose Lake* is thus in the composer's own hand.

Commissioned jointly by the London, Boston and Toronto Symphony Orchestras, its world première as part of the Barbican's month-long Tippett festival in February 1995 seemed to many the crowning achievement of his late years and an incredibly imaginative and innovatory work for a swansong. Tippett was quite taken aback by the ovations he received both for this work and by the packed audiences that attended this festival. What gave him even greater pleasure, though, were the performances of the work later that year by another splendid British youth orchestra, the Northern Junior Philharmonic, with whom he had recently formed an association.

The premières of Tippett's last three works were not without their hazards. The soprano Jessye Norman, booked well in advance to the give the world première of *Byzantium*, withdrew without explanation three weeks beforehand; Solti told the press that 'from now on, she is on my white list!' She was replaced by Faye Robinson, whose singing of the 'Hiroshima, mon amour' movement from *The Mask of Time* had propelled her into the fore-front of Tippett's vocal interpreters. Not long before the première of the Fifth String Quartet, Peter Cropper, leader of the Lindsay Quartet, suffered a heart attack; fortunately, he recovered in time, so the planned performances went ahead.

Prior to the world première of *The Rose Lake*, there was much debate over the practicality of the parts for three chromatic octaves of roto-toms (plastic-headed drums whose light, sharp sonority Tippett now preferred to the heavier, more resonant timpani). Laid out in a line across the concert platform, these drums occupied a considerable amount of space and the fast passages involved the players in an acrobatic sprint across the stage. In Boston and Toronto, the roto-toms were stacked vertically, but the players were still able to steal the show with their display of virtuosity.

After *The Rose Lake*, Tippett closed his piano, put away his manuscript-paper and removed his music-writing desk for ever – almost: for with the assistance of the present writer, he was able to produce 'Caliban's Song', a contribution to the tercentenary celebrations of Henry Purcell in 1995. But that was it.

In the autumn of 1995, he embarked on a two-month long tour of the USA and Canada, attending performances (eleven in all) of *The Rose Lake* in Boston, New York, Toronto and Hartford, dropping into Philadelphia for a BBC Symphony Orchesta tour concert that featured Symphony No. 2, attending a festival of his music in Tucson, Arizona, and taking vacations in Key West, Florida, and Carmel, California. Now physically far more vulnerable, when he returned to Nocketts, Tippett found living alone there both hazardous and depressing. So, in April, 1996 he sold up and moved to a rented riverside house in Isleworth, west London. There he has since received round-the-clock care and attention, has developed new routines, including daily trips to Kew Gardens and other scenic spots, continuing also to enjoy a varied social life. Suffering a mild stroke in October the same year, he astonished everyone with the speed of his recovery, though his speech remained to some extent impaired.

On a public level, Tippett came to be regarded in his eighties as the grand old man of English music – except that he was rarely grand. Quite the opposite: he gave up wearing dark suits, preferring more colourful ensembles; he also took to wearing sneakers, which he found more comfortable than shoes; and generally he gloried in the greater opportunities for irreverence which his status now allowed. Protocol he disregarded even more than in the past: and persons in positions of importance became prime targets for his mischievous, teasing humour. When it was rumoured in the late 1980s that plans for the refurbishment and commercial extension of the Royal Opera House, Covent Garden, might include the involvement of Disneyland, Tippett, immediately sent off a note to the Chief Executive, Jeremy Isaacs, offering to write an opera on *Snow White and the Seven Dwarfs*. The offer was welcomed, but seems unlikely to come to fruition. Having been made a Companion of Honour in 1979, in 1983 Tippett was chosen by the Queen to receive the Order of Merit (the highest British honour available). On the other hand, he remained outside the Establishment. He often spoke out against what he regarded as the evils of monetarism and denounced in the press the cuts in public spending that curtailed the teaching of music in schools. He made a particularly robust attack on the then Arts Council of Great Britain for removing its subsidy to the small, but enterprising Kent Opera Company, thereby causing its demise. Had he been of a different political persuasion, Tippett's protest might have had some effect, but during the Thatcher era there was not much chance. The landslide victory of the New Labour party under Tony Blair gave him unbounded delight.

From 1956 until 1978, Tippett served on the committee of the Vaughan Williams Trust. In 1979, he set up his own charitable trust, using the proceeds from the sale of the the bulk of his musical manuscripts to the British Library. All the manuscripts of his subsequent compositions have also been handed to the Tippett Foundation for sale to the British Library. The Foundation has thus been enabled to give grants to a variety of festivals, tours and educational projects involving contemporary music; it does not, however, subsidize performances of Tippett's own music.

For many years, Tippett himself contributed to the promotion of his music, conducting performances and recordings, undertaking talks and interviews and giving seminars at universities and colleges. If in recent years he has cut down on all this activity, it is partly because he has felt that the music must ultimately find its own way. To a much greater degree than many composers, he has taken the view that once a work is written, it is outside of himself, belongs to the performers and listeners. This detachment is sometimes found disconcerting. But he regards it as the best indication of its likely future survival when it is accepted into the repertoire of artists and ensembles of all kinds, without any promotional effort.

Some major projects have developed simply as a consequence of its appeal to artists in other disciplines. For instance, the Hamburg-based choreographer, John Neumeier, fell in love with Tippett's Triple Concerto in the mid-1980s and considered using it for a ballet. When, subsequently, he conceived the idea of a ballet based on *Hamlet*, he decided that all three acts would be supported by major Tippett works – Symphony No. 2 (Act I); two movements from the *Divertimento on Sellinger's Round* and the Triple Concerto (Act II): and Symphony No. 4 (Act III). Neumeier's *Amleth* was created for the Royal Danish Ballet in Copenhagen and enjoyed two runs there: it has now been re-created for the Hamburg Ballet. *Amleth* sustained its own independent choreographic narrative, based on pre-Shakespearean sources as well as Shakespeare's play; at the same time, it related very clearly to the architecture and thematic contrasts in Tippett's music, highlighting its intrinsic theatricality to a degree never before encountered.

Perhaps the most significant change in Tippett's late years has been the gradual acceptance of his music on the European continent. In the 1960s, 70s and early 80s, his works became part of the regular repertory in America, Australia and received frequent performances also in the Far East and Scandinavia. But in the last decade, it seems to have taken root in France and Germany. Previously, most of the performances in these territories had been given by visiting British artists. Critics favouring the modernism of the post-Darmstadt school were patronizing not only towards Tippett (whom they tended to label as a neo-classicist or unadventurous lyricist) but towards any contemporary non-serial British music. But since Colin Davis (as music director of the Bavarian Radio Orchestra) conducted *A Child of Our Time* in Munich in 1986 – a performance that was televised and issued on commercial video – there have been many performances by indigenous groups: some of them have been associated with educational projects aimed at countering the resurgence of Neo-Nazism.

The popularity of the oratorio in Germany was cemented in January 1995 when Vladimir Ashkenazy conducted two performances at the Berlin Philharmonie, not just to mark Tippett's ninetieth birthday, but to inaugurate a whole series of celebrations of fifty years of peace. Germany's belated but growing interest in Tippett has meant that his latest works, such as the Triple Concerto and *The Rose Lake*, have not had to wait very long before being presented there .

In France, Tippett's reputation – already in the ascendant there as a result of the success of the Triple Concerto at the 1984 La Rochelle Festival – was greatly enhanced by the highly praised Nancy Opera production of *King Priam*, in 1988. Six years later, *The Knot Garden* (translated as *Le Jardin labyrinthe*) received its French première in a striking production by L'Atelier de Recherche de l'Art Lyrique, an enterprising opera company based at an arts centre in Noisiel, outside Paris: the production was subsequently taken on tour to a number of French towns. Meanwhile, Strasbourg's contemporary music festival included a major Tippett retrospective in 1992; and the same year, *A Child of Our Time* attained its French première at the Quimper Festival: and as in Germany it is becoming the focus of special projects in France, such as one planned for 1998 in Besançon, involving twenty-five amateur choirs coming together for a month both to rehearse the work, study its background and significance, and give five performances in the region.

The fiftieth anniversary of the première of Tippett's oratorio was celebrated in March 1994, with a performance given in aid of the Save the Children Fund at the original venue, the Adelphi Theatre, with choirs from Morley College, Crouch End Festival Chorus and the recently formed Tippett Choir and Britten Sinfonia conducted by Nicholas Cleobury. The same forces gave the Polish première at the Wratislava Cantans Festival a few months later. In short, Tippett has lived to see *A Child of Our Time* become almost an icon.

In his eighties and early nineties, he has continued to enjoy travel, reading (or listening, when nearly blind, to cassette recordings of poetry and novels), going to the theatre, developing new tastes in gourmet food, wine and exotic cocktails, watching television, making new friends, falling in love. But as far as listening to music is concerned, his own works have remained a low priority. He hardly ever turns on radio broadcasts or recordings of his own music, preferring always to hear works by other composers – and even that in limited doses, as the task of listening stirs up compositional debate within his own mind. Tippett admits one exception – *The Midsummer Marriage*, the opera that brought so much radiance and warmth into the bleak atmosphere of the post-war world. It was the composition of his that had the longest gestation period and which was the most arduous to bring to fruition. Even he still succumbs to its spell, feeling that, without doubt, its exaltation of life, love, nature, humanity were worth all the effort and sacrifices to bring it to fruition.

4
Songlines

Folksong

Asked at a seminar with music students in Boston in 1989 which twentieth-century composer he most admired, Tippett replied, 'Gershwin: because in an age of experimentation with rhythm, percussive and fragmented musical textures, Gershwin kept song alive.'[1] A declaration of the same kind might be made about Tippett himself. Although he never ventured into the world of commercial musical theatre, or of 'hit' tunes, and although, on the other hand, he too explored new possibilities for rhythm, texture, percussiveness and so on, he has certainly kept song alive. One important feature of his work as a whole has been an enlarged concept of the nature and functions of melody. This has something to do, partly, with his sense that a composition must have a thread running through it – *il filo*, as Leopold Mozart called it. But it also derives from a fascination with melody at its most primal. During his childhood and student days, he took a great liking to The Skye Boat Song and the Londonderry Air (in an arrangement by Hamilton Harty). It was not simply the emotive directness and immediacy of such tunes that appealed to him: as a budding composer, he noted their phrase-construction and careful placing of climaxes. Songs were amongst his earliest unpublished works, and Tippett has since felt his first success in song-composition to have been the love-duet in his ballad opera, *Robin Hood* (*see* Example 1).

Most of Tippett's music in the early part of his career reflects his fascination with folksong and dance – though his interest was cosmopolitan rather than nationalist. How important it remained for him is evident in his Suite in D – or *Suite for the Birthday of Prince Charles*, (1948) – a rare instance of him writing music 'to order' – in which he drew from his early ballad operas both folk-

Example 1

melodies and composed thematic material of a related character. Tunes – chosen, invented and deployed for their sheer diversity of character, reference and association – are indeed the very lifeblood of this engaging, infectious, yet subtly constructed composition.

The five movements of the suite amount to a series of tableaux – scenes and idylls in the life of a mythical prince, each one encapsulated by an apt selection of tunes. It being customary in the England of the late 1940s for parents to marry before they had children, Tippett's opening *Intrada* evokes the celebrations for the wedding of Prince Charles's father and mother, the then Princess Elizabeth and the Duke of Edinburgh. Bow Bells can be heard ringing out at the start on the cellos and basses, defining the tempo and mood: above this Tippett builds an orchestral chorale prelude upon the hymn tune *Crimond* (which was sung at the actual wedding). The second movement, *Berceuse*, is a cradle-song based on a traditional French melody, which Tippett had used before as a boating song in his children's opera, *Robert of Sicily*. Played by the oboe, here, it depicts the newborn babe asleep and, at its climax (bar 36), crying.

The third movement, *Procession and Dance*, takes us into the world of children's initiation rites and games. Its outer sections quote from the little march for wind and side-drum which signals the entry and exit of the mysterious Ancients in Act I of his opera *The Midsummer Marriage*, while the dancing, whirling middle section is based on an Irish version of the fertility dance-tune *All Round my Hat*. With the fourth movement, *Carol*, the Prince grows up and enters into courtship and marriage: for this Tippett utilized the English medieval hymn, *Angelus ad virginem*, which he had used previously as a wedding processional in *Robin Hood*. In the Finale to the Suite, the Prince and his bride (unlike in real life) live happily ever after. Tippett made two attempts at this movement. At first, he tried to invent entirely fresh musical material, but was dissatisfied with the results. He then decided instead to extend the Overture to *Robin Hood*, elaborating upon its opening contrapuntally and rhythmically, and incorporating

into it a reference to *Early One Morning*. The contrasting central
episode, involving a change of tempo and key (from D to B flat),
also drew upon a folk-style melody he had composed originally
for the blessing of the lovers by Robin Hood (*see* Example 2).

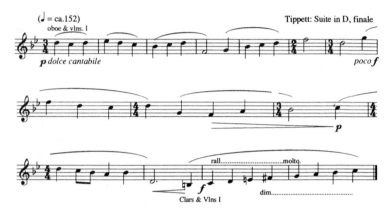

Example 2

In this movement in particular, we can note the contrast between
Tippett's early efforts, deploying a variety of popular melodies
for short, straightforward dramatic 'numbers', and the skills he
was now able to exhibit in his maturity, where the same materials
are made the basis of carefully balanced musical structures, with
rich textures and varied rhythms. The emergence of these purely
musical skills can be observed in works, such as the Piano Sonata
No. 1 and Concerto for Double String Orchestra, where folk-
music ideas are often incorporated into the framework of a
classically conceived structure: an aspect of his work that will be
explored further later on.

In *Robin Hood* and Tippett's other unpublished stage-pieces,
the alliance of words and music harnessed the immediacy and
directness of the vernacular. This remained a strand in his musical
make-up. Typically, later on, when commissioned by Bremen
Radio in 1956 to write his *Four Songs from the British Isles*, for
unaccompanied choir, Tippett picked one from each British

country so as to demonstrate the underlying plurality of the British cultural heritage, rather than any regional or nationalist rivalry. His version of the English tune, 'Early One Morning', at the start, places this classic tune within a firmly composed harmonic frame. The second (Irish) song, 'Lilliburlero' is turned into a rollicking scherzo. In the Burns setting, 'Poortith cauld' ('Cold Poverty'), Tippett added his own embellishment to the tune in its second and third appearances: and his arrangement of the final (Welsh) song, 'Gwenllian', released it from the 'four-square' straitjacket it had acquired within the context of eighteenth-century Welsh harp music.

When Tippett came to write his oratorio *A Child of Our Time*, and wanted a similar uncluttered simplicity of utterance, he clearly profited from his recent experience of writing and arranging vernacular music for amateurs to perform. A good instance is the tenor aria, 'I have no money for my bread' – a simple statement, sung against a tango accompaniment (*see* Example 3).

Example 3

But Tippett was trying also to express much more ambitious ideas and sometimes the verbal metaphors strained against an easily outlined musical format. The composer himself later acknowledged, for instance, that in the same aria, when the tenor has to sing, 'I am caught between my desires and their frustration/as between the hammer and the anvil' – a metaphor he may have picked up from Goethe's poem 'Koptische Lied'[2] – the words contradict, even distort, the melodic flow. He had still much to learn.

Part-songs and Madrigals

Discovering how to match verbal and musical metaphors of great complexity was to prove one of the cornerstones of Tippett's evolution as a composer. To some extent he was already profiting from the example of Elizabethan madrigals, wherein the composers often had musically to accommodate complex verbal conceits (cf. Weelkes's 'Thule, the period of cosmography'). Tippett soon became quite accomplished in this genre. His two madrigals, 'The Source' and 'The Windhover' (both dating from 1942) form a contrasting pair, one slow and the other fast. While 'The Source' (a setting of a poem by Edward Thomas, concerning 'the river in spate: the triumph of the Earth') is in essence a part-song whose melodic line is harmonized differently when repeated, 'The Windhover', is a more elaborate, through-composed treatment of a poem by Gerard Manley Hopkins, in which, Tippett remarks, he 'wanted to see how far I could carry the poetic imagery expressing a continuing experience (the bird flying on the wind) over into the musical imagery'.

Tippett's skills in this domain reached a peak when he later contributed to the anthology of madrigals, *A Garland for the Queen*, commissioned from ten composers to mark the coronation of Queen Elizabeth II in 1953. For this he used a text which had been 'tailor-made' by Christopher Fry, *Dance, Clarion Air*, enabling him specifically to start with vocal fanfares and their echoes, and, more generally, to recapture the rhythmic and contrapuntal vitality of the Renaissance madrigal tradition. The fluency that he developed in writing such part-songs was manifest also in his handling of Yeats's strophic poem 'Lullaby' (1960). Comparable facility is evident in his two rare incursions into liturgical music, 'Plebs Angelica' (1943) – a setting of a medieval Latin lyric from Helen Waddell's collection – and a Magnificat and Nunc Dimittis (1961), where the vocal writing is counterpointed against florid passages for the organ's trumpet stop (a special feature of the instrument at St John's College, Cambridge, for whose 450th anniversary these canticles were written).

Part-songs, interspersed with potpourris of existing popular tunes and art-music of the kind found in the *Suite for the Birthday of Prince Charles*, are a special feature also of two of Tippett's best pieces of 'educational' music, his cantata 'Crown of the Year' (1958) and the *Shires Suite* (1965–70). The cantata made use of an alternative text to *Dance, Clarion Air*, which Christopher Fry had given the composer when he was asked to contribute to *A Garland for the Queen* and which the latter had put aside.

The connection in this text between the cycle of seasons and the four great English Queens (Elizabeth I, Anne, Victoria and Elizabeth II) gave the composer an apt basis for a sequence of nine movements, starting with an instrumental evocation of Spring in the Golden Renaissance age of Queen Elizabeth I and a matching part-song, 'Hush, Nightingale', which is recalled at the end, after a 'Winter' prelude and a part-song, 'Hurl of the Wind', have evoked the horror of modern war, hinting now at the promise of another springtime in the modern Elizabethan age. The four instrumental preludes incorporate 'O mistress mine' from *Twelfth Night*, as set by William Byrd and Thomas Morley, 'Marlborough s'en va-t-en guerre' (a tune more familiar to the English as 'For he's a jolly good fellow'), an Austrian carol, 'O wie wohl ist mir am Abend' (known in English as 'O how lovely is the evening' and the song 'Frankie and Johnnie'.[3]

The three movements for voices and orchestra in the *Shires*

Suite were conceived to take account of the more limited capabilities of school choirs – in terms of chest resonance and projection – compared with the skills of instrumentalists the same age. Each vocal number is a canon: the Prologue is a setting of 'Sumer is icumen in' the Cantata, third in the sequence of five movements, contrasts two extrovert canons – Byrd's hunting song, 'Hey ho, to the greenwood' and Purcell's drinking catch, 'Fi, nay prithee, John' – with a more meditative one, an elaboration of a canon by Alexander Goehr to an epigram of William Blake, which had been presented to Tippett on his sixtieth birthday; lastly, there is an Epilogue featuring Byrd's canon, 'Non nobis Domine'.

The contrasts of jollity and reflection extend to the whole conception of the work. The festive Prologue is offset by a slow, purely orchestral interlude, conceived as a chorale prelude on the canon 'The Silver Swan', and again, after the uninhibited fun and frolics of the rather loosely constructed Cantata, comes an explosive, energetic Interlude II, utilizing the music that introduced the characters Dov and Mel at their entry in Act I of Tippett's opera, *The Knot Garden*, the major project on which he was engaged at the same time. But the movement also incorporates the canon, 'Great Tom is Cast', which appears three times: first on three trumpets, then three trombones and finally both groups in octaves. And after this dark, menacing piece, the Epilogue uses Byrd's canon to bring about a reassuringly serene end to the *Suite*.

Tippett's skills in madrigal writing were also put to memorable use in two much later works: first, in the fifth movement of *The Mask of Time* (1980–2), where the main dramatic exchanges for the four solo singers (characters in an imaginary Paradise Garden) are framed by settings for semi-chorus of lines from Milton's *Paradise Lost*; then again, in the choral writing of his subsequent opera, *New Year* – notably in the interlude between the first two scenes in Act I ('Is it science, is it love'), and in its use of echo-effects throughout. Madrigalian word-setting thus forms a second important strand in Tippett's musical make-up.

Art-song and Cantata

It was, however, neither through folksong nor madrigals that Tippett was able to achieve comprehensive mastery of word-setting or to discover a distinctive vocal idiom of his own. The real turning-point occurred with his first encounter with the music of Purcell.[4] When Morley College was hit by a landmine in 1940, Tippett found amid the rubble some library copies of the Purcell Society Edition. Studying these at leisure, he was stimulated by the various formal procedures in Purcell's music – such as the ground-bass with variations – and made use of the technique throughout his later music – from the slow movement of his Symphony No. 1 (1944–5) to the final movement of *The Mask of Time* (1980–2). Purcell's fantasias also offered new models for his musical structures. But what he found most riveting of all was Purcell's dramatic treatment of words: so also did Britten, who participated in Tippett's revivals of Purcell's music at Morley College. Thereafter, both composers emulated and in their own ways extended Purcell's vocal style – a style that was florid and flexible, sensitive to the finest nuances of meaning and accentuation.

Tippett was particularly impressed by Purcell's extended songs and cantatas, such as 'The Blessed Virgin's Expostulation' and 'Mad Bess' – vocal pieces which intermingled recitative, arioso and aria in a fluctuating sequence of moods and tempi – thus giving psychological veracity and depth to an essentially dramatic musical form. Taking advantage of his new friendship with Pears and Britten, Tippett wrote for them a Purcell-ian cantata, 'Boyhood's End' (1943), using as his text the eponymous chapter from W. H. Hudson's autobiography, *Far Away and Long Ago* (1918). Here, the writer, as an old man, recollects the crucial period in his life when, having reached the age of fifteen, he feared he might have lost the instinctive empathy with nature that he had known through boyhood.

Tippett charges this prose text with emotional intensity by presenting it within a flexibly planned musical structure comprising a continuous sequence of recitatives and arias. The piano fulfils a role comparable to the continuo in baroque music (except that it is, of course, composed in full, not improvised over a figured bass): and it also has quite often a pictorial function, e.g. in the dotted rhythms that introduce the lines 'To ride at noon on the hottest days ...' The layout of the cantata suggests a sonata-type scheme: introduction (recitative), first movement (aria), slow movement (recitative), scherzo (aria), finale (aria). But its chief characteristic is the use of vocal coloratura: indeed, the cantata is replete with subtle 'coloration' of the text and makes prominent use of Purcell-ian melismas on words such as 'uprising', 'dance', 'glist'ning', 'floating' and the final 'ecstasy'.

If 'Boyhood's End' proved to be something of a watershed in Tippett's setting of words to music, taking him into a realm where complex verbal images could not only be matched by appropriate music but could suggest suitably pliable formats, the composer remained capable (just as Purcell did) of writing simple, direct songs, especially for the theatre. For instance, his three *Songs for Ariel* – for a long time all that survived of his incidental music for a production, in 1962, of Shakepeare's *The Tempest* – were written for an actor who might be male or female and who might lack musical training: the tessitura of the songs is thus limited, and their lines unelaborate, but telling. In the play, Prospero sends Ariel to sing two songs to Ferdinand. The first, 'Come unto these yellow sands', is an invitation to dancing and to love. The second, 'Full fathom five', is a song of death and rebirth. (Tippett later incorporated references to these songs into his third opera, *The Knot Garden*, which at one level is a modern gloss on *The Tempest*.) The third song, 'Where the bee sucks' presages Ariel's freedom and the end of the play. When, in 1995, he added *Caliban's Song* to his incidental music to the play, he related it both to *The Knot Garden*, prefacing it with a 'Trumpet Tune with Boogie' (based on episodes in Act One of *The Knot Garden*) and to Purcell, building the main section of the setting over a ground bass.

If these songs are judicious in their choice of sung, declaimed or spoken phrases, 'Music' (1960), written for amateur singers, with an accompaniment of strings and piano, somewhat overstepped the mark: the Purcell-ian melismas in this setting of Shelley's poem are more easily projected by a solo singer than by a choir singing in unison.

The consummate example of Tippett's skill in song-writing is his song-cycle *The Heart's Assurance* (1951). The work brings all the skills he had learnt into play – vocal lines that vary from direct tunefulness to utterances that are florid, declamatory, or both at once; music that probes the deepest connotations of the texts; music that singles out and projects theatrically the most important words; piano accompaniments whose textures and colours carry a great burden of associations and references – suggesting, in fact, an implied orchestra (which was not the case with 'Boyhood's End'). The song-cycle is also the work of a mature artist tackling a theme close to his heart: for in setting poems by two young writers, Sidney Keyes (1922–43) and Alun Lewis (1915–44), both of whom died in the Second World War, Tippett was not only commemorating his close friend Francesca Allinson (whose suicide near the end of the war had left him devastated) but reflecting on the seemingly never-ending contest between the inhuman forces of war and destruction and a contrary, entirely human impulse towards love and compassion.[5]

Each song in the cycle is a kind of Purcell-ian cantata. While in 'Boyhood's End', the singer is 'the poet's voice describing', here it is 'an "I" talking'. *The Heart's Assurance*, however, has no underlying narrative thread, as is the case with Schubert's *Die Schöne Müllerin* or Schumann's *Frauenliebe und Leben*. Rather, it is a series of reflections on a theme which Tippett has referred to as 'Love under the shadow of death'. From first to last, the ironic counterpointing of love against death in the poetry is brought to the surface by Tippett's music. Ardent lyricism, rich in Purcell-ian melismas and word-painting, is thus offset by intimations of aggression and conflict. The radiant flow of piano demisemiquavers in the first song, for example, is sometimes jolted momentarily, as on the repeated word 'cruel' early on, or at the change of tonality on the word 'bad'. The most significant interruption to the singer's surge of melody occurs at 'And though Death taps down every street', where the rhythm of the accompaniment is dislocated and the voice-line reduced to brooding around a single low note (*see* Example 4a).

Tippett: The Heart's Assurance, song 1

Example 4a

Matching this is the intoning of a single high note in succeeding lines invoking the love that can transcend death (*see* Example 4b).

The remaining four songs build both upon this theme and its treatment. There is an ironic conflict between 'the heart's assurance' in the second (title) song and 'the heart's fear'; likewise, 'Compassion', is built on the contrast between 'she' (*her* actions,

Tippett: The Heart's Assurance, song 1

Example 4b

in the first stanza) and 'he' (*his* reactions, in the second), as preparation for what follows (death). Aware of the importance in the lieder
of Schubert and others of the 'secondary images' added to the poem
by the piano accompaniment, Tippett creates thus a miniature drama
out of each song. This is most obvious in the fourth song, where
the piano conjures up a dancer speeding, tripping towards and away
from points of rest. But the technique is at its most haunting in the
final song, where Tippett imagined 'a young woman singing out
over the Elysian fields to the young men beyond'. The song opens
with the singer, unaccompanied, evoking (to the words 'Young
men') the Last Post: this is the refrain that recurs three times in
Tippett's setting, culminating always in the words 'remember your
lovers', the piano's entry with repeated chords hinting at the poetic
opening of Beethoven's Fourth Piano Concerto.

Here, the composer undoubtedly had at the back of his mind
Purcell's highlighting of 'remember' at the plangent climax of
Dido's Lament. Later, whether setting other writers or putting
together his own texts for vocal music, Tippett sometimes picked
on the word 'remember' on account of this specific and powerful
association with Purcell. In *New Year*, not only does Jo-Ann's
opening aria in Act I gravitate towards this word, 'remember': the
fulcrum of the denouement in Act III is Jo-Ann's confrontation
with the 'Lake of Rememb'ring'. In the 'Hiroshima mon amour'
movement of *The Mask of Time*, the lines Tippett chose from
Anna Akhmatova's *Requiem* and 'Poem without a Hero',
emphasizing the act of 'remembering' brings his great threnody
for the oppressed and persecuted to a climax:

> I shall *remember* always and everywhere
> shall not forget come fresh evil days.
> And if they shut my tortured mouth
> through which a thousand million shout
> then shall you *remember* me
> on the eve of my *remembrance* day.
>
> [my italics throughout]

Voice and Theatre

Tippett's discovery of Purcell provided confirmation of the aesthetic principles concerning relationships between words and music which T. S. Eliot had recently clarified for him. These principles now became quite fundamental to Tippett's work. We should, therefore, summarize them here. The arts all depend for their expressive power upon metaphor: a 'trick' whereby the inner world of the human psyche and the outer world are made suddenly to correspond, producing a memorable image of actuality. In the mixed art forms – ballet, drama and opera – the metaphorical component of *one* of the ingredients will always be dominant; indeed, it will swallow up the rest. In each of these art forms, a kind of hierarchy obtains: in ballet, gesture and movement are more important than music and plot; in drama, the words and plot take precedence over gesture and music; and in opera, music comes first, the words, second, action and gesture, third. The result is invariably a unique fusion of elements carrying its own intrinsic power of metaphorical expression.

When words are set to music, the verbal metaphors are 'eaten up' by those within the music. It is almost unnecessary for the words to be heard individually: as long as the *situation* they express is embodied in the music, then all will be well. An 'inferior' text can be transformed by 'superior' music; conversely, an excellent piece of poetry will often be harmed by a musical setting, or will simply sabotage the musical operation which the composer has tried to perform upon it.

The good operatic librettist is not someone who offers the composer a self-sufficient play to set to music. He must, rather, write words that will fit the composer's pre-established notions of what the music will be doing at any one stage. The same principle applies in an oratorio and, at a more diminutive level, in songs, cantatas and other small-scale vocal forms. Not everyone agreed with Tippett's view. Peter Pears, for example, expressed his dissent thus ...

the relationship between poet and composer must not be regarded as a destructive one. True, the words exist first and it is for the music to fertilize them and generate the song, but the composer should court the passive poem and not offer her violence. A happy marriage is the proper relationship where each respects the other and takes it in turn to dominate. There has always been and will continue to be a need for every degree of music-domination or word-domination in its proper context ...

While appreciative of 'Boyhood's End' and *Songs for Ariel*, Pears felt that in *The Heart's Assurance*, 'it is perhaps a too strong feeling for the situation of the three big songs [1, 3, 5] which has driven the music to destroy the poem – by inflation. The same inflation can be seen affecting the *Songs for Achilles*.'

Pears's charge of 'inflation' may well have resulted from observing what Tippett produced vocally in his operas. Having begun writing his own texts and libretti, in his oratorio *A Child of Our Time*, Tippett held steadfastly to the aesthetic position he had developed initially through contact with Eliot. At the time of writing *The Heart's Assurance*, he took his Purcell-ian methods of word-setting, using texts of his own devising, into the opera house. In Act I of *The Midsummer Marriage*, Mark's aria, apostrophizing the lark and identifying its rhapsodic song with his love for Jenifer, is an early memorable example of his 'inflated', florid vocal style. What made this style possible was the trouble he had taken to produce the most apt and singable words. This point was rarely appreciated by critics of his libretto-writing, but in fact, it became part of his craftsmanship as a composer of dramatic vocal music.

The Purcell-ian cantata, with its flexibility of construction and vocal style, acted as the underlying model for the monologues that are the linch-pin of Tippett's next opera, *King Priam*. By the time he wrote this work, to create words and music as a single, inseparable dramatic entity was an essential element in his compositional make-up. Take, for example, Act I, scene 2 of the opera. During this hunting scene, the King is reunited with his son Paris, his order to have the boy killed in infancy having been subverted by the usual method in classical Greek stories – adoption by a shepherd. Priam's reflective monologue here stretches from his own birth to his own death – as such, a microcosm of the overall progress of the opera – and it suggests a shape for the cantata-like flow of text and music, each stage marked by the recurrence of the line 'I have a deepening anguish'.

The cantata-monologue also recapitulates the action so far and presages its consequences. Priam summons the 'shadows of the past that haunt his dreams' – i.e. the Nurse, Old Man and Young Guard who had each figured significantly in the action of the preceding scene – and predicts the fateful future consequences of Paris's survival: 'Let it mean my death!'

In Tippett's hands, this umbrella-like expressive functioning of the Purcell-ian cantata became an important theatrical tool. Subsequently, in all his vocal music, Tippett was able to uncover further potential within the form. The two extra songs (with guitar accompaniment) which he added to the one with which Achilles introduces himself in Act II of *King Priam*, to make a short cycle, *Songs for Achilles*, depict clearly defined dramatic situations. The first song (in the opera itself) is a song of intimacy and nostalgia: Achilles prefers to be alone in his tent with his friend Patroclus, rather than embroiled in the war between Greece and Troy. By contrast, the second song is about the warrior Achilles, boosting the efforts of Patroclus on the battlefield with his war-cry – a Purcell-ian ululation on the syllables 'Oi-o' as spine-tingling in the concert room as when it brought the second act of the opera to a conclusion of barbarity. In the third song, Achilles's mother, the sea-goddess Thetis, emerges from the ocean for a last meeting with her son. Addressing her, Achilles looks forward to the morrow, when he is destined to kill Hector and himself be killed subsequently by

Paris: then Thetis sinks back slowly again. Thetis's emergence
and return are portrayed in the extended guitar solos that frame
the song: aptly, the structure also of the song is palindromic.
Achilles's own vocal delivery is here at its most varied and
flexible.

Purcell's florid melismas are pressed to their limits in *The
Vision of St Augustine* becoming climactic wordless outpourings,
or *glossolalia*: likewise, now, the cantata concept blossoms into a
free-flowing organic design. Yet a newer dimension appears
within Tippett's third opera, *The Knot Garden*, where the cantata
format is made the vehicle for a kind of cinematic stream-of-
consciousness technique, leaping from one textual and musical
idiom to another and encompassing parenthetical quotations and
references. More of this in a later chapter: but just here to
establish its significance, we might consider the opening of the
second song in the cycle, *Songs for Dov* – which extends the
character of Dov outside the context of the opera.

Dov, a young musician, is sexually ambivalent and immature
in his dealings with fellow human beings: these aspects of his
personality are explored in the opera. At the end he leaves, as an
artist and loner, to discover a new life: and Tippett's song-cycle,
now focusing on Dov the creative artist, takes him on an
imaginary journey through time, place and culture in search of
his true vocation. The opening section of this three-stanza song
illustrates well Tippett's filmic jump-cutting expansion of the
Purcell-ian cantata. After Dov's cry of anguish (quoted from the
opera), the orchestra alternates phrases from the refrain of
Beethoven's setting of Goethe's 'Kennst du das Land', the vocal
line taken over by a trumpet, with Tippett's own original music.

The process is repeated as the singer enters, with the opening
of the Beethoven/Goethe setting (sung in English translation),
again countered with original music of Tippett's own: and the two
elements are superimposed as this section leads into an
instrumental refrain, replete with 'travel' imagery in both text and
music – the percussive clatter of horses hoofs and of train-wheels

turning ('The live horse, the iron horse'), wild glissandi for piano and harp and piccolo trills, interrupted by a Wagner quotation ('Pegasus, the flying horse/(Or that Flying Dutchman)) all gathering pace as Dov 'rides off into the sunset'; there are two further recurrences of this refrain later in the song. Disjunct sequences of words and music deployed in this cinematic manner are a notable feature of most of Tippett's later works and affected his compositional procedures generally, as will be seen later. It is in truth hard to imagine vocal writing of this type coming successfully to fruition if the tasks of producing text and music had not been accomplished by one and the same person.

Nevertheless, in an apparent contradiction of all that he had previously advocated, Tippett in fact turned in 1990 to a poem by a great writer, Yeats's 'Byzantium' (1930), and proceeded to set it to music for soprano and full orchestra. It would have been an irony indeed if, thus late in his career, he had been hoist with his own petard, so to speak. But this was not an act of wayward genius, for by now Tippett had such uncanny instincts about how words and music might relate that he knew he would not come unstuck.

Tippett wrote later that he could have chosen to set Yeats's earlier poem, 'Sailing to Byzantium' (1927), 'whose vivid images have perhaps more obvious musical implications': what attracted him to 'Byzantium', on the other hand, was its structure – 'a five-stanza format which led me straight off to plan a continuous work in five sections. Furthermore, the advantage, it seemed to me, of this particular poem over its predecessor was its sheer compression and condensation, allowing me, the composer, to apply *techniques of musical extension* [my italics].' Although Tippett also declared that 'he was not writing a song, a dramatic *scena* or a cantata, or one or other known genre of vocal music ... [but] a work that was *sui generis*',[6] the end-result was really a synthesis of all these genres – another way in which he was able to push Purcell's flexible cantata concept towards new horizons.

The five stanzas of this Yeats setting are linked with brief orchestral interludes. In general terms, the first two stanzas are preparatory, while the next two bring into the foreground the key images of song and dance, after which all the various strands are drawn together. Tippett's extension of Yeats's highly compressed imagery was perhaps suggested by the final lines of the poem – for which he confessed an abiding fascination:

> Those images that yet
> Fresh images beget
> That dolphin-torn, that gong-tormented sea.

Their 'convergence of the mythological and the actual ... prompted the return of the opening music of the piece and a final ambivalent resolution.'[7] Indeed, this opening preludial music – an explosion of gong sounds, duetting trumpets and angular violin melody, recapitulated in modified form at the end – certainly propels the listener into a world in which the musical images instantly beget fresh images and stream forward in an inexorable organic flow.

Tippett's *Byzantium* thrives on the Yeatsian polarity between the actual and the visionary. At the start of the poem, we have a picture of the historical Byzantium – the holy city later known as Constantinople, later still to become modern Istanbul – whose intermingling of diverse religions and cultures so appealed to Yeats: 'unpurged images of day' and 'night resonances' recede, horn-calls echoing the voice leaving an image of the star-lit dome of the Santa Sophia mosque. The opening gong-motif, minus its trumpets and violins, is succeeded by a passage of exquisite lyricism for voice and strings, the voice-line curving upwards and back down again to outline a dome-like shape (*see* Example 5): Such pictorialism is incidental: the same motifs reappear elsewhere as purely abstract elements in the design.

The first interlude mirrors the poet's ascent into the tower – the concrete symbol of Yeats's poetic activity – where the soprano evokes the poet's visionary state in long melismas on single vowels, floating beneath a pulsating motif for two harps:

Example 5

thereafter the invocation of an elemental spirit increases the urgency of the music. After another interlude, we again encounter a dual image – that of the golden nightingale created (as Yeats tells us in 'Sailing to Byantium') by Grecian goldsmiths. The golden bird doesn't sing in Yeats's 'Byzantium', but it obviously has to in Tippett's setting, as it 'sings better than the actual bird'. After a stanza centred on song, the next one emphasizes both dance and trance (a 'rite of purgation') – hence the linked musical extensions of these words and the oscillation between rhythmic movement and stasis. The fusion of musical motifs and visionary poetic metaphors reaches a climax in the final stanza, where the sea is present for the first time – 'not the sea rippling by the shore that appears in Yeats's earlier Innisfree poetry, but a powerful symbolic force; hence the concentration of Yeats's imagery'[8] – and it also brings about the final coalescence of musical images in Tippett's score.

If *Byzantium* was Tippett's ultimate extension of the Purcellian cantata genre in the domain of vocal music, it yielded yet more potential in his last two instrumental works, the String Quartet No. 5 (1990–1) and *The Rose Lake* (1991-3) – the latter subtitled (at this writer's suggestion), *A Song without Words for Orchestra*. Like the monologues of *King Priam*, the five song-sections in *The Rose Lake* are its core-element, each one given a pictorial caption: 'The lake begins to sing', 'The lake song is echoed from the sky', 'The lake is in full song', 'The lake leaves the sky' and 'The lake sings itself to sleep'.[9] They indeed sit within the musical structure like five contrasting cantatas. Moreover, the song-like character of all save the central climactic song is defined not in terms of separate single lines, but by a texture of what Tippett calls 'lyrical heterophony'. This technique was something he initially tried out in the first movement of String Quartet No. 5. In the centre of this movement there is a kind of epiphany, or an unexpected moment of illumination: the main thrust of the musical argument is suddenly suspended and the four instruments converge on a single strand of melody,

Example 6a, 6b

played both by the violin and cello, three octaves apart, while simultaneously the second violin and viola, an octave apart, present an embellished version of it. The melody in question derives from the ardent wordless vocalizations sung by Pelegrin, the spaceship pilot, at his first entry in Act I of *New Year* (*see* Examples 6a, 6b).

In *The Rose Lake*, Tippett writes similar cantata-colloquies: each of them elides differences between song and accompaniment; each now accommodates the changing emotions, previously presented in sequence, as a network of intertwining song-lines, already reconciled and supportive of each other. Thus in his last major work Tippett produced an unusual sort of swansong – one that suggested new lyrical horizons, whilst simultaneously summing-up a compositional career devoted to keeping song alive.

5

Protest and Polemics

A Child of Our Time

Within Tippett's compositional career one can discern two
parallel tendencies: one is concerned largely with technique, with
the discovery of an individual voice and with the expansion of his
musical language; the other brings all his experience – musical
and non-musical – to bear upon a humanitarian message.
Throughout the 1930s, Tippett was preparing himself for the first
of these artistic 'manifestos' – his oratorio, *A Child of Our Time*.
The gestation period for this was a long one and cost him a great
deal of effort. But when he eventually became clear as to his aims
and intentions, he was able to carry the work through to its final
stages with some facility. He began composing the music a few
days after the outbreak of war in 1939. Fearing that he might be
wiped out in an air-raid, he wrote at great speed.

Examining Tippett's *Sketch for a Modern Oratorio*[1] – the title
he gave the draft scenario which he took to T. S. Eliot when he
was hoping the poet would provide him with a text – we can see
that certain key decisions regarding the shape and content of the
work underlie its success. First, his choice of genre – oratorio
rather than an opera – ensured that there would be an overriding
emphasis on *reflection*. The incidents that provoked the writing
of the piece are absorbed into a larger framework wherein the
actions and reactions of people in general could be considered. At
every stage, we are invited to step back from events and regard
them in a wider context. Whereas the focal point of Handel's
oratorios and Bach's Passions is always a named individual, the
'child of our time' here is nameless, though no less significant. As
with the Unknown Soldier, we are in no doubt as to who and what
the 'child' represents – the eternal scapegoat, a figure present in
all periods and all societies.

The link between Tippett's oratorio and Odon von Horvath's eponymous novel[2] is limited to the title; neither is the oratorio tied to a particular place or period. Even at its most specific, any protest or polemic element could still be applied to situations other than those in the pre-Second World War epoch. When the composer's response to the immediate political situation surfaces, as it certainly does in (for instance) the Spiritual of Anger, 'Go down Moses', its relevance to many other contexts of oppression is obvious. Tippett, in fact, encountered this spiritual for the first time on the soundtrack to the film *Green Pastures*,[3] where its context was different – Moses leading the Israelites away from the persecution inflicted upon them in Egypt by Pharaoh.

Modelling his oratorio on Handel's *Messiah*, Tippett uses a tripartite scheme to move from the general (in Part I) to the specific (in Part II) and back again (in Part III). As the composer has stated, 'Part I deals with the general state of oppression in our time; Part II presents the particular story of a young man's attempt to seek justice by violence and the catastrophic consequences; while Part III considers the moral to be drawn, if any.'[4] The change to the specific in Part II is also indicated by the actual naming of the soloists for some of the episodes as Mother, Aunt, Boy and Uncle. Tippett adopts devices common to the Handelian oratorio and Bach Passions: narrative in recitative; choral description and reflection; contemplative arias; and the congregational hymn. *Messiah* is explicitly evoked in the Chorus of the Oppressed (No. 5) – cf. Handel's 'He trusted in God that he would deliver him' – and in the opening chorus of Part II, comparable to 'Behold the Lamb of God' at the start of Part II of Handel's oratorio (*see* Examples 7a, 7b).

The indebtedness to Bach is overt in some of the choruses of Part II: 'Let Him be crucified' from the *St Matthew Passion*, for instance, is mirrored in Tippett's 'Away with them! Curse them! Kill them!' (no. 11); and this same Double Chorus of Persecutors and Persecuted owes its questioning 'Where? Why? How?' to Bach's opening double chorus in the same work. Again, Tippett's

Handel: Messiah, Part II

Tippett: A Child of Our Time, Part II, No. 9

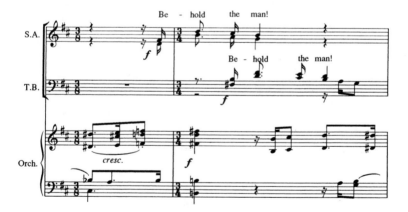

Examples 7a, 7b

Chorus of the Self-Righteous echoes 'We have a law' in Bach's
St John Passion. Nevertheless, we are here manifestly not dealing
with something comparable to the feeble imitations of baroque
oratorio and Passion that proliferated especially in Victorian
England. Tippett always renews and revitalizes his models.

The chief mode of renewal is that of irony. The Jewish villains,
for example, of Bach's 'We have a law', mentioned above, are
here the *victims* in Tippett's equivalent chorus. Again, a line from
the Book of Isaiah (14.4) is distorted to become 'When shall the
usurer's city cease'. But the newest, most ironic slant came from
his use of Negro spirituals for the congregational hymn element
in the oratorio. Originally, it seemed an odd decision: even Eliot
asked Tippett if the chorus would have to 'black up' when they
performed them. The composer's view was that all races
everywhere could identify with the sentiments of Negro spirituals
– and this has certainly been borne out by the recent history of
performances of the work. By comparison, the appeal of
Lutheran chorales or Jewish melodies (which he had considered
using) would have been more limited.

Tippett observed that the spirituals themselves 'have turned and
twisted Bible language into a modern dialect: the stories they tell
of Bible Jews are used to comfort Negroes in the bitterness of
oppression.'[5] They could thus serve to symbolize 'the agony of
modern Jews in Hitler's Europe' along with any who are 'rejected,
cast out from the centre of our society onto the fringes; into slums,
into concentration camps, into ghettos'[6]: and, more recently, that
would include Vietnamese boat people, the many refugees from
civil wars in former Yugoslavia and tribal wars in Africa, and AIDS
victims.[7]

Tippett first heard spirituals in a radio broadcast in 1938, when
his planning of the oratorio was already under way. When, in
'Steal away', the singer reached the phrase 'The trumpet sounds
within-a my Soul', he was 'shot through with the sudden
realization that the melody was far greater than the individual
singer and had the power to move us all'. He then obtained from

America a volume of spirituals and incorporated five of them into his *Sketch* for Eliot. Outlining a suggested basis for the text that Eliot might have written for the rest of the oratorio (on the right-pages of the the *Sketch*), he tried to match the 'lapidaric' verbal style of the spirituals derived from folk-idioms. Often he succeeded, as in the powerful declamatory line 'Let them starve in No-Man's Land' for the Chorus of the Self-Righteous (no. 13).

Tippett managed quite successfully, in fact, to integrate a wide range of ingredients into his design. Taking its cue from the Prologue in Heaven from Goethe's *Faust*, the opening chorus and alto solo offer a view of the world as if from 'some point in insterstellar space'.[8] Seasonal metaphors also mark the structural progress of the oratorio: 'The world turns on its dark side/It is winter', at the start is balanced by 'The moving waters renew the earth/It is spring', at the end. Most important of all, it is the Jungian references in the text that were of critical importance in widening the scope of the oratorio beyond the immediate and the specific, notably in the three alto solos – 'Man has measured the heavens' (no. 2), 'The dark forces rise like a flood' (no. 24) and 'The soul of man' (no. 27). The last of these, suggested not only by Jung, but one of the illustrations in Blake's *Book of Job*[9] leads to a question-and-answer sequence (no. 28) between the uncertain, vulnerable Chorus and the oracular bass soloist, whose aphoristic utterances enable the tenor to lead off the final ensemble for the soloists, joined eventually by the chorus, with the a Jungian-ly expressed vision of reconciliation:

> I would know my shadow and my light
> so shall I at last be whole.

– after which the final spiritual, 'Deep River', enables the oratorio to end with a Bunyan-esque vision of paradise.

If the text is thus rich and multi-layered, so almost deceptively, is the music. Its sustained directness and limpid simplicity were qualities Tippett tried to emulate from Berlioz's *L'Enfance du Christ* (which he had heard on the radio at the time). The choral and orchestral writing are both distinctive and unusual. Tippett's consistently linear approach, the fruit of his interest in Renaissance music, is evident throughout, and heavyweight performances can easily undermine the impact of the tensions engendered by the flow and clash of lines. The linking interludes in Nos. 3 and the Praeludium before no. 29, again challenge the canonically imitative flutes and viola to float their lines across the bar-lines: and here the harmonic movement against a sustained B flat on the cellos is implied rather than overt (as in the 'open', transparent textures encountered so often in Berlioz).

Tippett rejected the harmonization of the spirituals in the published versions he had obtained and re-worked them so as to pit the soloists dramatically against the chorus. This technique he learnt from the singing of the Hall Johnson Choir on the soundtrack to *Green Pastures*. But the general musical style of the piece was also affected by the presence of the spirituals. As Tippett himself later commented: 'I used the interval of a minor third, produced so characteristically in the melodies of the spirituals when moving from the fifth of the tonic to the flat seventh, as a basic interval of the whole work – sometimes on its own, sometimes superimposed upon the open fifth below the whole note. These intervals (minor third, fifth and flat seventh) could lead on the one hand to a kind of sliding chromatic fugue (cf. no. 5, Chorus of the Oppressed); and on the other to a Weill-like tango (cf. no.6, the tenor solo, "I have no money for my bread")'; or even to a dance-like accompaniment (cf. no. 27, the alto solo, "The soul of man").[10]

Tippett has always heard as one and the same thing the blues inflexions of jazz and the expressive chromaticism of Wilbye, Monteverdi and Purcell. Even before he had encountered Purcell, in fact, he was beginning to use harmonic 'false relations' to give a bitter-sweet, bluesy twist to essentially diatonic harmony. The poignancy that emerges from the soprano solo 'How can I cherish my man', for example, arises from a combination of two elements. One is the gently lilting, berceuse-like gait of the soprano line, whose initial simplicity is chromatically intensified as the self-questioning continues, and which culminates in a wordless threnody, only relieved when it leads into the spiritual 'Steal away' – one of the most inspired, most deeply affecting passages in the whole of Tippett's music. Secondly, the surge of pathos is emphasized by the bluesy clashes of major and minor in the accompaniment (*see* Example 8).

Example 8

On a rhythmic level, also, Tippett discovered in the spirituals a kinship with his own music which, as it had recently flowered in his String Quartet No. 1 and Piano Sonata No. 1, was replete with jazzy syncopation and an uneven spread of accents in defiance of the barline (a feature to be discussed in more detail in Chapter 7). In his version of the spiritual 'O by and by', the lilting lightness lifts the listener out of the brooding intensity of the alto's preceding recitative in a way that suggests that the whole sequence had been freshly *composed*. Preceding it, the mother's solo 'What have I done to you, my son?' (no. 23) derives its anxious mood from the alternations of triple and duple time.

  There are some aspects of *A Child of Our Time* which Tippett, had he been writing the work a decade or two later, might have handled somewhat better. The recitatives for the solo bass, for example, are musically not particularly memorable : on the other hand, the composer hardly intended them to be on a par with the arias and chorus, as their function is very largely to tell the story and link the different episodes – a task that can easily be undermined by singers who adopt a portentous, melodramatic delivery. In the two scenas (nos 15 and 17) in Part II, the successive contributions of the four soloists are well differentiated – but the later, operatically experienced Tippett would perhaps have devised a subtler interaction at this point.

What is most impressive, however, from a purely compositional standpoint, is the sense of discipline and clarity of purpose that underlies the work. Having decided on the oratorio genre, Tippett is never tempted to introduce theatrical gestures that would distract from his reflective stance. Thus, when the alto and bass (in no. 17) report the shooting of the official, there are no spurious histrionics. It is succeeded only by a quiet (Jungian) observation by the alto, 'But he shoots only his dark brother/And see he is dead'.

Rare amongst the many composers wanting to emulate Handel in oratorio, Tippett displays a true Handelian directness, breadth and variety of utterance, endearing his work thus to amateur and professional choruses worldwide. Early on in its history, the dramatic power of his compositions was often subverted by lethargic articulation, especially in numbers like 'Burn down their houses!' (no. 19). Much of the impact of the piece depends on the ability of the chorus to identify in turn with the oppressors and the oppressed, as well as to paint the scene and meditate on its deeper significance. As the work proceeds, the choral writing becomes ever more spacious and flexible: for example, at the start of Part III, 'The cold deepens', there are telling contrasts between homophonic statements and contrapuntal responses. And when the chorus takes over from the soloists in the final General Ensemble, it is as if everyone taking part (as in the great choruses of Beethoven's *Fidelio*) is now asserting and identifying with its aspirations toward inner peace.

Postwar Polemics

After *A Child of Our Time*, the polemic element in Tippett's artistic make-up remained important and was often associated with an explicit use of vernacular styles – particularly jazz and blues – or quoted popular tunes. It came to the fore again particularly in his later operas, in his Third Symphony and in *The Mask of Time*.[8] Amid the personal entanglements of the characters in *The Knot Garden*, the character of Denise – the archetypal freedom-fighter, her name derived from the martyr St Denys – stands out. She finds a kindred spirit here only in Mel, the black writer: in her eyes, he is essentially a representative of an oppressed race, for whom

> Words are weapons
> In the fight
> For freedom, justice, dignity.
>
> (Act II scene 7)

As they reach out to each other, the anthem of the freedom movement, 'We shall overcome' surfaces in the orchestra and the singers join in at the climax, 'O deep in my heart.'

In *The Ice Break*, the music for the race riot of Act II is built up out of a montage of competing popular tunes, defined and sharply contrasted from the standpoint of their racial and religious origins.

The vernacular ingredient in his fifth opera, *New Year*, is more celebratory – albeit a celebration that goes awry – than a vehicle for polemics or protest. There is, for instance, in Act II a reggae-based trance dance for a Shaman: later, 'Auld Lang Syne' is sung (against a montage of loud bell-notes, percussion, and dancing violin lines) to greet the New Year. Among the characters in *New Year*, the rebellious Donny is more a representative of a lost, orphaned group in society rather than someone with a particular political or revolutionary standpoint. Nevertheless, he is predominantly characterized by means of allusions to reggae and rap. It is the Presenter who, just before the opera ends, suddenly articulates the composer's humanitarian stance with a passionate cry –

> One humanity
> One justice

– which might at first seem tangential, but in truth serves to encapsulate the general message of the opera.

Tippett's Third Symphony, coming not long after *The Knot Garden*, is by far his most confrontational work. The mood is set by the abstract first part, built out of explosive contrasts of thematic material. The second part, ostensibly celebratory and playful at first, builds up a great tumult of ideas, that lead, by way of Beethoven's raucous presto opening to the finale of his Ninth Symphony, to a sequence of blues and dramatic scena for voice and orchestra. Tippett's text for these songs crystallized out of his feeling that the ecstatic celebration of the brotherhood of man in Beethoven's setting of Schiller's 'Ode to Joy' could no longer – after two World Wars, the horrors of the concentration camps, Siberian labour camps and Hiroshima – be taken at face value.

The ironies of *A Child of Our Time* are now developed to the extent that they are an unavoidable component in the modern sensibility, qualifying its hopes and dreams. The blues, a means both for expressing anguish and for curing it, embody this duality. Tippett's four blues, with instrumental breaks, and a Miles-Davis-inspired flugelhorn obbligato, outline a human progress from birth and innocence to experience. Each verbal metaphor looks back to Schiller and ironically contradicts his rejoicing in a future brotherhood of man. Thus, for instance, 'They sang that, when she waved her wings, the goddess Joy would make us one' is given a modern slant:

> And did my brother die of frostbite in the camp?
> And was my sister charred to cinders in the oven?
> We know not so much joy for so much sorrow.

The blues alternate slow-fast, slow-fast, but are not 'authentic' – that was never Tippett's intention – except in pace, in general outline and in the use of characteristic motifs, e.g. the piano triplets and pizzicato bass in the first fast blues. The blues inflexions are experienced more as an outgrowth of Tippett's harmonic language – now much more chromatic, indeed freely atonal – compared with that of *A Child of Our Time*. The cradle-song accompaniment to the second slow blues culminates three times in a quotation from Act II of the *The Knot Garden*, where Dov is comforting the distressed Flora – (*see* Example 9) – which is finally extended to lead into a second fast blues, where wind fanfares hint at the sorrow beyond the lovers' bed.

Example 9

All of this all precipitates an accusatory episode in which quotations from the Ninth Symphony and the 'Ode to Joy' are subject to musical and verbal commentary and contradiction culminating in the searing line – 'My sibling was the torturer'. Although the final scene that follows makes reference to Martin Luther King's dream of a more just society, the work ends as bleakly as it had begun.

The Mask of Time, too, reaches its emotional apex by staging a confrontation between the 'progress' represented by the triumphant rise of science and its perversion in the technology of modern warfare. The last of three instrumental interludes is interrupted at its climax by triumphant choral cries:

> Fire and arithmetic
> flash upon flash of mirrored mind to mind
> unbind the structured atom
> to a whiteness that shall blind the sun.

But then it goes into reverse with –

Or Shiva dancing our destruction.

The ultimate in destruction – Hiroshima – is pictorialized here.
As the tumult dies down, a chorus hums a hymn-like introduction
to a solo soprano threnody, setting words from Akhmatova's
'Requiem' and 'Poem without a Hero'.

The Mask of Time, written late in Tippett's career, thus widens
its polemic against destruction beyond anything that had been
experienced in Europe. (It makes a sharp contrast, for instance,
with Britten's *War Requiem*, which is overtly centred on the First
World War, using poems by Wilfred Owen as ironic extension of
the Latin Mass). In *The Mask of Time*, Tippett had thus also to go
beyond the vernacular, in musical terms, to find a medium for his
expression of hope and compassion and to find a vehicle for a
dream of human survival. The final two movements of the work
focus on individuals, past and present, mythological and actual –
Orpheus, returning from hell, a group of anti-Nazis in Japanese-
occupied Peking, and a young actor in classical Greece (a character
in one of Mary Renault's historical novels, *The Mask of Apollo*)
responding to a proclamation from Zeus. Their aspirations
culminate in a final outburst of wordless choral singing – suggested
by a poem by Siegfried Sassoon, 'Everybody Sang'. But this is not
the aspiration towards paradise encountered at the end of *A Child
of Our Time* so much as an assertion of humankind's ability to
overcome the aggressive, destructive elements in a universe that
knows no limits.

6
Illusion and Actuality

The Midsummer Marriage

Tippett's deliberate attempt in *A Child of Our Time* to distance himself from everyday events, to reflect upon them and uncover some durable meaning, affected deeply his approach to the writing of opera. He thus steered clear of making stage-versions of well-known plays and books, preferring – with one exception – to fashion his own plots and characters, deploying them with the subversive theatrical freedom of an innovatory playwright. None of his operas was created with specific singers in mind: whilst giving guidance as to the casting, he has always trusted in the conductor and director – with their more up-to-date knowledge and awareness of the potential of individual singers – to make the right choices. What mattered more to Tippett was the magical aura of theatre in its widest sense, its capacity for self-renewal and its potential to illuminate the darkest recesses of the human psyche. His plots are often concerned with what Jean Cocteau (writing about his dramatic and film treatments of the Orpheus legend) called 'frontier incidents'. Many of Tippett's characters thus move freely backwards and forwards between their actual selves and mythological or other prototypes: or, alternatively, they are defined in contrasting groups – some inhabiting the everyday world, others coming from an imagined domain in the past or future – and generate excitement and tension by invading each other's territory. Intriguing, but dangerous ploys, these: but by the time he came to write his first published opera, *The Midsummer Marriage* (1946–51), Tippett had accumulated sufficient experience – musical and dramatic – to be ready to take big risks.

Early on, working with amateurs, Tippett had experimented in four (unpublished) pieces, with different dramatic genres: *The Village Opera* (1929) and *Robin Hood* (1934), both ballad operas; *Robert of Sicily* (1938), a children's opera to a text by Christopher Fry; and *Seven at a Stroke* (1939), a play by Fry with music arranged by Tippett. Wanting eventually to produce a full-scale opera for professional performance, Tippett was prepared to wait until he was ready and to allow it a proper period of gestation. But the outcome, as with *A Child of Our Time*, was a composition that welled up inside him, took over his entire existence and demanded objectification in some concrete form outside himself. Like Stravinsky, writing of *Le Sacre du Printemps*, Tippett could say, 'I am the vessel through which [they] passed...' Later, he viewed the process in Jungian terms: 'I hold for myself that the composition of oratorio and opera is a collective as well as a personal experience. While indeed all artistic creation may be seen in that way, I believe the collective experience, whether conscious or unconscious, is more fundamental to an oratorio or an opera than to a string quartet.'[1]

The gestation period for Tippett's first opera was a very long one. Preceding the writing of the opera, which took six years, were at least six years spent exploring various avenues. In 1941, he outlined to Francesca Allinson a scenario for a comic opera entitled *The Man with Seven Daughters*.[2] Tippett's collaboration with Douglas Newton yielded another different concoction, entitled *Aurora Consurgens or The Laughing Children*. A foreword in their sketch for this declares its origin in Aristophanes 'as postulated in F. M. Cornford's *Origin of Attic Comedy*'.[3] The Latin part of the title was adopted from an alchemical treatise discovered by Jung – *Aurora Consurgens: a Document Attributed to Thomas Aquinas on the Problems of Opposites in Alchemy* (ed. Marie-Louise von Franz). The subtitle was suggested by Edric Maynard (another of the conscientious objectors working at Doolittle Farm; he worked in a bookshop and was nicknamed 'The Book Boy') and refers to lines in Eliot's 'Burnt Norton':

> Go, said the bird, for the leaves were full of children
> Hidden excitedly, containing laughter.

The treatise contained symbolic representations of pyschological wholeness and had some peripheral relevance to Tippett's ultimate operatic intentions. But, as Willy Strecker observed, to use its title would have been disastrous and so the composer wisely abandoned it, continuing on the project alone. The 'laughing children', however, survived into the text sung by the chorus at the end of Act I of *The Midsummer Marriage*. Moreover, Eliot's image of children able to rejoice in transcendent beauty, something denied to adults, recurs later at the denouement of Tippett's fifth opera, *New Year* – 'Laughter will come with the children'.

The Midsummer Marriage, as it took shape, stirred new life into an art-form that had all too readily become encrusted with routines and formulae. While Tippett utilizes the standard apparatus of opera – arias, duets, ensembles, choral episodes and orchestral interludes – he also places a new emphasis on the symbolic power of stage-illusion. This is most obvious here in the fact that the main working out of the drama (in Act II) and the climax and denouement (in Act III) are articulated through ballet – a sequence of Ritual Dances – lending a new dimension to the action.

Ballet is, in fact, fundamental to Tippett's dramaturgical conception here. For one of his main models is Shakespeare's *A Midsummer Night's Dream*, wherein there are two sets of characters, the mortals and the fairies. Tippett writes that, likewise, 'Part of my entertainment is the interaction of two worlds, though the supernatural world I conjure is not a fairy world but another.'[4] As with Shakespeare's Bottom, when he acquires an ass's head, so, too, in Tippett's opera, the principal characters – two lovers who fall out on their wedding-day – are able to enter 'a different range of experience from anyone else'.[5] The 'other' world is represented by a temple 'peopled by a wise priest and priestess [He-Ancient and She-Ancient], to whom I gave a chorus of neophytes in the shape of a group of dancers [led by Strephon] who are silent.'[6] Dance is thus integrated into the action, and is not merely a *divertissement*.

The Midsummer Marriage begins where *A Child of Our Time* leaves off. Its point of departure is the final prayer for renewal and regeneration in the oratorio – 'I would know my shadow and my light'. Tippett's aim is now to communicate *on the stage* a vision of wholeness, an integrity of mind, heart and body. He does this by devising a modern version of the traditional plot about the unexpected hindrances to an eventual marriage. The old hindrances – social ones – he felt to be no longer relevant: it is no longer unusual, for instance, for a king or prince to marry a commoner. The real hindrance in present-day society is 'our ignorance or illusion about ourselves'.[7]

The point at which the opera crystallized in Tippett's mind came as a kind of dream, a moment of illumination that suggested the stage-metaphor he could use to show the falling apart of the two lovers, Mark and Jenifer, when they meet (in Act I) on their wedding-day. Tippett tells us that he saw

> ... a stage picture (as opposed to hearing a musical sound) of a wooded hilltop with a temple, where a warm and soft young man was being rebuffed by a cold and hard young woman ... to such a degree that the collective magical archetypes take charge – Jung's *anima* and *animus* – the girl, inflated by the latter, rises through the stage – flies to heaven, and the man, overwhelmed by the former descends through the stage-floor to hell. But it was clear they would soon return. For I saw the girl later descending in a costume reminiscent of the goddess Athena ... and the man ascending in one reminiscent of the god Dionysus ...[8]

All this might seem over-fanciful, self-indulgent, even, were it were not the fact that Tippett had created a valid dramaturgical context.

Tippett felt that opera, to survive and remain a vital force, must relate to the contemporary theatre. This meant, to the Tippett of the 1940s, the verse-drama of Auden, Eliot and Christopher Fry. Thus, the magical genre of *A Midsummer Night's Dream* is now linked to Eliot's concept of the theatre as one 'whose stage is generally a stage of "depth" – by which I mean that we sense, especially at certain designed moments, another world within or behind the world of the stage set.'[9] Moreover, the characters in Tippett's opera, like those in *The Family Reunion*, only become aware of their real selves in the course of the plot.

Tippett's stratification of the action affects the names he has chosen for the characters: royal Cornish names for the 'marvellous' couple, Mark and Jenifer, the lovers who are capable of entering the 'other world'; functional names for Jack (the mechanic) and his girlfriend Bella (secretary to Jenifer's father, King Fisher), whose perceptions are purely earthbound. The other characters' names have important resonances, too: King Fisher is up-to-date American (like Duke Ellington) but also evokes the impotent Fisher King of the Holy Grail legends discussed in Jessie L. Weston's *From Ritual to Romance*; the mysterious intermediary between the two worlds of the opera, Madame Sosostris, is the fortune-teller in Weston's book (and she and the Fisher King figure in Eliot's *The Waste Land*). Such care in the choice of names has always been essential to Tippett's strategy in building up a multi-layered theatrical conception.

Classical precedent also shapes the opera. Tippett structured the piece originally like two Aristophanic plays, the first an *agon* (or contest) between the sexes and the second an *agon* between age and youth. These were to be separated by an interlude that consisted of a set of dances : but (at the suggestion of Eric Walter White), he expanded the interlude into what is now Act II. Almost every scene, in fact, can be considered an *agon*. Tippett thus establishes at the start of the opera a musical division between the worlds of the actual and supernatural. The chorus burst on stage to join in the exuberant orchestral music that opens the opera. The magical 'other' world then takes over and everyone is still. A celesta motif, answered by flutes and accompanied by a single note tremolo on the violas, signals the appearance of the mysterious temple (*see* Example 10):

Tippett: The Midsummer Marriage, Act 1

Example 10

Immediately, our disbelief is suspended and we are ready to go 'within or behind the world of the stage set'. A little march marks the entrance of the dancers and the ancients (*see* Example 11).

The telling contrast between lyrical and hieratic music here is the clear basis of the *agon* in this scene: and it is a point of reference throughout the opera.

The music for each of the characters is equally well-defined in theatrical terms. Mark – whose first appearance in Act I culminates in his rapturous hymn to the ascending lark and to his future bride on midsummer morning – and Jenifer, whose arrival stems his flow of lyricism, compete on the same declamatory level at this initial encounter. When they return, later in Act I, from their respective 'other' worlds, they are sharply distinguished. She is like St Joan (according to Tippett's sketches)[10], her soul wafting high in a visionary trance. He is even more intoxicated with passion. Tippett sets them apart from each other in a singing competition. Jenifer's aria, at first introverted, takes off into Queen of the Night-style coloratura, embellished by a trumpet obbligato: this aria aligns her with the inhabitants of the

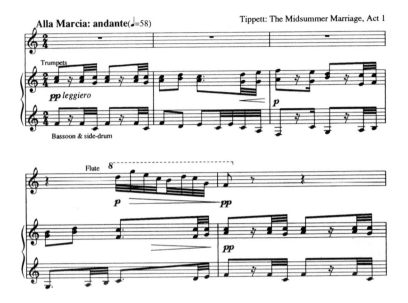

Example 11

temple (and in production, this association can be made to register if the aria is supported by choreography). Mark's aria, proudly rhetorical, is accompanied by a Verdi-like thrumming on strings, assisted by woodwind, and it draws him even closer to the young mortals around him. When the two lovers reappear in Act III, now reconciled, these musical distinctions are swept away.

What has happened meanwhile? The libretto offers one clue: 'She must leap and he must fall,' sing the chorus before the Ritual Dances – but later (in Act III), as Jack and Bella renounce servitude to King Fisher and take responsibility for their own actions, the personal pronouns are reversed. Two complementary processes are embodied here: growing up – what Jung called the 'individuation process' – and acceptance of subconscious drives; and also growth to social maturity. In everyday life, individuals or couples who need assistance seek psychiatric counselling or take part in group therapy or meditation. On the stage, there is an age-old tradition of initiation rites that serve essentially the same purpose (cf. *Die Zauberflöte*).

The Midsummer Marriage also involves a contest between the generations. King Fisher, a Shavian capitalist and staunchly Victorian father, is able neither to comprehend the world of the Ancients, nor the attitudes of the friends of Mark and Jenifer (the singing chorus). Communicating at first primarily through his secretary Bella, he is immediately at odds with the Ancients. Failing to persuade them to open the temple gates and allow him access to Jenifer, he sends Bella to fetch Jack and in her absence tries to win over the chorus (friends of Mark and Jenifer) with money, addressing – in a magnificently proportioned aria – first the men (who are susceptible) and then the girls (who rebuff him).

Unsuccessful in Act I, King Fisher renews his confrontation directly with the Ancients in Act III: this time it results in his death – which is more a ritual necessity than a death motivated by the actualities of the plot or by an inherent villainy. King Fisher, a representative of an older, impotent generation and its values, has to 'die' in order that a new generation, led by Mark, and new values, respectful of the inner life represented by the Ancients, can take over. As such, his death is essential to the emotional development of Mark and Jenifer.

Linking the two worlds of the mortals and the Ancients is the mysterious figure of Madame Sosostris. Erda-like in Act I, she warns King Fisher of the likely consequences of his actions. Her appearance in Act III is even more extraordinary: here she sings a spacious aria which unburdens the creative artist's dilemma of being able to offer spiritual nurture to others but not himself. For the action to stop, thus, for about fifteen minutes, presents a great risk to the stage-production: on the other hand, the aria is one of Tippett's most sustained, impassioned and riveting utterances – and, perhaps paradoxically, one of the set-pieces for which the opera is always remembered. After King Fisher's challenges have failed, and with his death imminent, the chorus echo Sosostris's final couplet (quoted from a Schiller essay that Beethoven kept on his desk):

> I am what has been, is and shall be,
> No mortal ever lifted my garment.

As her veils are removed, Mark and Jenifer are disclosed in a pose of hieratic contemplation. Their union is a concrete manifestation of the Sosostris's mysterious symbolic creative integrity.

Even more than in *A Child of Our Time*, nature metaphors are essential to the action of *The Midsummer Marriage*. Its time-span takes us from dawn to noon on Midsummer Day (in Act I), through the heat of the afternoon (in Act II), to starry night and the chilly mist-enveloped dawn with which the opera ends. Nature takes over, symbolically, also in the Ritual Dances of Acts II and III.[11] The first three dances interrupt the courtship of Bella and Jack in Act II. Each of these dances entails animal transformations – a mythological sequence which Tippett drew from the Mabinogion story of Gwion and Cerridwen, as reported by Robert Graves in *The White Goddess* – a familiar component in the mythology of the sex-chase and in various other contexts, such as Jungian psychology.[12] As the two lovers go off to make love in the shadows of the wood, the prelude to Act II – a rich texture of woodwind figurations, romantic horn-calls and a string theme taking the music to a voluptuous climax (all of this opening redolent of Ravel's *Daphnis et Chloë*) – returns to introduce the dances. The music subsides and the dancers come out of the temple to their usual glockenspiel motif. Then, preceding the first dance and thereafter separating each dance from the next, are episodes of 'transformation' music. These three dances are, in fact, all built on ground-basses and use concentric structures that are characteristic of the opera in general. They merit description in some detail, for within them

Tippett achieves his foremost aim of taking us into a symbolic realm beyond the world of actuality, even that represented by a stage-set. If the starting-point of the music is pictorial, it summons up unsuspected power and passion. The tensions between masculine and feminine, of Jungian *animus* and *anima*, first acknowledged by Mark and Jenifer in Act I, are thrust into the foreground.

The first dance, 'The earth in autumn: the hound chases the hare', begins softly on harp, cellos and basses, and the chase sequence is led by a flute in scurrying semiquavers. At the end the hare eludes the hound, the scene is re-set and the transformation returns, leading as before to assertive repeated chords and a pause on an open fifth for horns. The second dance is called 'The water in winter: the otter chases the fish', and grows from its slow, murky opening towards a cadenza for two clarinets. As the otter dives into the stream, the chase gets under way again – twice in the original uncut version of the ballet. With difficulty, the fish escapes (cadenza for clarinets again), the otter returns and the scene is once more transformed. The third dance, 'The air in spring: the hawk chases the bird', begins with preparatory music as before, which now comes to rest on a soft D major chord for four solo violins, and the dance starts with these four soloists. The appearance of the bird is marked by soft plucked lower strings supported by staccato bassoon notes. The hawk flies down (descending woodwind scales) and the bird hops into shelter. The hawk retreats and the rite begins again a second and third time, finally with evident defeat in store for the bird. The dance is interrupted by a scream from Bella – as if awakening from a nightmare – and the dance is broken off.

In Act III, after Sosostris has vanished, and King Fisher has been carried to his grave, the dancers return (introduced by essentially the same transformation music as before) for the final ritual dance, entitled 'Fire in summer: the voluntary human sacrifice'. This fire-dance is a ceremony of the kind described at length by Frazer in *The Golden Bough* (e.g. South German fire ceremonies in which lovers leapt over the flames hand in hand, the higher they leapt and the higher the flames, the better their marital prospects). Here, Mark and Jenifer reappear, singing ecstatically (and in canonic imitation); the duet continues until the couple are hidden from view, still singing; the pace quickens and the chorus joins in pace to intone praises of the 'carnal love through which the race of men is everlastingly renewed'. There is a rapturous climax that leads to a return of the music to the opening of Act II.

Back in the 1950s, some people took the view that the opera should have ended at this stage. But Tippett always felt that after the dream-like experience of the opera, we have to exit from the theatre into the street. There follows, therefore, an extended coda, as the chorus awaken from the dream to a new dawn and Mark and Jenifer return – their re-entry mirroring the manner of their first encounter in Act I, no longer prompting dissension but happy harmony. And as everyone leaves, they sing a couplet from Yeats that encapsulates the new-found hope and regenerative impulse underlying the opera:

> All things fall and are built again
> And those that build them again are gay.[13]

The stage is left empty, as the orchestra alone sweeps towards its final cadences.

If much of *The Midsummer Marriage* is on a high-flown symbolic level, it is equally convincing when dealing with the down-to-earth couple, Bella and Jack. In Act I, their readiness to flirt with each other at the slightest opportunity and their courtship in the first scene of Act II, help to place the other elements in the drama in a proper perspective. Bella's concluding set-piece in Act II, sung as she is combing her air and putting on make-up, has a poise and delicacy that must be the envy of every composer who has attempted a comic opera. They too, however, are integrated into the main action: for when in Act III, Jack defies King Fisher's order to unveil Sosostris, opting instead to go out into the world with his beloved Bella, he prefigures that integrity of mind and body which are at the heart of the relationship between Mark and Jenifer, shortly to be revealed.

The libretto and the music in *The Midsummer Marriage* contain ultimately a richness of reference and symbolic meaning that can only be touched upon here: indeed, there is possibly too much for any one production to do it complete justice. This is certainly not an opera to be trotted out as a repertory piece. On the other hand, every re-staging of it, each re-engagment with its issues, is bound to be stimulating: and critics and opera-lovers alike tend to come away stunned by the sheer miraculous freshness and vigour of Tippett's musical invention, his control of pace and mood and his incomparable sureness of touch in matching voices and orchestral colours. There are a couple of places in Act III where the story is re-told too often, or the repetition of felicitous musical ideas causes them to outstay their welcome (this is true particularly in the final scene of the opera). But *The Midsummer Marriage* has a unique, uncanny capacity to ensnare the listener in its dreams, its celebrations and its grandeur of conception.

King Priam

In Act III of *The Midsummer Marriage*, when Mark and Jenifer attain the illumination for which they have searched, the He-Ancient (in the final Ritual Dance) sings:

> Fate and Freedom are a paradox,
> Choose the fate but yet the God
> Speaks through whatever fate we choose.

This is Tippett's point of departure for his next opera, *King Priam*. Each time Tippett has embarked on a new operatic project, his first impulse has been to tackle a different genre. This time he wanted to write a tragedy, in the Racinian sense in which the outcome of the action is determined by unavoidable destiny. Tippett's decision to do so arose partly out of reading a book on Racine and Pascal by the literary critic and philosopher, Lucien Goldmann, *Le Dieu*

Caché. Goldmann, a Marxist, held that tragedy in the modern epoch was an impossibility, since whether one chose a Christian view of the world or a Marxist one, the outcome was always eventual happiness – either in the after-life or in some ideal society of the future. For Tippett this was demonstrably false. *King Priam* thus shows us 'the absolute solitude of the tragic characters under the gaze of the hidden God'[14] – the hidden God being, of course, fate or destiny: not just an up-to-date retelling of a story out of Homer, but an opera of relevance to any period, not least our own war-torn century.

Once he had settled on Homer's *Iliad*, Tippett was able to articulate his intentions quite clearly:[15]

> 'At the very beginning, there was a series of scenic titles, like eight ages of man: Birth, Boyhood, Young Love, Warriors, Women, Judgement, Mercy, Death. In each of these the characters (now one, now the other) are presented with some problem of choice and action, but in the early scenes given little knowledge. Yet the tragedy flows from one such choice, honourably made: Priam and Hecuba at the cradle of Paris. So that this first scene is truly the key to all – exactly crucial. Not birth itself, but what will flow into the world through the child that is born.'

Tippett's overall theme in the opera is 'the mysterious nature of human choice', as exhibited in the relations between Priam, King of Troy, his wife Hecuba, their sons, Hector and Paris, and their wives, Andromache and Helen. Whereas in Homer, war is in the foreground, here it is only a backcloth to the main action. Our attention is focused upon the six protagonists, three male, three female, all of them preoccupied with a series of choices that involve the need to distinguish between personal desire and the fulfilment of social and political duty – choices that admit less readily of easy solutions than might at first seem to be the case. The internal conflicts experienced by the main characters are crystallized within the monologues that are the core of the work.

Thus, at the outset, Priam has to decide whether or not he should put to death his baby son Paris. According to the Old Man, brought in to interpret Hecuba's dream, Paris is destined to cause the death of his father. Priam, as his first monologue makes clear, is torn between the impulses of 'A father and a king'. And although he orders the child to be killed, Paris is saved from death, is brought up by a shepherd and eventually reunited with his family (in scene 2), at which point Priam reverses his decision in another monologue that counterbalances the first. Paris goes on to abduct Helen (scene 3), thereby provoking a war (Act II) and his father's death at the hands of Achilles' son, Neoptolemus, at the end of the opera.

The emphasis upon monologues and a hard-edged style of presentation brought with them a slant towards vocal declamation rather than lyricism. Paris and Helen, for example, are not allowed a love-duet in which to unburden their passion. Paris is instead made to ponder the catastrophic consequences of his involvement with Helen in a self-questioning monologue (Act I, scene 3).

King Priam also differs from Tippett's other operas in that its characters are not linked explicitly with any external prototypes, theatrical, historical or mythological. Tippett's sole ploy of that sort – and it is a brilliant one – is a new version of the Judgement of Paris. He fuses together the three female protagonists and the three goddesses, to one of whom Paris is invited to give the golden apple in the final scene of Act I. For Paris, the goddesses Athene, Hera and Aphrodite closely resemble the three women in his life – respectively, Hecuba, Andromache and Helen: thus Tippett contrived for the roles so that they are taken by the same three singers. Hecuba/Athene offers to inspire Paris on the battlefield; Andromache/Hera offers the warmth of a secure marriage: but Paris rejects them in favour of the illicit passion promised by Helen/Aphrodite.

By such methods as these, *King Priam* avoids becoming an

The composer on holiday in Spain with Wilfred Franks, *circa* 1932 *(David Ayerst)*

Michael Tippett (right) aged about seven, with his brother Peter

Tippet in Zambia in 1975
(Anna Bush Crews)

Top: Michael Tippett conducting the Leicestershire Schools Symphony Orchestra in the late Sixties *(W.E. Hall)*
Below: Tippett conducting the English Chamber Orchestra in a Queen Elizabeth Hall rehearsal on 9 January 1980 *(Malcolm Crowthers)*
Right: San Francisco Opera production of *The Midsummer Marriage* in 1983 *(David Powers)*

Act I of *The Knot Garden* in the 1970 production at the Royal Opera House, Covent Garden *(Mike Evans)*

Michael Tippett with Colin Davis after the première of the Third Symphony in 1972 *(Mike Evans)*

Right: Kent Opera production of *King Priam* in 1985 *(Malcolm Crowthers)*

Bottom: European première of *New Year* at Glyndebourne in 1990 *(Guy Gravett)*

Sir Michael with Sam Wanamaker, the director of the 1977 production of *The Ice Break*, and Ralph Koltai, the designer *(Donald Southern)*

A scene from the Hamburg Ballet's production of *Hamlet (Holger Badekow)*

A page from the manuscript score of *The Mask of Time*
(*Sir Michael Tippett/Schott & Co.*)

Tippett giving an outdoor seminar Aspen, Colorado in 1978

Tippett with NJPO roto-tom players at a summer course in 1995 *(Schott & Co.)*

historical documentary or pageant. It highlights instead the factors contingent to the Homeric epic – factors that are none the less important because they are the eternal problems of the human heart, of human destiny. In Tippett's words, the opera is concerned with 'the values that arise from the past staged with an intense sense of the Present'.

The male protagonists in the opera have contrasting attitudes to war. Hector and Paris are polar opposites, the former aggressively virile, the latter romantic and self-indulgent. In Act II, scene 1, Priam, who has no desire for war at all, tries to reconcile and unite them. Providing a counterbalance to them in the next scene – and in the Greek camp – are Achilles, unwilling to fight, and his friend, Patroclus who, 'in the nick of time' restores some sense of manhood to the great hero. All are brought together in the great climactic ending of Act II, where Priam and his sons pray to the gods for assistance. Their prayer is interrupted by Achilles's blood-curdling war-cry – Patroclus having been killed – echoed by the chorus.

The female protagonists (counterpointed against their maids, in an Upstairs/Downstairs-style presentation) take the stage at the start of Act III. Hecuba is still concerned with the outcome of the war and the fate of the city, Andromache still trusts in the marriage bond (in Tippett's words, 'she echoes down the centuries as the proud, passionate, grieving widow'). Helen remains the one character who never has to choose. Fatal in her public and private involvements, she is faithful only to some mysterious unavoidable passion. Insulted by Andromache, Helen shows her true colours, reminding us of her divine birth – 'for I am Zeus's daughter, conceived when the great wings beat above Leda'; love with Helen 'reaches up to heaven, for it reaches down to hell'. Helen's monologue is the longest allotted to a female character in the opera.

After attending the Jean-Louis Barrault company's production of Paul Claudel's *Christophe Colombe* (with music by Milhaud), which he saw in London in 1956,[16] Tippett realized that the best

way to structure his new composition was as an opera that
emulated Brecht's 'epic theatre' and Shakespeare's history plays.
Thus he shaped the piece as a sequence of operatic scenes and
commentaries. Immediately after the opening scene, and elsewhere
in the opera, the subordinate figures – the Nurse, the Old Man and
Young Guard – combine to form a chorus commenting on the
action. Their initial function is to act as an extension of Priam's
mind. In addition, they signal changes of time and place.

Also there to provide continuity between scenes is Hermes the
Messenger or 'Divine Go-Between', as he announces himself in
Act I – meaning that he connects up the inner world of human
beings and the outside factual everyday world. Taking over the
'death motif' (*see* Example 12) –

Example 12

– that follows upon the Old Man's reading of the dream in the
opening scene, Hermes precipitates Paris into making the choice
that is crucial to his father's future: the choice of one of the three
Graces (or Goddesses). In Act II, Hermes oils the action further,
effecting the changes from one side to another in the war. But in
Act III his ironic nature comes to the fore as he presides over
Priam's imminent death. Interpreting the final scene for the
audience, he steps outside the action to sing a hymn to music. This
contemplative, visionary moment in the opera precedes the death
of Priam, who now sings only of his awareness of the inner world:

> I see mirrors
> Myriad upon myriad moving
> The dark forms
> Of creation.

Of necessity, in this opera, Tippett altered his musical style and formal procedures to serve his freshly defined theatrical aims. In *The Midsummer Marriage*, the voices are supported by a homogeneous flow of orchestral sound. In *King Priam*, the orchestra is fragmented into a heterogeneous mixture of solos and ensembles, bringing forth a mosaic of instrumental gestures that are rigorously related to the personalities and situations in the drama – Wagner's leitmotif method carried to an ultimate level. From the echoing trumpet-calls and off-stage choral cries at the start, which return at the end of the opera, each motif in the score is etched by means of distinctive instrumentation. The cry of the child Paris in scene 1 is allotted to the oboe and this instrumental association is retained throughout the opera. Priam's regal strength is expressed by two horns set between high and low piano octaves. The Old Man interpreting Hecuba's dream is given ominously murky music for bass-clarinet, bassoon and contrabassoon. Only when the dream has been interpreted and Hecuba and Priam have to choose between killing the child or immediately accepting Fate by letting him live – only then do the strings enter. Hecuba's response – 'Then am I no longer mother to this child' – is declaimed against fast figurations on violins (never divided into conventional firsts and seconds). Priam's anguished conflict of loyalties – 'A father and a king' – is uttered above sadly plodding violas, cellos and basses. In the theatre, the listener adjusts quickly to such spare, telling instrumental gestures and identifies the motifs at each recurrence.

Unless told in advance, few will notice that the strings are omitted altogether from Act II. On the other hand, in their absence, Tippett provides relief from the abrasive violence of the war-music for wind and percussion with an intimate solo song for Achilles accompanied only by guitar: its entry, after the war-music has reached a climax, is one of the composer's theatrical master-strokes. The nostalgic mood of Achilles' song is enhanced by the sad tones of cor anglais and two horns associated with Patroclus. When Achilles decides to allow Patroclus to fight Hector, aggressive piano, percussion and horns take over. All this is recalled in the scene in Act III when Priam comes to Achilles' tent to beg for the body of Hector – probably the most poignant scene in the whole opera.

Tippett's prime task in *King Priam* was to emphasize immediacy, actuality and inevitability. The clarity with which the narrative unfolds is exemplary. The very opening scene offers in microcosm its overall progress from Paris's birth to Priam's death; Priam recapitulates this also in his monologue in scene 2, while the story is again recapitulated and its outcome foretold at other points in the action. Likewise, the pinpointing of character and motivation is almost deceptively precise. *King Priam* offers stunning stage-craft and an extraordinary discipline, quite unexpected in a composer deemed so often at the mercy of an over-fertile imagination. Successive productions have confirmed it as one of the composer's finest achievements. But Tippett had yet more radical operatic ideas in store.

The Knot Garden

Actuality is all but ignored in *The Knot Garden*. In this opera, we focus exclusively on the inner life of seven individuals. A plot as such hardly exists. The action takes place within the span of a single day. The knot garden that forms the set is a dream-world conjured into existence at the very start by Mangus, a psychiatrist. Comparing himself to Prospero in Shakespeare's *The Tempest*, he imagines he has the power to solve people's problems and set the world to rights. The knot garden is thus a magical place, like the island in *The Tempest*, or, for that matter, the wood in *The Midsummer Marriage*. At the point in Act III where Mangus realizes he lacks the powers he claimed for himself, that 'Prospero's a fake ... this island's due to sink into the sea', the knot garden disappears briefly from view.

The libretto and music of *The Knot Garden* are thus steeped in allusions. The title itself is an allusion to the formalized gardens of French origin popular in Elizabethan times, usually made up of tiny box-hedges and low shrubs, and intended to relate the layout of the garden to the architecture of the house it adjoined. It could also be thought of as a maze, or as a rose-garden in which, according to Persian tradition, lovers meet. The entire action of Tippett's opera takes place in a garden which changes with the inner situations, and in the central act it turns explicitly into a maze.

Tippett indicates the different functions of the knot garden by giving each act a title. In Act I, called 'Confrontation', it is simply the place to which Mangus (his name a variant of the Latin *magnus*, suggesting greatness and power) has brought six people whose relationships are in disarray. The most important of them are Faber (his name chosen because of its Latin origin – man, maker, engineer) and Thea (the Greek for a goddess) whose marriage is at breaking-point. He is preoccupied with his business affairs, his factory papers; she withdraws to the dream-world of the garden. Their ward, Flora, still a 'flower' – an adolescent and virgin – is obsessed with the half-real, half-imagined sexual threat of Faber. Two of their friends now appear: Dov, a homosexual musician (his Jewish name chosen because of its association with David, a psalmist and musician in the Old Testament) and Mel, a bisexual black writer (his name derived from a Latin term of endearment, meaning honey). Their love affair also has broken down. Lastly, there is Thea's sister, Denise, a freedom fighter and revolutionary. She stands apart from all the other characters in that her psychological difficulties are more a product of her political and social activism. Her scarred countenance and declamatory rhetoric add a special dimension to the drama. Tippett manipulates his characters in the manner of Shaw in *Heartbreak House* or Edward Albee in *Who's Afraid of Virginia Woolf?* In Act II, entitled 'Labyrinth', these games are intensified, the characters interact in a fast-changing sequence of pairings, but are drawn away again when their encounters attain a climax of possible violence or love. In Act III, called 'Charade', the characters play at Mangus's instigation, a further series of charades and games aimed at achieving self-awareness and reconciliation. Act III also brings into the foreground its links with *The Tempest*, which are an important feature of the work overall.

The Knot Garden begins with a 'storm' prelude, even more of a psychological storm than the one that opens Shakespeare's play. Some of Tippett's characters are modelled on Shakespearean prototypes: Mangus dreams he is Prospero; Faber is a reincarnation of Ferdinand; Flora, Miranda; and Mel and Dov, right from their histrionic first entry in the opera, pretend to be Caliban and Ariel. In the charades they play in Act III, they revert to these prototypes: and their anticipated resolution of their problems is underlined by Ariel's song of invitation – Tippett's own setting of 'Come unto these yellow sands', originally as part of his incidental music for an Old Vic Theatre production of *The Tempest*.

If *The Tempest* is the main link with past theatrical tradition in Tippett's opera, the techniques of television, cinema and the twentieth-century popular musical are used to ensure a sense of immediacy, modernity and psychological truth. Tippett had nurtured the idea of using such techniques for some time. In his essay, 'The Birth of an Opera', he had noted that in the film *Citizen Kane*, 'the cutting and the shots themselves (that is scene-changing *in excelsis*) become part of the artistic experience and put the old-fashioned scene-changing of the operatic stage to shame.'[17]

By the time he came to write *The Knot Garden*, he felt that his opera had to relate to the important new genre of contemporary theatre, now central to everyone's lives – television. Thus, the action of the opera often moves at the sort of pace more generally experienced in TV or cinematic presentations. Moreover, instead of cumbersome transitions between scenes, Tippett produced 16 bars of purely schematic 'non-music' (as he calls it, picking up a term he had heard Harrison Birtwistle use) that recur throughout to effect the cinematic 'dissolves' (as they are called in the libretto) from one scene to the next.

Like *King Priam*, *The Knot Garden* is built like a mosaic out of little blocks of musical material – leitmotifs which remain in the memory because their scoring is never changed, e.g. Thea's gently swaying motif, symbolizing her absorption with the garden and her inner world (*see* Example 13) –

Example 13

– is always scored for three horns and high strings. Examined in detail, they turn out mostly to be brief song-and-dance routines, entirely apposite to an opera in which the characters are acting out dreams and fantasies. Faber's sexually provocative stance is encapsulated in a jaunty, angular trumpet tune (*see* Example 14):

Example 14

When they enter, Dov and Mel, dressed up as Ariel and Caliban, dance round Flora and taunt each other. Only Thea and Mangus never dance. Sometimes the dances are built into big song-and-dance numbers, such as the slow blues and fast up-tempo boogie that form the basis of the final ensemble of confrontation in Act I, or the scene between Mel and Dov in Act II.

More fundamentally, dance figures prominently on a metaphorical level in the opera. The 'storm' prelude at the start of Act I is thus really an angular, distorted dance which keeps breaking down and starting up again (*see* Example 15). This music recurs in Act II, linking the different pairings-off of the characters in the labyrinth; and at the end of the opera, when Thea and Faber have reached the stage where they might once more communciate, the storm-motif, slowed down, goes into reverse and finally concentrates its chromatic intensity within a final upward-sweeping chordal aggregate, starting from the bass note B, as at the start of the opera. When the characters line up together at the climax of Act III and join hands in an expression of reconciliation, Tippett's libretto also quotes from a poem by Goethe, 'Magisches Netz', which depicts the comings and goings of a group of people dancing with a net.

Knowing that *The Knot Garden* is anchored in *The Tempest* and being aware of the use of dance imagery, literal and metaphorical, are the two essential lifelines for those navigating their way through a production. But it is also worthwhile noting that the piece is not just a multiplicity of abruptly curtailed interactions between the characters. The opera does have an overall shape and trajectory. Up until about two-thirds of the way through, it appears that the relationships are in permanent disarray, indeed free fall. But, then, suddenly near the end of Act II, the two most innocent figures in the opera, Dov and Flora, find themselves flung together in the maze. Both are in a state of considerable distress. This is the turning-point of the work: one realizes that things now can only get better!

ex.15

Tippett: The Knot Garden, Act1

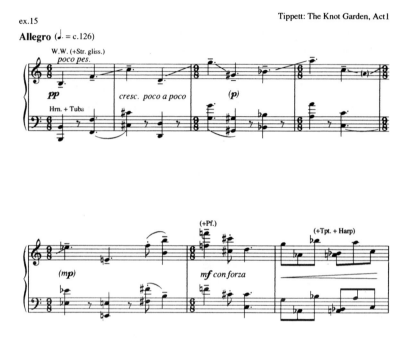

Example 15

Dov comforts Flora and persuades her to sing. In her immaturity,
in her inability to connect with the tension-ridden modern world
which she inhabits, she can only retreat into a past dream-world
through the medium of a Schubert song. Dov counters with a
song of his own, a modern-style piece, with electric guitar and
throbbing pop-style rhythms, in which he first tells of his
boyhood amid the skyscrapers of a big city, in a home without a
garden. After this first stanza, sung to Flora, he now stands up and
– *as an artist* – sings to the audience and to the world: he dreams
of the warm south and of the 'golden Californian west'; he
dreams of eternal youth and of love 'in the fabulous rose-garden'.
Suddenly, the hostile labyrinth flowers into a rose-garden. From
now on in the opera, there is some likelihood that the tensions
that divide everyone will be resolved. For a moment though,

there is a rude awakening as Mel appears to remind Dov that this dream of love had been learnt from him; Dov comes down to earth and dismisses it bitterly as false.

To a degree quite rare in opera, *The Knot Garden* forces its characters to confront their sexuality. For Thea it is largely a symbolic inner world, expressed in her absorption with cultivating her garden and in the protection of her 'seedling' Flora from the lechery of Faber. Thea is only half aware of her reversion to a Circe-like role of seducer, when – having brought out a tray of cocktails – she draws Mel away into the garden, leaving Dov isolated and shattered by the supposed betrayal inflicted by his partner; he goes down on his knees and howls like a dog. In Act II, provoked by Faber's continuing pursuit of Flora, Thea reverts to another classic prototype, appearing as one of the Furies to correct and 'cleanse' him, attacking him with a horse-whip. Meanwhile, Faber, in Act I, when he unexpectedly stumbles on the howling Dov, is intrigued to hear of his friendship with Mel and is half-consciously attracted. In Act II, Faber, tempted by an inner urge to explore further, angles for a kiss from Dov.

Flora's childlike innocence is consistently stressed, as when (in Act I, for instance) she day-dreams, singing a children's counting song, as she picks flowers: at its climax – 'catch a nigger by his toe/If he hollers ...' she is brought back to reality by the entry of Dov and Mel. Bewildered by their camp appearance and behaviour, she immediately affects the studiously polite tones of Alice in Wonderland. Similarly, in Act II, her singing is interrupted by Faber, attempting to bully her into womanhood. Her confusion about her own sexual identity is manifest also when she sings Schubert's 'Die Liebe farbe' (from *Die Schöne Müllerin*) to Dov – for as Dov points out, it is a boy's song.

Meanwhile, in Act II, there is a crucial sexual confrontation scene for Dov and Mel, stylised as a song-and-dance number with refrains. Mel ruthlessly denies any validity in Dov's love for him and observes that Dov is infatuated only with the attributes of manhood – physical beauty – not man as a totality: in their case a relationship is impossible, for Mel asserts that 'there's no family/between black and white'. Giving Dov the best advice he could ever receive, he declares:

> Stop howling now.
> Become yourself.
> Go turn your howls to music.

That is literally what Dov, the singer, the creator of songs, ultimately has to do: it is what Tippett, after his own sexual crisis and Jungian self-analysis had to do – 'turn his howls to music'.

Sexuality is not the problem that concerns Denise, but *power*: regarding sexuality largely as one of many power struggles, she thus acts as a catalyst to the action, intervening crucially in these turbulent relationships. On her arrival, she recalls the horrors and brutality to which she and other freedom fighters were subjected – and which she refuses to forget or forgive – offering thus a glimpse of those realities beyond the garden which the others hardly dare mention.

Their collective response to her is stylized in a blues initiated by Mel, and imitated by Dov and Flora. Moving into a fast boogie-tempo, Faber enacts the traditional role of the man escaping from the domestic problems by going off into town –

> 'cause I'm gonna play the high-class joints,
> I'm gonna play the low-class joints ...

– which prompts an even firmer rejection from Thea, retreating into her inner world:

> I walk, talk – but all by myself.
> Alone in my garden.

As the slow tempo resumes, Mel, Dov and Flora assert the role of the blues both to articulate pain and to assuage it; Thea and Faber remain apart, and Denise can only utter wordless anguish. Mangus, above the mêlée, impotently quotes from *The Tempest*:

And my ending is despair
Unless I be relieved by prayer
Which pierces so, that it assaults
Mercy itself, and frees all faults.

The related themes of sexuality and power are united and interwoven in the charades of Act III. But matters are not sorted out as easily as Mangus imagines. Mel, crawling around submissively as Caliban, and Dov, imprisoned (as Ariel) in a tree, when they are both set free, 'go beyond the script' and attack each other. Denise, lost amid so much personal confusion, reacts uneasily when Thea recommends the warmth of love, possibly a close relationship with Mel. True, in Act II, she had found common political ground with Mel. Their relationship was cemented with the emergence of the civil rights song, 'We shall overcome', within the orchestral texture, which Mel joins in singing at the climax, 'O deep in my heart ...'. But Denise is ill at ease with Mel's sexuality: and she is distraught when Mel-Caliban (in Act III) tries to rape Flora-Miranda. Ironically, now, Dov, acknowledging that he doesn't belong any more with Mel, urges him to make it up with Denise, which he does reluctantly. Rather than a full union, there is a final truce between them.

In a game of chess set up by Mangus, symbolically representative of the devious power games in which the characters are involved, Flora-Miranda finds the strength to resist Faber-Ferdinand's deceptions and leaves exultantly. In another chess-game, Thea begins to communicate with Faber: her fears evaporate and she sings of the mutual self-awareness that has brought them together again. Mangus attempts to reconcile Dov-Ariel and Mel-Caliban in a mock trial scene with Faber as jailer. Set free from servitude, Dov-Ariel identifies completely with 'Music, my muse': Dov's future life lies only with his art. After the opera, Tippett followed him into the future in a song-cycle, *Songs for Dov*.

Dealing with Mel-Caliban proves to be a bigger task than

Mangus can accomplish. The issue of racial superiority surfaces, as Mel-Caliban asserts his rights and Mangus treats him as an underling. The continued taunting of Dov-Ariel by Mel-Caliban prompts Mangus to give up his efforts at setting things right. He strides to the footlights to end the illusion (as does Prospero) that he has power:

> Now that I break my staff and drown my book.

Like the rest of us, he is foolish and fond, 'whistling to keep my pecker up'. Throughout the opera, Tippett has depicted his characters

> Whistling to a music
> Compounded of our groans and shrieks
> bitter-sweet and wry
> Tender yet tough: ironic
> Celebration for that trickster Eros.

The exultant affirmations of love in *The Midsummer Marriage* are not possible here. At the most, it is a question of whether

> For a timid moment
> We submit to love
> Exit from the inner cage
> Turn each to each to all.

Nevertheless, there is a whiff of hope in the air. Dov, Mel and Faber – reinforced by offstage voices – allude to Ariel's two songs, 'Full fathom five' and 'Come unto these yellow sands', intimations, in turn, of death and rebirth and of song and dance. The scene reaches its climax with an allusion to Goethe's

> ... magic net
> That holds us veined
> Each to each to all.

Exiting in succession, Denise and Mel together find common ground politically, Flora leaves radiantly for her 'brave new world', Dov, the loveless loner, arouses pity. Finally, Thea is impelled to 'put away the seed packets' and Faber 'puts away the factory papers'. As the curtain falls in the opera, it rises in their lives. A *tour de force*, dramatically and musically, *The Knot Garden* is exactly the kind of uninhibited discourse on love, sexuality and power that the contemporary opera-house always needed. Its depth of insight, dazzling theatricality and concentrated musical potency have yet to be equalled, let alone superseded.

The Ice Break

The Ice Break takes onto a large canvas the themes of forgiveness and reconciliation present in *The Knot Garden*. Tippett declares in the preface to the libretto that its subject is 'stereotypes – their imprisoning characteristics – and the need for individual rebirth'.

The title of the opera embraces both actual and symbolic references to such rebirth. On the one hand it refers to 'the frightening but exhilarating sound of ice breaking on the great northern rivers' which signals the arrival of spring. Such extreme seasonal transformations are best known to Russians and others in the more northern latitudes where they form part of the whole experience of living from one year to the next. Stravinsky, asked by Robert Craft what he had loved most in Russia, replied: 'The violent Russian spring that seemed to begin in an hour and was like the whole earth cracking. That was the most wonderful event of every year from my childhood.'[18] Galina von Meck (grand-daughter of Tchaikovsky's patroness), recalling in her memoirs her time in a labour camp, notes that when spring comes to Siberia, 'it comes so intensely that one can positively watch things coming out of the earth.'[19] The ice-breaking sounds are therefore naturally prominent in the deathbed recollections of Nadia, one of two Russian émigré figures in Tippett's opera. But the breaking of the ice – the motif that starts the opera and recurs three times later on (it consists of a brass and percussion chord and rhythmically manipulated major and minor thirds) (*see* Example 16) – signifies more than a background context in nature or the seasons. It draws

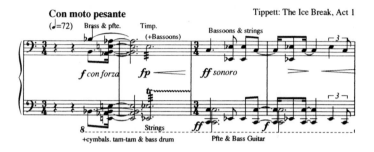

Example 16

our attention to the main concern of the opera – 'whether or not we can be reborn from the stereotypes we live in'. That is what Tippett calls 'the central problem of our time' and it manifests itself in the plot through the struggles between racial groups (black versus white) and opposing generations (young versus old).

The first two acts delineate the tensions that arise between Lev, a Russian teacher newly released into exile to join his wife Nadia, and their son Yuri, who finds it difficult to accept him. Their discord is exacerbated by the racial strife in which Yuri becomes involved. Yuri sustains serious injury when it turns into a riot. His survival in Act III, after a successful hospital operation, is immediately interpreted by the chorus as a spring-like portent of reconciliation in the world at large:

> Spring comes to you at the farthest
> In the very end of harvest.

– *The Tempest* once more supplying Tippett with an apt point of reference. Sadly, but inevitably, this is a dream: reconciliation is only temporary, and Tippett ends the opera with a scene between Lev and Yuri that echoes what he had read in Goethe's novel *Wilhelm Meisters Wanderjahre* some fifty years earlier. Wilhelm, by this time in his career, a country doctor, has to save his son's life. He bleeds him and as he looks at his naked, sleeping body, remarks: 'Yet you will always be brought forth again, glorious image of God, and likewise be maimed, wounded afresh from within or without.'[20]

These are closing words of the opera: a perception that (metaphorically) spring may be followed by many more winters, necessitating an even greater effort to achieve rebirth. The cycle of conflict and resolution is eternal. Tippett drives the point home musically in the hieratic motif which ends the opera – held chords decorated by harp arpeggios – whose first appearance in Act I accompanied Lev's recollections of imprisonment, when he comments: 'Poetry upheld me [quoting from Mandelstam]: "The earth was worth ten heavens to us' (*see* Example 17).

Tippett: The Ice Break, end of Act 3

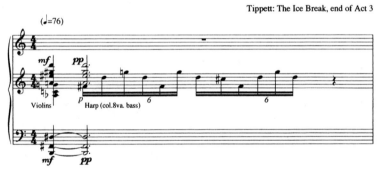

Example 17

The Ice Break differs from Tippett's previous three operas in giving the chorus a variety of roles. One reason for this was his fascination with *masks*, dating back to his attendance at a production in the 1920s of Ernst Toller's play *Masse Mensch*, in which the rows of chorus figures with their backs to the audience suddenly turned round and disconcertingly revealed that they were faceless. Tippett's interest in masks was re-activated during a continental holiday in the early 1970s, when he attended a performance in Paris by the great mime Marcel Marceau. Reporting on it, Tippett commented, 'The most vivid of Marceau's creations that evening was of the mask-maker. By a quite fabulous technique, Marceau with his hands and facial expressions alone presented to our visionary eye the masks being tried on and taken off. The one grinning mask could not be taken off and the desperate struggle began, until it had to be wrenched off in a soundless agony. I think that here again we were being moved by archetypal feelings never far below the surface of our modern world. What masks indeed does this world force us to wear? And who then are *we*?' In Paris, on the same trip, he was also greatly affected when he saw the film *Orphée Nègre* in which the legend of Orpheus and Euridice is transferred to a new context, the Rio de Janeiro Carnival. 'There is the sense of contemporaneity; the modern city, the lorries, the power station, the slum shacks or the hills above the town. There is the sense of the primitive; the dancing and the music and of course the masks!'[21]

The chorus in *The Ice Break* became a metaphor for people in real life who, basically anonymous, are capable of wearing many masks that indicate the particular stereotype they have adopted. Their activities cut across the narrative in a manner for which Tippett uses the term 'surreal' – inhabiting a realm beyond actuality. (This notion crystallized in his mind as he observed the choral interpenetrations of the action in the 1968/9 Covent Garden production of Berlioz's *Benvenuto Cellini*.) At the start of the opera the masked chorus are the crowds of fans that gather at the airport to meet the black champion, Olympion – a mixture of blacks and whites, collectively supporting their idol with uninhibited slogan-shouting and sexually chauvinist behaviour. In Act II they polarize into rival black and white mobs, and eventually come to blows. Off-stage during Act III, they represent Nadia's friends from her childhood, calling to her as she dies. Then they become another stereotypical group, seekers for Paradise invoking their guru, the androgynous Astron (a role sung jointly by mezzo-soprano and counter-tenor, following the example of Britten's music for God in his canticle 'Abraham and Isaac'); later, the same group rushes through the hospital where Yuri has survived his operation, heralding a new spring.

A consequence of these choral interpolations is to accelerate the pace of the opera, making it Tippett's shortest and fastest. There are no transitions between scenes. The action shifts back and forth between exteriors and interiors, presenting the stage director with a formidable task, though not, in these days of sophisticated theatrical technology, an insuperable one. More of a risk is the implied requirement that the chorus should be capable of fast movement, even dance, 'to obtain the imperatively necessary histrionic vitality in the chorus scenes'. Tippett writes in his libretto, 'non-singing performers may have to be used'.

Just as there is an archetypal sound for the ice breaking, so, too, with the chorus, whose music relies mainly on basic chanting, shouting and hymn-like motifs. Against the anonymity of the chorus the nine characters in the opera have to assert their individuality. This is quite a test for them, as some are by their very nature stuck in stereotypical postures, while others die off in Act II and three of them – a police lieutenant, Luke the doctor and Astron the Messenger – make appearances that are far too brief for them to have a chance to grow and develop. In fact, in an early draft of the scenario, Tippett contemplated bringing back a number of them as ghosts (so to speak) in what was to become the Psychedelic Trip scene of Act III, as a way of clinching their inter-relationships. Disappointingly, perhaps, he never followed up that option. Some of the characters in the opera are thus sketchily developed.

Aside from the three peripheral figures just mentioned, there are two main groupings of characters, with one person in common: the first comprises a family – Lev, Nadia and Yuri; the second, two pairs of young people – Olympion, 'a black champion', and Hannah his girlfriend; and Gayle, Hannah's white friend, whose boyfriend is Yuri. The two girls cross sides, as it were: Hannah finds Olympion's violent, divisive personality increasingly intolerable; Gayle, on the other hand, identifying with the black cause, enrages Yuri by prostrating herself before Olympion, his fans egging him on to take sexual advantage of her, thus triggering off the tensions that lead in Act II to a riot. Lev and Nadia stand apart from it all, as if paralysed.

The speedy exposition of Act I is followed by a second act of overt confrontation. In the dense opening quartet, Gayle, Nadia, Yuri and Lev each moralize from their own entrenched positions: no one will budge and the ensemble simply ends with the younger figures being lured away into the crowd of whites outside by some sinister chromatically duetting trumpets. Olympion, too, must abandon his love-making with Hannah to join the rival black group. Hannah, in an aria (whose bluesy character is defined by the electric guitars in the orchestra), searches for some hint of sanity amid the wrought-up situation that prevails outside, and asserts an attitude of calm compassion as an alternative. Stepping back from the tumult, thus, Hannah, a nurse by profession, is the first character in the opera to grow in stature.

Now the black and white mobs strike up ritual poses of aggression. The cries of the black group, 'Burn, baby, burn' are superimposed on the barber-shop harmony of the white group's distorted hymn tune (an original Methodist hymn appropriated by the Ku-Klux-Klan and now given new words). Taunts and provocation are articulated by means of an (authentic) voodoo tune on the clarinet for the blacks and a hoedown on the violin for the whites; these, too, are then superimposed, and with rival vocal groups added, the totality becomes a wild montage of competing musical strands.

A brief withdrawal into the intimately reflective world of Nadia and Lev precedes an eruption of crudely explicit violence. The Police Lieutenant, discovering the carnage on the streets – which has cost Olympion and Gayle their lives and left Yuri maimed – offers only a standard response: he sees only human trash, bodies to be removed to the mortuary or hospital. At the end, Hannah, left alone with Lev, shares with him a mood of unspoken sympathy, signified by the soaring violin line that sustains its lyrical course throughout the orchestral epilogue.

The death of Nadia at the start of Act III denotes simply her withdrawal from the conflicts about her. Only her memories matter now. Lev, on the other hand, has an inkling of the reconciliation that may be possible between himself and Yuri: he reads to Nadia on her deathbed the very scene in Goethe's *Wilhelm Meister* from which he will once more quote at the end of the opera. Nadia's death, symbolizing the passing of an older generation of attitudes and ideas, makes way for a new beginning. And this is the underlying purpose of the Psychedelic Trip scene that follows.

Seekers after paradise exist in every generation and in virtually every culture. Their notions of Eden vary: sometimes they find it in a return to Nature (naturism, even) and organic foods; or in the re-enactment of prehistoric rituals (cf. the Stonehenge hippies); sometimes paradise can be a gambler's heaven (Paradise, California, derives its name from 'pair of dice'!); or it might be found in Zen and other oriental cults, or in the hallucinations induced by drugs. Behind the trendy jargon of Tippett's Psychedelic Trip, an age-old aspiration finds expression.

It is here that the chorus are faced with the need to break out of stereotypes. For when Astron appears to them and hands down a Jungian adage –

Take care for the Earth
God will take care for himself.

– they still naïvely acclaim him as a god or guru, a status he
ironically disowns:

Saviour?! Hero?! Me!!
You must be joking.

This is germane both to the message of the opera and to Tippett's
own stance as an artist. The common fault of the crowd is to
worship a prominent figure one day and seek to demolish him or
her the next. Hero-worship is suspect, guru adulation risky,
deification deadly. As an intellectually alive, socially committed
composer, Tippett has encountered all three and has invariably
sought to disabuse those inclined to put him on a pedestal. Astron
(like the messenger-figures in the earlier Tippett operas and the
Presenter in his next one, *New Year*) reflects the composer's
desire only to be treated as a messenger, not as a divine figure
whose message is sacred: for the alternative usually leads to
dogmatic self-righteousness and intolerance.

The intentions behind Tippett's Psychedelic Trip scene are
clear: but it needed much stronger invention – and extension,
maybe – at the start, into a proper vernacular set-piece to
establish the context of the episode rather better. Tippett's
emphasis on televisual conciseness let him down here.

In the succeeding hospital scene, Yuri is the centre of attention,
as Luke, assisted by Hannah, frees him from the plaster in which
he is encased.[22] After a choral eruption (with its invocation to
spring from the masque in *The Tempest*), Hannah brings Yuri to
meet Lev, and with their uncertain reconciliation the opera ends.

New Year

With *New Year*, written a decade after *The Ice Break*, Tippett
allowed himself far more room to manoeuvre. This was
appropriate in what turned out very much to be a summatory

work, compounded of ideas and images that had absorbed his attention from his earliest days right up to the present, as well as a lot of more recent experiences. Its genesis could credibly be dated as far back as 1919 when the composer's parents went to live in France and Tippett at the age of fourteen felt himself to be effectively 'orphaned'. Hiking around Germany in the aftermath of the First World War, he also became aware of the many abandoned children lost and starving in Berlin and other cities.

About sixty-five years later, at the time he was considering the possibility of a new stage-work, Tippett read about the French-Canadian composer, Claude Vivier – murdered in Paris in 1983 – who had lost both his parents in early childhood and was so traumatized as to be unable to speak for several years, thereafter harbouring such deep fears that (for instance) he could only live and work in an environment where there was an excess of electric light. Tippett has always been aware of such wounded or dispossessed 'children of our time'. The coalesence of these memories of his youth and later experiences produced the two disturbed figures that were quickly to become the main focus of *New Year*: Jo-Ann, the young trainee children's doctor, herself an orphan, and her foster-brother, Donny, also orphaned, both of them brought up by a foster-mother, Nan.

New Year contains further links between past and present. As a student, Tippett had read a recently published story, *Men Like Gods* (1921), by H. G. Wells. In this story, a sub-editor on a liberal magazine, Mr Barnstaple, decides to take a recuperative holiday from his work, leaving behind his book, his overbearing wife and three noisy, galumphing children, to drive off into the countryside. During the drive, he skids, bangs his head and wakes up in a kind of socialist utopia of the future – a world in which there is no evil. Wells's story fascinated Tippett then, mainly because of its conjectures on the nature of time: and one of his earliest student compositions was an attempt to set one of these didactic episodes to music (it remained unfinished).

Time remained a major intellectual preoccupation, as

numerous later works attest – from *A Child of Our Time*, and *The Vision of St Augustine* to *The Mask of Time*. It so happened that in 1984 Tippett re-read the Wells story. By chance, also, he came across a recently published book on the Russian novel containing a chapter on three post-revolutionary novels of utopia: Aleksei Tolstoy's *Aelita* (1923), Konstantin Fedin's *Cities and Years* and Marietta Shaginyan's *Mess-Mend* (both 1924).[23] Even more crucially, he saw Jeremy Paul and Alan Gibson's two-part BBC television film entitled *The Flipside of Dominick Hyde* and *Another Flipside for Dominick*.[24] Wells's story and the Russian novels impelled him to envisage a set of characters living a different existence from Jo-Ann, Donny and Nan: an existence that was literally *utopian* (a word deriving from the Greek *outopos*, meaning 'nowhere' or 'radically elsewhere', in a different world, in a distant future). Hence the division in the opera between the three characters from 'Somewhere today' and those from 'Nowhere tomorrow'. Such a division was also manifest in *The Flipside of Dominick Hyde* and Tippett chose to model his two 'utopian' characters – Pelegrin and Merlin – on two corresponding figures in the film. Pelegrin, the handsome young spaceship pilot, is a reincarnation of Dominick, and is so called partly because when Dominick arrived on earth in the spaceship he wore a pilgrim's hat. Merlin is a new version of Caleb, the computer controller, and his name obviously draws on links with the Arthurian legend.

There are some other connections between the film and the opera. The relationship that develops in the film between Dominick, who is living in the year 2130, and Jane, whom he meets by travelling in a flying saucer back to 1981, is re-formulated in the opera, so that the protagonist is now the woman Jo-Ann rather than the man Pelegrin. Of immense importance was Tippett's decision to use a voice-over, a characteristic element in *Dominick Hyde*, as in many television presentations, but new to the opera house. He named this character the Presenter, when it was suggested to him that an unseen voice-over character would be difficult to give credible form in the theatre. The Presenter's role is to conjure up the world of dreams on which the action subsists and to comment on the action. The only utopian character not so far mentioned, Regan, the boss, emerges as a conflation of Rider Haggard's *She* and the singer Servalan in the sci-fi TV series *Blake 7*. Regan is the archetypal iron maiden – 'She Who Must be Obeyed'. (Journalistic rumour at the time of the production of the opera suggested that she was modelled on Margaret Thatcher. That was inaccurate, though the ex-Tory Prime Minister certainly had some of Regan's traits).

At the same time as he put together two sets of characters inhabiting different realms, Tippett made some crucial decisions regarding the theatrical genre he would explore. *New Year* was ultimately the nearest he came to writing a musical. A key factor was the chorus, which he wanted to have both singing and dancing. For a single chorus to do both, as in *The Ice Break* was unsatisfactory, so Tippett now decided to return to having two choruses, one singing, one dancing, as in *The Midsummer Marriage*.

Whereas Tippett still drew to some extent on television and cinematic techniques, he reinstated the transitions between scenes – using the Presenter and chorus to assist in linking the two worlds of the action. Moreover, he wanted to create a fresh new sound-world appropriate to this genre. Thus, for the first time in thirty years, he excluded the piano from his orchestration. Also, instead of using the heterogeneous mixtures of instruments that he deployed from *King Priam* onwards, he decided on homogeneous groups – three flutes (doubling three piccolos), three saxophones, four horns, and so on. The special colour possibilities of electric guitar seemed to him of value in a work full of bizarre fantasy. The orchestra for *New Year*, totalling about 53 players, closely resembled the standard band for a West End or Broadway musical. Moreover, electro-acoustic effects – for the ascent and descent of the spaceship, the voices of a computer, a fountain and a lake – were incorporated as additional 'magical' elements in the score.

New Year is constructed around the dreams and aspirations of its main characters. Jo-Ann dreams of summoning up the strength and determination to go out into the 'Terror Town' in which she lives, to help the abandoned children. Donny's dream is a confused one: he desires to be united with the parents he lost, to discover his Caribbean or African roots, to find some kind of communion with nature and animals, find a real family to which he could belong. Merlin has fantasies of ever-greater feats of technological wizardry, while Regan dreams only of the voyage into a farthermost future in time and space. Above all, there is the dream-love which Pelegrin and Jo-Ann nurture for one another and which will eventually help her realize her professional ambitions. Set apart from them all is Nan, who lives hardly at all in a world of dreams. She injects a note of down-to-earth common sense.

The fulcrum of the action is the most hopeful ritual to be found anywhere in the world: the ritual that greets the arrival of any New Year and which repeatedly intimates that the unhappy or unfortunate experiences of the present and past will give way to better things in the future – especially (we imagine) if we make New Year resolutions. Tippett was attracted by the idea partly because it meant that a particular *sound* – the New Year bell – could symbolize a turning-point in the events of the opera – which it does, in Act II. Having discovered also that 'Auld Lang Syne' is sung in many parts of the world at midnight on New Year's Eve, he decided that it should be sung in the opera when the great bell strikes at the end of Act II.

Re-reading the appropriate sections on New Year rituals in Frazer's *The Golden Bough*,[25] he observed that the oldest ceremonies regularly began with a shaman (or medicine man) dancing himself into a trance (this was to 'cure' people afflicted by evil spirits). After this dance, the local community hunted for a Scapegoat, representing the Bad Old Year, and symbolically beat him out, so that the Good New Year could come in. In Act II of the opera, Tippett has a comparable ritual sequence: a shaman's dance, the chorus hunting for a scapegoat (who turns out to be Donny) and symbolically – later on, actually – beating him out. Tippett's opera thus has as its backcloth the most primal form of drama.

The opera opens with an instrumental introduction – one that recurs at the start of each act and at the crucial point in Act III at which Pelegrin has helped Jo-Ann overcome her fears and inspired her to dance – not just literally, but metaphorically or spiritually. The introduction, dominated by guitars, percussion, clarinets and saxophones, evokes a mood of suppressed violence and tension (*see* Example 18) –

Tippett: New Year, Act1, Prelude

Example 18

– appropriate to the Terror Town; although distant wordless voices hint at a faraway world beyond (another recurrent motif in the opera) (*see* Example 19) –

Example 19

– the Presenter and chorus sing of a wicked world which needs reformative action.

Their song takes off into a dance number, introducing Jo-Ann, whose task will be to 'dance nightmare away'. As the violence reaches a peak, Jo-Ann is almost blown into her apartment, where she now sings of her sense of safety and security with her books and dreams. As her 'dreamsong' reaches a climax, the chorus drive her towards the door, to go out and meet the children of the town. But now Donny bursts in and whirls her into a wild dance. Donny, ever delinquent and rebellious, provokes amusement and sympathy in equal doses. He is one of Tippett's extraordinary operatic creations, threatening (especially in Act III) to upstage Jo-Ann as protagonist. His music throughout the opera is replete with rhythmic motifs and vocalizations from Caribbean music; here, flapping his arms, strutting and crowing like a cock, he takes off into a parody nursery rhyme:[26]

> Co-co-ri-co!
> Cock-a-doodle-dandy
> Who stole the sugar candy?
> Co-co-co-cori-co!

When Nan arrives to try to take charge of him, he bursts out with a 'skarade' – a dance-sequence, punctuated by choral refrains, in which his orphaned situation and rejection in the countries where he thinks he has roots (the Caribbean and Africa) are graphically depicted, even caricatured.

Left alone, Jo-Ann conjures in her imagination the world of Nowhere and in a poignant, bitter-sweet interlude for the Presenter and echoing chorus, the scene changes to Nowhere Tomorrow. The characters here, too, are finely differentiated: Merlin, proudly declamatory in demonstrating his new computer; Pelegrin entering with a burst of florid, rapturous wordless melody, anticipating the journey out into space; Regan, steely and incisive in asserting her authority. In a scene emulating one in *The Flipside of Dominick Hyde*, Pelegrin has managed to capture on the computer screen the harrowed face from the past of Jo-Ann. Fascinated, Pelegrin vows to visit her. Led by the dancers, Merlin, Regan and Pelegrin define their ambitions in a finely structured ensemble that culminates in the unison declaration (echoed by the chorus), 'New Year is come'. Pelegrin takes off on the spaceship to visit Jo-Ann and in the final scene of Act I, they meet, but cannot touch: for each of them, it is only a dream-vision. Pelegrin leaves again. Merlin, musing on the situation, attempts to monitor the spaceship's flight.

Act II of the opera is dominated by the ritual celebrations on New Year's Eve, introduced by the dancers and the Presenter. The discovery of the scapegoat – the Bad Old Year – is everyone's objective: and after initial attempts to identify who it might be, the shaman comes to dance his trance-dance – a virtuoso piece for electric guitars, saxophones and percussion. The shaman's dance is continued by the crowd and becomes a hunt, with Donny picked upon as the prey, then symbolically 'beaten out'. As the hand-clapping by the crowd and percussive violence from the orchestra reach a peak, everyone gets ready to greet the New Year.

But an immense bell-stroke signals instead the descent of the spaceship. Merlin steps out as a kind of Master of Ceremonies, eloquently saluting the skills of navigation that have conveyed him and his fellow travellers into their presence. Pelegrin, in his pilgrim's hat, appears – the orchestra recalling his florid wordless song from Act I – and, spotting Jo-Ann in the crowd, heads straight towards her. The red carpet is rolled out for Regan, who, spectacularly attired, appears and indignantly, repeatedly demands an explanation as to where they have landed. Only Donny is prepared to respond, and he sends her up in imitation rap, to which she responds in kind. Regan realizes she has been tricked into travelling into the past not the future. She denounces Pelegrin and Jo-Ann. Nan intervenes to dismiss Regan's power as a figment of her imagination. Muted horns now introduce an ensemble for Nan, Regan, Jo-Ann and Pelegrin – its canonic imitations taking their cue from the quartet in Act I of Beethoven's *Fidelio*. Their collective lyric rapture is interrupted by Merlin, attempting to control the crowd that has now tried to invade the spaceship. Donny's rebellious exhibitionism causes him always to identify with the unfettered expressive freedom of the animal world. In Act I, he struts about like a cock and roars menacingly like a lion. Now, he imagines he is a bird, dancing around flapping his arms and making bird-calls.[27] When he attempts to join Regan on board the spaceship and she spits in his face, there is mayhem. The spaceship takes off and the crowd return to their violent hand-clapping, this time blaming Donny for what has occurred and beating him up literally. When the great bell sounds again, New Year really has arrived and everyone sings 'Auld Lang Syne' – except Jo-Ann, who is left to drag off the injured Donny.

The predominantly extrovert, wild activity of Act II ('rough theatre' in Peter Brook's parlance) is now followed by the restrained ceremonials of Act III ('holy theatre').[28] At the start of Act III, the Presenter and chorus depict a world still wicked and cruel after the celebrations of the night before. Jo-Ann and Nan now consider what to do about Donny. Jo-Ann does not want to lose him, but her love for him is insufficient – inevitably he has to be taken under firmer control. The injured Donny wins some sympathy with his pathetic attempts at a dance (corresponding to the skarade of Act I) recalling the disappearance of his parents and his early delinquency. Sombrely submissive, as he goes off with Nan, he leaves with Jo-Ann a video-cassette in which he has tried to depict for her his dreams. Each of the three stanzas of Donny's dreamsong – whose enactment on the video screen adds another dimension to the staging – is linked by schematic 'dissolve' music of the kind Tippett had used in *The Knot Garden*. The first two stanzas define a metaphorical association with a bird of prey (the condor) and a beast of power (tiger), with which Donny had always identified. Jo-Ann, a potential victim or subordinate, however, recoils from them all. Donny's dream (in the third stanza) of finding a metaphorical family amongst the whales that 'boom their love-song in the deep' is clearly more congenial to her.

The opera leaves open Donny's fate: reflecting on it later, Tippett felt that Donny's future life might entail some kind of group therapy, rather than submitting to 'the ministrations of some Mangus figure'; but he feels that 'he is bound to remain a wounded figure, an oddball, an outsider'.[29] Probably for this reason, he is the most moving character in the opera: and the composer himself, writing the last act, had to be careful to ensure that Jo-Ann re-asserted her position as protagonist in the drama.

Thus, after Donny's song has ended, Pelegrin appears and takes Jo-Ann off in his spaceship. Their mood and aspirations are depicted, in another Interlude, by the Presenter and echoing chorus. The dark place at which they arrive is the scene for another ritual. Here, Jo-Ann has to choose between drinking the blissful waters of a fountain that will enable her to forget the abandoned children and her worries, or sampling the bitter waters of a lake that will ensure she remembers her orphaned past and her duties to the children. She tries both, but rejects the fountain in favour of the lake. Whereas the fountain is conjured musically with rippling, dancing semiquavers for high woodwind, strings and glockenspiel, around a single, sustained, sung note (*see* Example 20) – the music for the lake is almost static, shimmering with harp triplets and with an unforgettably plaintive oboe melody (*see* Example 21).

Tippett: New Year, Act 3

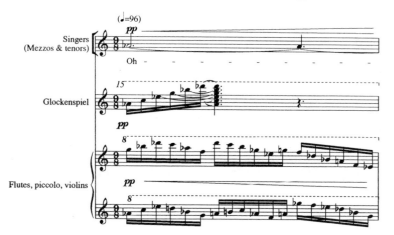

Example 20

Tippett: New Year, Act 3

Example 21

Illusion and actuality could not be more finely contrasted in musical terms. In a florid duet, Jo-Ann and Pelegrin now pour out their love for each other – a love more mystical than sensual : and this is the source of strength that enables Jo-Ann to overcome her fears and to dance.

The stage set flowers into a Paradise Garden and Jo-Ann participates in a dance number – a slightly re-scored version of the stately Sarabande for flutes, harp, lower strings and high percussion, which Tippett had composed a few years earlier for the Paradise Garden scene depicted in the fifth movement of *The Mask of Time*. After a climax of jubilation, Jo-Ann has to return to the world of actuality and the Presenter, in an interlude, intervenes in the action to urge on the change of scene. Pelegrin has picked a rose from the Paradise Garden and this he leaves with her when he bids goodbye (a significant incident that Tippett had taken from Wells's novel). At his instigation she holds it high and dances towards the door of her apartment: the scene switches to Nowhere, briefly, as Regan and Merlin condemn Pelegrin's trickery. But he declares that their world is – for the time being – finished, no longer needed: it was in any case a figment of Jo-Ann's imagination and has served its purpose. Now she is strong enough to carry on alone. As the Presenter and chorus once more enact the scene-change, the sounds of Terror Town (recapitulated from the introduction to Act I) become a barrage: the Presenter declaims what is probably the motto of all the Jo-Anns in this world –

> One humanity;
> One justice.[30]

– and the protagonist steps out, her head held high, slamming the door behind her. So, as in all the Tippett operas, with the exception of *King Priam*, the end of *New Year* marks a new beginning: not as confident and optimistic as that of *The Midsummer Marriage*; not as bleak as that of *The Ice Break*; not as tentatively hopeful as that of *The Knot Garden*: rather, a prodigious phalanx of possibilities.

7
Form and Fantasy

Sonata Strategies

Tippett has often told aspiring composers who send him scores
and tapes that he could never give a truly objective judgement on
their work. At best, he himself would learn from them, maybe
even 'stealing' their ideas. This is not entirely true. In many
informal seminars over the years, Tippett has provided a lot of
guidance to creative musicians, generally by asking them the
questions that he would ask himself in the course of his own
compositional processes. At the same time, the intellectual
jackdaw in his make-up was always on the alert for new pickings.
Musically, throughout his career, he seized upon a lot from other
people's music. But the end-result was never a superficial
eclecticism. Some musical experiences provided him with
definite formal and stylistic models. Others enabled him to
pinpoint a musical image or motif needed to start or end a work,
or to allow some specific part of it to take wing; and many others
simply indicated what not to do.

He described the genesis of his Symphony No. 2 thus: 'The
exact moment when the symphony began was when listening to
a tape of a Vivaldi concerto for strings in C, while looking out
over the sunlit Lake of Lugano. I was specially moved in that
situation by some pounding Vivaldi C major bass arpeggios. I
knew them to be the beginning of a new orchestral work. I do not
any longer remember the Vivaldi arpeggios, but four pounding
bass Cs are in fact the notes that begin the symphony – and they
return at the end of the work. Their function is not so much to
establish any key, but to act as a kind of point of departure and
return.'[1]

Likewise, the poetic playing of Walter Gieseking at a rehearsal
of Beethoven's Fourth Piano Concerto suggested the character of

the piano concerto Tippett was about to create himself. Sometimes such stimuli are the result of a conflation of two separate musical influences: e.g. the sarabande interlude in the middle of the fifth movement of *The Mask of Time* owes its delicate filigree character and instrumentation to the interlude for flutes and harp in Berlioz's *L'Enfance du Christ*, but its rhythmic gait derives from Ravel's Sonatine for piano. Such fusions are integral to Tippett's creative temperament.

At the outset of his career, Tippett's instinctive cosmo-politanism caused him to distance himself from Vaughan Williams and nationalist notions of composition based on an allegiance to native folk-song. At the same time, his consuming interest in the music of the past did not lead him towards the 'neo-classicism' associated with Nadia Boulanger and her pupils. In Tippett's music, early or late, a variety of formal procedures collide and interact, producing a dualism that runs deep and a pluralism that had always to be disciplined.

Tippett shares Stravinsky's belief, as enunciated in *Poétique musicale*[2] – that music has its own ontology: that attempts to impose upon it, either in advance or in retrospect, some descriptive or ideological content, can only undermine its effect and significance, indeed, will strike at its very roots. On the other hand, he has often enough felt impelled to contradict the abstract element in his work with music bearing an explicit message: Symphony No. 3 is an outstanding example. Furthermore, once he became absorbed in writing music for the theatre, pictorialism became an essential feature, though only as a way of shaping and animating his ideas.

Tippett's strongest allegiance was, and still is, to Beethoven. Along with it came various other affiliations – to the Elizabethan madrigalists and to Purcell; to Stravinsky and Bartók; to jazz and all forms of vernacular music. Early on, it issued in a kind of tension in his make-up – between the exigencies of classic formal procedures and the lure of inventive fantasy. This tension has been a productive one, directing his creativity often along fresh, innovative paths.

In all his early instrumental works, Tippett was preoccupied with the formal aspects of composition. From the start, the example that meant most to him in this respect was Beethoven. 'When I was a student,' he writes, 'I submitted entirely to the music of Beethoven. I explored his music so exhaustively that for a long time later on I listened to every other music but his.'[3] His first target was mastery of the Beethovenian sonata-allegro. His String Quartet No. 1 and Piano Sonata No. 1 each contain a movement in sonata-style format; String Quartet No. 2 contains two. The kernel of the musical argument in the first movement of the First String Quartet (substituted, in 1943, for two original opening movements) is embodied in its two thematic groups, offering Beethovenian contrasts of tension and lyric grace. Another Beethovenian feature – and a very effective one – is encountered in the way contrapuntal episodes are offset by chordal suspensions of the rhythmic flow.

Tippett brings to an end his exposition and recapitulation with a dramatic gesture – a declamatory cello solo that seems to dismiss what has gone before. The second cello solo at least acts as a link to the slow movement (its E flat taken over and resolved upwards onto F by the viola), wherein all four instruments burgeon into song. The lyrical ardour and deep conviction of this movement compensate for an occasional uncertainty in the handling of chromatic harmony. With his fugal finale, Tippett was absolutely in his element. The main subject and counter-subject, outlined in octaves, establish an exemplary clarity of texture that is sustained throughout. The robust violin solo that suddenly starts up – conceived in a style echoing the violin writing in Stravinsky's *L'histoire du soldat* and his Violin Concerto – is better integrated into the structure than the cello solos of the first movement, initiating a new fugal episode that trails through a succession of tonalities before settling finally in the main one of A major.

In Tippett's Piano Sonata No. 1 we find the young composer's invention in full flood, given the stimulus of various kinds of popular music. Not for nothing was it originally entitled

'Fantasy' Sonata. In its outer movements the notes pour out. The variations on a theme that grows from an initial line of clashing octaves between the hands are essentially decorative at first: though two later variations take off into stranger realms – one of them imitating the sounds of Indonesian gamelan orchestras, which Tippett had recently heard on record. The rondo-finale has a similar unstoppable energy, its extrovert character sustained particularly by jazzy syncopations and hints of boogie-woogie.

The slow movement contrasts two types of music: a lyrical outpouring based on the Scottish folksong 'Ca the yowes tae the knowes', and more severe, almost Hindemithian two-part counterpoint. Tippett developed this contrast further when he based the slow movement of his Concerto for Double String Orchestra on the same folk-theme. But it is the scherzo, coming third in the sequence of movements, that pulls the musical design into shape. Its toughness of statement and inexorable forward momentum are poles apart from the discursive character of the other movements. Laid out as a sonata-allegro, it transforms the competing octaves of the first movement into a tense ongoing counterpoint between left and right hands. Tippett's melodic ideas now acquire a Beethovenian terseness. Without a scherzo of this type, the sonata might have become an indulgent sprawl. Its inclusion anchors the overall structure and alerts the listener to *all* the dimensions of the work.

In an early review of the first (private) recording and score of this sonata and the score of Tippett's String Quartet No. 2, William Glock drew attention to the 'new sense of rhythm gained chiefly from a relationship with music outside the Viennese period and all that can be connected with it'.[4] Tippett's buoyant rhythms are indeed an important idiosyncrasy in all his music. Their derivation is twofold: from folk-music outside the Austro-German tradition and from the techniques of the Elizabethan madrigal. Contact with the music of Stravinsky and Bartók before and after this time only reinforced his fascination with a type of rhythm conceived as a flow of unevenly distributed accents, as distinct from that type of rhythm which relies on regular metres.

'Additive' as distinct from 'divisive' rhythm: these are the terms Tippett uses (they come from the ethnomusicologist Curt Sachs) to define his approach. Additive rhythm became a powerful shaping force within his music, affecting the nature of his musical invention, often giving a new lease of life to the classic forms he utilized, and implying new formal directions which his music might take. Tippett's discovery of his own personal 'voice' hinged on his exploration of a predominantly linear musical texture. What lifted it on to an entirely fresh plane is, however, his deployment of additive rhythm. Without it, the fugal finale of the First String Quartet – headed by a quotation from Blake's *The Marriage of Heaven and Hell*: 'Damn braces. Bless relaxes' could easily have become a fussy exercise. As it stands, the harmonic tensions between the two pairs of instruments are the springboard for a stream of irregular metrical patterns (*see* Example 22).

Tippett: String Quartet 1, 1st movement

Example 22

The Beethovenian trick of increasing or decreasing tension by tapering or spreading out the phrase-lengths is underlined here by varying degrees of rhythmic interplay. For instance, as the movement reaches its final climax (between Figs 48 and 49), the time-signatures, which just beforehand had alternated 3/4 and 3/8, now alternate between 2/4 and 5/8: and at the climax (fig. 49), much broader phrase-lengths are outlined by the cello playing a line of crotchets tied across the bars.

This interaction between irregular rhythmic cross-currents and phrase-structure was an important feature in two subsequent works, the Concerto for Double String Orchestra (1938–9) and String Quartet No. 2. In both Tippett had difficulty in notating additive rhythms. (He was not alone: Stravinsky, Janáček, Bartók and others experienced similar problems when writing down music that needed to feel improvised.) Thus in the first movement of the Concerto he uses an 8/8 time-signature for music whose basic pulse is *alla breve*, so as to be able to group the quaver beats in different ways – sometimes 4 + 4, sometimes 3 + 3 + 2 (in which case he asks the conductor to give three beats in the bar) – and so on. Within that 8/8 time-signature, the Concerto springs into action with two rhythmically independent, but complementary (rather than competing) themes in octaves for the two orchestras (*see* Example 23).

This interplay, instead of sonata-style conflict, is the life-blood

Example 23

of the movement (though it certainly has a sonata-type *sub-*structure): and it engenders a new metamorphosis of the contrasts between *concertino* and *ripieno* groups which he admired in Handel's Concerti Grossi. Tippett builds up to the recapitulation of the opening exposition in a highly characteristic way, by setting a long flowing melody shared between the lower strings in each orchestra against continuous quaver-movement in the higher registers.

Beethoven's influence is actually uppermost in the slow movement, which is explicitly modelled on the slow movement of his String Quartet in F minor, Op. 95: here, too, the overall shape consists of a song ('Ca' the yowes', as in the slow movement of Piano Sonata No. 1) followed by a fugal section, at whose climax the song returns. The rhythmic excitement which is very much in the foreground of the finale is generated by hemiolas – alternations of 3/4 and 6/8 time – whose regularity is further disturbed by extra incidental cross-accents, changes of time-signature to 2/4 and notes being grouped across the bar-lines, e.g. in the main second theme.

Allied to the rhythmic and polyphonic traits in Tippett's music now is a greater freedom of invention. This alliance he was eventually to relate to the fantasia (or fancy), as exemplified by seventeenth-century masters such as Purcell or Orlando Gibbons. When he did manage to hear and study their music, it affected his own technical approach profoundly. He later launched the first movement of his *Divertimento on Sellinger's Round* (1953–4) with a buoyant theme from the eighth of Gibbons's *Nine Fantasias in Three Parts* (*c.* 1620) : and its flow of accents across the bar-lines attests to his natural affinity with Gibbons (*see* Example 24).

The freedom to digress, to introduce new ideas and immediately argue them to their limits – a characteristic of the fantasy genre – was germane to Tippett's compositional aspirations early on, and remained so. Much later, in his Symphony No. 4 (1976–7) his overall one-movement sonata-style layout is elastic enough to accommodate a number of such

Tippett: Divertimento on Sellinger's Round, 1st movt

Example 24

deviations: and the one that digresses furthest, interpolated between the scherzo and the recapitulation, is a contrapuntal re-working of the very Gibbons fantasia-theme he had deployed in the *Divertimento*. At the time of the Concerto for Double String Orchestra, however, Tippett had still not heard Purcell or Gibbons: he was able to use fantasia-style procedures as if by instinct. Thus the last movement of the concerto suddenly flowers into a 'new' theme – actually a Northumbrian bagpipe tune,with characteristic rhythmic decoration.

Tippett's preface to the score of his String Quartet No. 2 states that the first movement 'is partly derived from madrigal technique where each part may have its own rhythm and the music is propelled by the different accents, which tend to thrust each other forward. The bar-lines are thus sometimes only an arbitrary division of time and the proper rhythms are shown in the notation by the groupings of the notes and by the bowings.' A different solution is adopted in the third movement where 'the bar lines correspond to the rhythmical accents of the music' and the time-signature changes throughout very frequently.

Although, again, the first movement preserves some sonata features, its real vitality stems from a well-balanced scheme of thematic statement and development, oscillating between tension and repose: and when played with real understanding, its poise and grace are nothing short of miraculous. The detailed bar-by-bar interplay of lines and rhythmic accents tends to occupy the musical foreground. But when the exposition and recapitulation each come to a close, the cello line straddles several bars, unfolding spaciously with almost Wagnerian appoggiaturas: thus all four instruments are enabled eventually to converge in octaves, with ever longer note-values (*see* Example 25).

The two central movements of the work draw from both Beethoven and Purcell. But some of the subtlety of the fugue comes from the contrasts between two kinds of string bowing, giving the main subject a distinctive character that makes every one of its subsequent appearances and extensions unmistakable. In the first four bars of the subject, each crotchet is played *marcato* and slightly separated from the next note (the *tenuto* markings in the first two bars are intended to counter a natural tendency to weaken the second beat of each bar); the remaining three bars are bowed *legato*. This contrast clarifies the impact of Tippett's richly chromatic harmonic scheme – indebted to late Beethoven (e.g. the fugue in Op. 131) and echoing the multiple false relations he had found in Purcell's fantasias.

Tippett's mercurial third movement – ingeniously laid out as three statements of the same music, presented each time a third higher and subtly modified at the second and third repetitions – is one of his many attempts to re-create the typical Beethovenian scherzo, with its one-in-a-bar pulse and surging, forward momentum. Integrating elements from folk-music and pre-classical dance music, Tippett breathes new life into them, without letting either become dominant: stylistically the music is tightly knit.

Beethoven also dominates the sonata-style finale. Its two main subject groups are far more sharply differentiated than in anything earlier that Tippett had attempted along these lines. His success can be measured by the way he manages briefly to combine them (Fig 78, 5th bar to Fig 79), subduing the forcefulness of the opening theme, while decorating it with the imitative lines of the lyrical second group theme. The transitions are not so well managed, however, relying on a certain amount of obvious passage-work: and there are even the occasional rhythmic hiatuses (e.g. in the first bar of Fig 72 and the corresponding passage later on, one bar before Fig 81). What is

Tippett: String Quartet No. 2, 1st movt.

Example 25

extraordinarily convincing, however, is the controlled and lengthy unwinding from a fortissimo climax down to the slow final bars, reaching eventually a cadence in the main tonality of F sharp. In this felicitous concluding colloquy, Tippett displayed a rare instinct for what really works well in the string quartet medium.

While Tippett's studies of Handel proved fruitful in *A Child of Our Time*, and in the Concerto for Double String Orchestra, his *Fantasia on a Theme of Handel*, for piano and orchestra, begun before the oratorio and completed immediately after it, has elements of the romantic concerto genre, in which Tippett never really felt at home. Thus the cadenza-like links between episodes and the passage-work for the solo pianist appear slightly gauche. More fundamentally, the internal formal disciplines are ill-defined. Ostensibly, a set of variations on a sequence of Handelian chords – taken as quoted at the end of Samuel Butler's *Erewhon* – it goes off too readily at tangents, making reference to the finale of Mozart's 'Jupiter' Symphony and the *Dies irae* theme, but never really exploring their potential. Even the eventual transformation of the Handel motif into a fugue subject fails to lift the music to a higher level. Although not an unattractive piece, the Handel *Fantasia* remains one of Tippett's least well formulated. *Little Music* for strings (1946), on the other hand, is a safer, more limited enterprise, but certainly more assured and successful. Cast as a suite of four movements which follow each other without a break, it opens with a declamatory prelude, followed by two fast fugues, which enclose an air over a repeated ground-bass. There is an echo of the unwinding of the finale to the Second String Quartet in the way the first fugue here slows down gradually over a seven-bar span to merge with the slow air. The second fugue also has a characteristic Tippett-ian ending in which the brilliant cadential sequence is repeated exactly, but *pianissimo*, as if evaporating into thin air.

In Tippett's String Quartets No. 3 (1948) and 4 (1978), his models again come from late Beethoven, but allude to sonorities he had lately encountered in Bartók's works for the medium. Having earlier observed and emulated Beethoven's habit, in his late sonatas and quartets, of alternating lengthy fugal episodes or movements with song-like utterances, Tippett made this the structural basis of his Third Quartet. Its three quick-tempo fugues enclose two movements whose successive outpourings of lyricism bring the work to an emotional peak. Just as Beethoven conceived of his multi-section quartets as a single span of music, so also did Tippett: and of late, he has sought to emphasize the effect by modifying the original published score so that the finale begins on the last chord of the fourth movement.

Each of the five movements has its own profile. The first burgeons from a slow introduction into a fugue on a thematic subject of some dimensions (the fugue-subject of the finale of Beethoven's 'Hammerklavier' Sonata could well have been at the back of his mind): and the introduction is recalled later in the movement to provide a brief respite from the energetic thematic interplay of the fugue. By contrast, the third movement is a dancing fugal scherzo, whose lines disport themselves with the utmost rhythmic freedom: while the fugal finale is a more relaxed affair, an attempt to bring the listener gently back to earth after the effortful strivings of the preceding movement.

Sandwiched between these fugues are two lyrically efflorescent slow movements. The first seems deceptively simple in construction: its main, gently flowing theme is presented four times – on first violin, second violin, viola and cello in turn; while the folk-like musings of the viola that introduce it, supported by thrummed pizzicato chords on the cello, return halfway through and at the close. The movement exemplifies perfectly the art that conceals art: for Tippett's metric and contrapuntal schemes conspire to allow the music to float across the bar-lines in a spontaneously lilting melody and accompaniment (*see* Example 26).

A less accomplished composer would undoubtedly have made the same kind of texture sound crabbed and calculated. Even more extraordinary is the *lento* fourth movement, which consists simply of three statements of thematic material of similar character and shape, starting from absolute stillness and gradually culminating in pace, power and rhetoric. It would be difficult to pin down an exact exemplar for such music – let alone analyse it – but there is perhaps a link here with the variations or 'divisions' of sixteenth-century keyboard music, with its note-values getting progressively shorter as decorative embellishments of the original lines accumulate. More important, Tippett uses such techniques to bring the entire work to an ecstatic climax: after this, the finale fulfils its role of bringing us 'out into the street again' after the song has finished.

Strings – either in chamber music or orchestral genres – were a natural medium for Tippett's linear approach to composition. Although his string-writing was always technically challenging, the rewards were great because of his ability to etch so strongly the character of each line within the texture. Never was this more true than in his *Fantasia Concertante on a Theme of Corelli* (1953). Faced with the task of celebrating Corelli's tercentenary, a lesser composer would have turned out a neo-classic concoction, spiked with modern flavours. Not so Tippett. Everything about this composition seemed to activate his deepest creative impulses. The piece flowed from the same musical impulses that produced *The Midsummer Marriage*, which he had recently completed: certainly, the dawn music of its final scene, with high-register, divided strings pouring out endless birdsong rapture, still lingered in his mind. But Tippett was in any case a composer who wanted to keep song alive, and in the work by Corelli from which he drew his thematic material – the Concerto Grosso Op. 6 no. 2 in F – he discerned a kind of archetypal Italianate lyricism. 'The most fascinating thing about this theme,' he noted, 'is that, if Corelli's bass in F minor is put into the relative major and somewhat extended, it produces a melody of pure Puccini!' This is precisely what Tippett was able to achieve

Tippett: String Quartet No.3, 2nd movt.

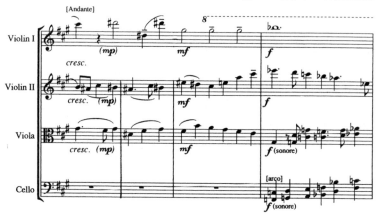

Example 26

in a slow, lyrical episode in the middle of the Fantasia (Figs 39–46). Tippett also provides a counterpart for this effulgent strain of melody in the concluding pastorale section, which echoes Corelli's own pastorale style in the so-called *Christmas Concerto*. (The lilting, *siciliano* rhythm of this section, incidentally, is all too readily lost in those interpretations that adopt a slow tempo, lingering over it, languishing in it, instead of allowing it to dance.)

The general format of the Fantasia re-creates the characteristics of the baroque original in Tippett's own terms. Corelli's division of the orchestra is emulated in the tripartite layout of *concertino* (two solo violins and cello), *concerto grosso* (the main string body) and *concerto terzo* (a section of the string orchestra playing, at first, the continuo role, but later regarded as equal to the *concerto grosso*). Rather than blandly lifting a theme from Corelli, Tippett structures two segments from the original to sustain sharp contrasts of passion and brilliance. He takes Corelli's short contrapuntal *adagio* theme and tacks on to it a *vivace* passage, all on the one chord of C major. These are the polarities that form the basis of the subsequent variations. There are other nuances within the variations. In the second of the variations (Fig 10), Tippett emulated a device in Monteverdi's vocal music – the repeated notes in a (so-called) 'goat's trill' (*see* Example 27).

The third *vivace* variation (beginning at Fig 22) takes off into a fast 'divisions' as in a fantasia by Purcell or Gibbons – though this is also meant as a spur to the Paganini instinct of the soloists.

For the fugue, Tippett's starting-point is a transcription of the opening of Bach's Fugue in B minor (BWV 578) for organ, itself a re-working of the theme from the second movement of Corelli's Trio Sonata in B minor, Op. 3 No. 4: an odd prefiguration of the medieval parody techniques subsequently revived in the music of Peter Maxwell Davies and others. But this is no ordinary fugue. Initially, it counterpoints three types of string bowing: lyrical on-the-string bowing for the second violas playing the Corelli theme;

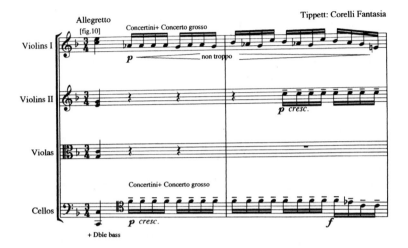

Example 27

off-the-string for the first violas playing Tippett's counter-subject; and, for the cellos playing Bach's counter-subject, *louré* bowing – i.e. each note slightly separated, but still smooth and singing (*see* Example 28).

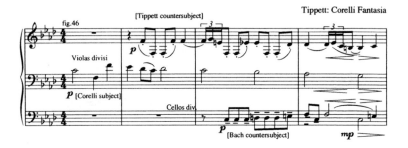

Example 28

Tippett embellishes these basic components with increasingly elaborate, swirling lines that are eventually so dominant as to cause the music to surge to a climax of great passion, with the Corelli fugue-subject, in augmented rhythm, proclaimed on the lower strings. Far from being staid or academic, this fugue rekindles the eroticism of the final Ritual Dance from *The Midsummer Marriage*, whose infinitely prolonged de-tumescence at dawn is also echoed here in Tippett's ardent pastorale section.

Roughly contemporary with Boulez's *Le Marteau sans Maître* (1952–4) and Stockausen's *Kontrapunkte No. 1* (1952), Tippett's *Corelli Fantasia* might seem by comparion to be the ultimate in backward-looking nostalgia. It is nothing of the kind. This is a score that deals with *essences*, with artistic values that remain unaffected from one century to another: and as such, a paean to the art of instrumental lyricism, springing from the very nature of stringed instruments, as understood by Corelli, as understood now. When realized with sensitivity to style, the *Corelli Fantasia* communicates a rapture and perfection rare in music: and it remains one of the composer's exceptional achievements.

Tippett's *Divertimento on Sellinger's Round* is a lesser affair, an enjoyable potpourri, rather than a carefully planned entity.The charge of nostalgia certainly holds in the case of the second movement – actually the first to be written – in which Tippett superimposes a decorated version of *Sellinger's Round* over his transcription of Dido's first aria, 'Ah Belinda!', in Purcell's opera.

Similar processes occur in the other movements, utilizing a Gibbons fantasia in the first movement and some of the composer's favourite British tunes – by Arne, John Field and Arthur Sullivan. The only movement which is really characteristic of Tippett himself, however, is the fourth, whose declamatory outbursts on the strings are redolent of *The Midsummer Marriage*. The finale, though deftly constructed, is the thinnest in musical content.

Tippett's obsession with Beethoven led him inevitably to write symphonies. Yet with each one – as in his concertos – he was naturally impelled to modify established notions of content and format. Being by instinct a contrapuntal composer, he needed the possibility of extra strands in the orchestral texture: thus, his Symphony No. 1 (1945) required three flutes (all doubling on piccolos) and three trumpets. They are prominent especially in the slow movement, where the flutes have an episode of their own, and in the scherzo, where the trumpets are particularly highlighted amidst the kaleidoscopic play of instrumental contrasts. Formally, classic Beethovenian procedures are qualified here by techniques from pre-classical music. Thus, the slow movement is a passacaglia based on an eight-bar theme (introduced by bassoon and strings), which is repeated beneath, or in conjunction with, a variety of musical material; and the finale is a double-fugue.

Although the first movement has a sonata-style structure it is difficult to differentiate within it first and second thematic groups, as the musical ideas crowd in upon one another in rich abundance. Indeed, no fewer than six thematic groups compete for our attention. They seem less well suited to an abstract symphonic argument than they might be for a stage-work: and in fact, there are many prefigurations here, and elsewhere in the symphony, of Tippett's next large-scale composition, *The Midsummer Marriage*. The ideas are nevertheless marshalled quite well. The climax of the development section and its progress towards the return of the opening thematic material are particularly commanding: they involve a repetition of an ascending phrase intensified by trills, with the phrases tapering shorter and shorter to create excitement.

What produces insecurity is Tippett's polyphonic writing for an orchestra whose internal balances were conceived originally for the vertical harmonic schemes of the Viennese masters. Musical textures marvellously suited to strings alone are more difficult to manage with a full orchestra, despite the additional instruments demanded. A better match occurs in the next two movements.

The craggy climaxes of the passacaglia-style second movement are magnificent: so also are its luminous episodes for the three flutes, giving way to moonlit magic in the exchanges between the three piccolos, oboe and trumpets. The scherzo is an astonishingly original re-creation of the typical Beethovenian scherzo. Imitating what Tippett recalled as the 'flying hocquets' he had encountered in transcriptions of some vocal music by the thirteenth-century Parisian composer, Pérotin, the impetus of this movement comes from the rhythmic 'hiccuping' that helps define the exchanges between contrasting groups of wind and strings. The full orchestra intervenes every so often to provide punctuation and pull together the various strands into cadential phrases. The timing and proportions of this movement have the breathtaking precision of a conjuror. To offset this spine-tingling wizardry, Tippett provides a more sober trio, a freely flowing fantasia for strings alone. In the finale, sonata and double-fugue seem to be forced into marriage: the clinching of the relationship is undertaken by sudden intrusions from the bass drum and trills for woodwind and violins that produce not so much a final cadence as a dramatic suspension of the action – as such, a foretaste of methods deployed even more extensively in *The Midsummer Marriage* and continued thereafter in the Piano Concerto (1955).

A comparable dramatic gesture occurs, for instance, in the slow movement of the Piano Concerto. Throughout it, the violins and violas are silent. Out of an evocative introduction by the horns and bassoons there flows a continuous sequence of canons for the woodwind, against which the pianist pours out an endless stream of arabesques. Lower strings add yet another strand to the disjunct rhythmic relationships here. Overall, the musical texture looks on paper quite ungainly and initially baffled its interpreters. But when properly realized, it comes across as something of a technical coup – a multi-layered written-down improvisation, setting rubato fluctuations for the pianist against firm, if uneven pulsations from the orchestra. This movement ought to be the envy of every disciple of Boulez, Ligeti or Lutoslawski!

Shortly before the close, however, this colloquy is interrupted when the violins and violas burst in with a passionate rhetoric to which the piano opposes its own ruminative reflections – and these ultimately remain in the ascendant. The relationship between piano and orchestra at this point lifts into a new dimension encountered in the slow movement of Beethoven's Fourth Piano Concerto (by which it was inspired). The general poetic emphasis in Beethoven's concerto affected Tippett's conception elsewhere in this work: and the connection is further cemented by the celebratory dance-like mood of each composer's finale.

Without the very specific example of Beethoven's Fourth Concerto, it is unlikely that Tippett would have attempted a concerto that embodied the standard opposition of soloist and full orchestra. While he admired many works in that genre, he always felt that his own notions of concerto-writing led elsewhere. Here, in order to achieve the kind of poetic emphasis he was emulating from Beethoven, Tippett added an extra dimension to the scoring – an ensemble consisting of solo viola, celesta and muted horns. The interpolations of this group counter the assertions of power by the full orchestra in the first movement, and sets a precedent for the splitting up of the orchestra into smaller groups in the slow movement. The celesta, in particular, appears like an ethereal extension of the solo piano sonorities: this relationship achieves greatest prominence in the rondo-finale, where the third episode, an absolute contrast to the gigue-like main theme and the jazz hemiolas of an earlier episode, harmonizes the magical aura of high-register celesta with the deeper resonances of low-register piano chords – their dialogue floating along in characteristic rhythmic disjunction.

Knowing how much the Piano Concerto is indebted to *The Midsummer Marriage* certainly helps our appreciation of it. The opening theme of the first movement, for instance, is a clear offshoot of the music in Act III of the opera for the continuation of Sosostris's aria (Fig 387 *et seq.*): its opening bars, seeming to start as if already in mid-flow (very difficult to achieve in performance), culminate towards its first rapturous climax for piano and orchestra, paralleling the opening of Act II (the music that recurs at the start and close of the Ritual Dances). The tintinnabulations of the celesta in the outer movements also seem to relate to the 'temple' music in the opera. On the other hand, the evocative horn-writing finds a place throughout Tippett's entire oeuvre – from his unpublished Concerto in D (1928–30) through to his final major work, *The Rose Lake*. Tippett was even tempted to write a Sonata for four horns (1955), whose four strophically structured movements distil much of his fascination with the traditional hunting-calls and romantic enchantment associated with the instrument (inspired specifically by its use in the music of Weber and Berlioz). In short, the Piano Concerto demonstrates that by this time in his career, Tippett had marked out his own sonorous territory. Aside from all that, of course, the work stands perfectly well as an original and distinctive contribution to the repertoire.

New Forms, New Idioms

With his Symphony No. 2 (1957), Tippett began to move towards fresh concepts of orchestration and harmony, foreshadowing the quite radical changes that were to occur in his second opera, *King Priam* (1959–62). Its most unusual movement is undoubtedly the slow one, coming second. Its song-format runs in close harness with a symmetrically balanced scheme of instrumental groupings. Anything resembling sonata-style development is absent. Instead, we encounter a pattern of restatement and recapitulation – sometimes fragmentary – whose transformations of the thematic material most fundamentally affect colouring and register. The most prominent themes are an introductory trumpet solo and a heavily ornamented duet for divided cellos. These are both later recapitulated a tone higher, with different instrumentation and in different registers. The trumpet motif is taken over by a trombone; the cellos relinquish their duet to divided violins, and the luminous, downward-spread woodwind chords that accompany them are transformed into murky, upwardly climbing trombone chords – stalactites changed to stalagmites, as it were. Three elements supply continuity within these changing patterns of colour and texture. One is the presence of the piano and harp, adding incidental punctuation and embellishment. The others are an extended theme for the entire string orchestra, heralded by trumpet fanfares that stir a pizzicato salute from the strings. Only a fragmentary glimpse of these remains at the end. The mosaic shatters and we are left with a mysterious mumbling coda for the four horns – a sonority absent from the colour-scheme of the movement until now.

The third movement of the work is an even more brilliant metamorphosis of the Beethovenian prototype than Tippett had so far achieved. He himself describes it as 'a kind of mirror form scherzo, whose undeviating idea is the play between long beats

(of three quavers) and short beats (of two quavers). The climax ...
is where this play is closest and most abrupt [i.e. Figure 105 *et
seq.*]. The beginning and end are on the other hand gentle and
cool.' A sophisticated use of additive rhythm is clearly thus the
basis of the musical structure.

The whole of the symphony, however, contains a further
tightening-up and elaboration of Tippett's symphonic methods:
and one should not be deceived into regarding it merely as an
example of backward-looking 'neo-classicism'. Stylistically, the
symphony marks a turning-point in Tippett's music.

Although the initial inspiration for the opening movement and
its pounding Cs came, as we noted earlier, from Vivaldi, there is
no point in searching through the six-hundred-odd concertos by
the baroque master to find further links. Less peripheral is the
influence of Stravinsky's Symphony in Three Movements
(1942–5). Its ethos of ritualized violence balanced against a
lambent lyricism is accepted here as a way of decisively
modifying Tippett's own musical identity. Like Stravinsky,
Tippett also includes a piano in his score, on account of its
capacity for rhythmic and percussive incisiveness, as well as its
actual timbre: and the piano remained an essential ingredient in
his orchestration for almost thirty years – only excluded from his
compositions from *New Year* (1985–8) onwards. Both the
Stravinsky work and Tippett's Symphony have C as their main
tonality, but thereafter the comparison ceases, for Tippett
certainly provided his work with an identity of its own.

Tippett regards the first movement of his Symphony No. 2 as
his most successful attempt at a Beethovenian sonata-allegro. It
certainly has the feel of an inexorable piece of musical argument;
its overall proportions are well conceived and the Vivaldi-ish
'pounding' rhythm propels it forward from first to last. The
musical argument subsists ŏn an intricate pattern of tonal
tensions, wrought initially between sharp and flat keys, both of
which seek resolution in the 'neutral' home tonality of C. The
tonal conflict is expressed at the outset in clear linear terms, as a

Example 29

clash between C major and D major (*see* Example 29) – and
vertically, in dancing semiquavers for the divided violins which
stretch our understanding (as listeners) of C, constantly
gravitating towards a chord (marked 'x' below) that is ultimately
accepted as a consonance (*see* Example 30).

Towards the end of the finale, Tippett harks back to the bitonal
conflict at the start of the symphony. Against the pounding
assertion of C in the lines for the lower instruments (reinforced by
timpani), the brass and strings try repeatedly to pull the music
towards other tonalities: ultimately, the 'x' chord becomes the final
point of rest, accepted as an acoustic extension of C. (Berg ends the
first half of his Violin Concerto with a similar type of chord.)

Tippett's expansion of his tonal and harmonic schemes had, to
date, been very gradual, but was now increasingly empirical. The
'x' chord above is very much the product of a composer
'discovering' harmonies in the course of composition at the
piano. Back in the 1930s, his capacities as a contrapuntist had
blossomed under the influence of R. O. Morris. But any prowess
he was to show in the harmonic, vertical dimensions of
composition remained latent. Rejecting the pedantries of C. H.
Kitson, he turned first to Schoenberg's *Harmonielehre* and later
Hindemith's *Unterweisung im Tonsatz*. Neither of them satisfied
or stimulated him; both seemed academically 'alphabetic' . What
he needed was something that dealt with the living emotive force
of harmony and tonality. Eventually, he found it in Vincent

Example 30

d'Indy's *Cours de Composition Musicale*,[5] especially the chapter entitled 'La Sonate de Beethoven'. Tippett learnt essentially two things from d'Indy. One was that in a classically conceived composition (especially its development section) the music was either in a state of '*immobilité*', '*en repos*' or in a state of '*translation*' or '*en marche*'. It was important not to confuse the two: at one level, the music asserted its territory – especially in tonal terms; at another level, it was moving towards some new experience, both tonally and thematically.

In most of his music, Tippett demonstrated his understanding of this contrast of what one might call 'structural intention'. One possible instance of failure is the first movement of Symphony No. 1, where from the outset the musical invention is too much *en marche*. In general, however, Tippett has shown a remarkable instinctual understanding of what a composition needs in these respects at different stages in its unfolding. The trouble and effort he always took to ensure that the openings of major scores were exact in character and emphasis paid great dividends: from the Concerto for Double String Orchestra right through to *Byzantium*, he retained a capacity for seizing and riveting the listener's attention with a thematic gesture which – like an 'establishing shot' in a film – ensures that one is drawn into the piece, understanding in a moment its essence and its potential implications. Thus, with the opening of Symphony No. 2, we encounter immediately the tonal confrontations that are to remain as the core of the musical argument up to the resolution effected in the finale.

The other lesson Tippett learnt from d'Indy concerned *tonality in action* within a musical structure. Using Beethoven as his model, d'Indy defines tonal modulation in terms of ascending and descending cycles of fifths, each with a contrasting emotive connotation: key-changes that ascend through a cycle of fifths tend towards *'clarté'*; those that descend tend towards *'obscurité'*. There are, of course, intermediary gradations: and understanding their relationships made it possible for Tippett to gauge with some degree of precision the expressive impact of his musical structures. D'Indy did not provide him with a set of dogmas, or a theory to be rigidly applied, so much as general principles that could be adapted to new contexts, modified, but never entirely disregarded.

The conflict between sharp and flat keys that is the *raison d'être* of the whole of Symphony No. 2 is best comprehended through an awareness of the transitional episodes, where the music is explicitly *en marche*. Thus, after the initial tension between C and D has been decisively articulated as in Example 31, the dancing semiquaver figurations take over – the strings being joined by duetting trumpets – moving the tonality gradually towards the flat keys in which the woodwind can eventually introduce the second thematic group (Figure 9). The pull back to sharp keys is begun by the oboes (in canonic imitation) and lower strings (Figure 11 onwards), so that the development section starts with a conflict between E and B, similar to that of the opening. The dancing figurations retain their re-orientating function (so to speak) throughout. When the development section attains a focal point of *immobilité*, they are temporarily subdued: they take over again (at Fig 30) only after this flat-key territory has been firmly established, their task now to effect a return to the C-D tonal orientation of the opening – something they achieve in a matter of 22 bars. An enlarged version of this process enables Tippett to round the movement off with a lengthy coda that has the culminative power of those he admired so much in Beethoven (e.g. in the first movements of the 'Eroica' Symphony or Symphony No. 7). Likewise, Tippett's strategy in the scherzo is to build from initial sharp-key territory towards a climax in flat-key domain which generates the most tonal conflict in the piece – the point where the conflict is most decisively, most resolutely *en repos*.

The finale ritualizes the conflicts further, its opening gestures even more balletic, its clash of tonalities yet more compressed: and the ground bass theme that emerges encapsulates the contrast of sharp and flat keys, moving from A to A flat within its nine-bar stretch (*see* Example 31).

Again, as in the scherzo, Tippett's dramatic plan is to take us as far away as possible into flat key territory: thus, its climax is an entirely new musical idea, a long theme in A flat – accompanied by what the composer called *Petrushka*-esque

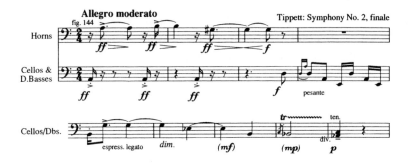

Example 31

'blazes of colour' for wind, harp and piano – which descends gradually from the highest register of the violins to the lowest register of cellos and double-basses: at which stage the pounding Cs of the opening of the work return, making several strenuous efforts to bring us back to the original tonality. The theatrical twist at the end entails rather too many stops and starts, in performance, thus demanding a final surge of momentum to ensure that it finishes convincingly.

If the first, third and fourth movements of Symphony No. 2 were the climax of Tippett's re-creation of Beethovenian sonata-style methods, the slow movement pointed towards the future. The key factor was its mosaic-style presentation of ideas and scoring – inspired in part by hearing Stravinsky's *Agon* in London in 1958. With *King Priam*, Tippett made this the cornerstone of his structural processes: and it changed for ever his whole attitude towards the orchestra. His retrospective comments on all this are apposite:

> The dramatic nature of this opera forced me radically to reconsider the standard orchestra. I began to realize that the sound of the standard orchestra had become so strong a historic archetype that contemporary music written for it gets inevitably drawn back in history by analogy to the

period when the archetype was produced ... I realized that use of the string body within the standard orchestra was the crux. This body is historically the string quartet blown up, as it were, so that there is a terrifically strong historic archetype embedded within it. I was at last ready to let go of this archetype and replace it with a body of stringed instruments whose number and layout would be entirely conditional on the piece to be composed. Essential to this understanding was the realization that there were to be no first or second violins, but just violins.[6]

The outcome, the mosaic scoring of *King Priam*, suggested new possibilities not just for orchestral music, but for musical forces of all kinds.

Immediately after the opera came two works that were derived stylistically and structurally from it: Piano Sonata No. 2 (1962) and Concerto for Orchestra (1963), both of which contain actual quotations from the opera. In the sonata, the fantasy procedures of Purcell and Gibbons are given a fresh lease of life. Tippett's musical thought flows uninhibitedly within this concentrated, tightly organized format.

As in the opera [the composer stated in his programme note], everything in the sonata proceeds by statement. The effect is one of accumulation – through constant addition of new material, by variation and repetition. There is virtually no development and particularly no bridge passages. The formal unity comes from the balance of similarities and contrasts. The contrasts are straightforward ones of timbre and speeds. But there are also contrasts of function. Music can appear to flow; or to arrest itself especially through the devices of ostinato; or temporarily to stop in silence ... But the work is for one player and one instrument and there is little opportunity for the 'climax' or 'jam session', i.e. when the contrasting sections or bits from them, instead of being just sequential, are made to appear together. These 'climaxes'... are more appropriate to an orchestral piece in this form. But the sonata nevertheless has a kind of 'climax' coda where the bits of addition and repetition are made very small and the resulting mosaic therefore more intense.

The table on pages 174–5 shows the format deployed in the piece.

Of fundamental importance is the definition of each idea by a tempo indication retained whenever the idea recurs, whether it is in any way altered, extended or contracted (something all performers should strictly observe). There are thus eight main sections to the work (A–H), in which only the vestiges of classic sonata-style presentation remain: exposition (A), development (B–G) and recapitulation (H); and even then sections E and G introduce new material. Although Tippett disowns sonata-style presentation, some of the same d'Indyesque expressive functions as those uncovered in Symphony No. 2 still determine the character and balancing of ingredients.

The harsh rhetoric of the opening two ideas stresses both its initial C major orientation and its undertow towards B flat. These tendencies are mirrored in the lyrical fourth and balletic fifth ideas, reached by means of the fast sequence of octaves serving as the third idea. In its highly concentrated format thus, the sonata develops to a high degree the contrasts of *clarté* and *obscurité* that shaped Tippett's previous Beethoven-inspired compositions. The most original device is the final shattering of the mosaic (in section H): and the compression of the original contrasts makes possible a cyclic conclusion of the utmost power. The opening idea (*see* Example 32 overleaf) – which has not been heard since the start of the piece, now returns, is repeated five times and extended by quiet, tonally flattened phrases that are steadily shortened until ultimately just a single note is left hanging in the air. As at the end of *King Priam*, we are left to reflect on an abstract musical situation which seems as pre-ordained as the King's death at the end of the opera.

Example 32

Section	Musical Material with associated Tempo indications	No. of bars
A	1 (Lento = c.100)	4
	2 (Allegro = c.112)	3
	3 (Molto piu mosso = c.200)	7
	4 (Pachissimo meno mosso = c.138)	7
	5 (Adagio = c.54)	8
B	4	12
	5	4
	4	15
	2	8
C	6 (Andante = c.58)	67
D	3	7
	4	5
	3	7
	4	8
	5	12
E	7 (Allegro = c.132)	33

F	4	18
	2	8
	3	7
G	8 (Lento = c.40)	9
H	2	9
	3	7
	4	2
	6	2
	7	3
	6	2
	7	1
	6	1
	4	4
	7	2
	6	2
	7	2
	6	2
	3	4
	8	2
	7	4
	3	3
	1	16

In a number of later works, Tippett leaves the listener with a similar final question-mark, though its inevitability is not always so assured. Each of the three movements of his Concerto for Orchestra, for instance, has what the composer calls a 'non-ending': the first two relate organically to the musical structure; the third one is more of an abandonment.

The Concerto for Orchestra starts at the opposite end of the spectrum from the Second Piano Sonata. Although the 'building-block' method of construction is the same, and the mosaic style of orchestration is manifestly an extension of that deployed in

King Priam, it has a fresh slant. The hard-edged musical material
that dominated Sonata No. 2 is now part of a carefully devised
plan of expressive gradations.

The first movement, in some ways the most original, is based
on nine thematic 'blocks', each individually scored: and within
these we find that music emphasizing 'line and flow' is allotted
equal importance alongside music that is ostensibly 'heroic or
martial' or which overtly stresses 'speed and energy':

A	1	Flutes and harp	
	2	Piano and tuba	line and flow
	3	Three horns	
B	1	Timpani & piano	
	2	Oboe, cor anglais, bassoon & contrabassoon	heroic and martial
	3	Trombones and percussion	
C	1	Xylophone and piano	
	2	Clarinet, bass-clarinet & piano	speed and energy
	3	Trumpets and side-drum	

In the exposition of these nine ideas, each group of three is linked
to the next by a few bars superimposing fragments from the three
ideas just introduced (e.g. A is linked to B with a few bars of
A,1,2 and 3 heard simultaneously). Thereafter, the entire
movement is composed of juxtapositions of all this material, or
extensions of it. These occur in three stages, with the opening
theme for flute and harp returning to act as a signpost: this in
itself is deftly managed, for the theme itself is in three sections,
so each time it returns, it starts at the next entry point. At the end
of the movement, just its opening bar returns – to be cut off,
leaving only a bar of silence to follow: it is as if we are meant to
continue the musical processes in our mind, conjuring a further
sequence of juxtapositions and superimpositions of the material.
Listening to the interaction of these heterogeneous groups of

soloists, or *concertini*, leaves us with a quite new impression of what a symphony orchestra can sound like overall. Yet its radicalism is not anarchic: Tippett sticks rigidly to his mosaic scheme, as he did in *King Priam*, so that the only new sonority to appear that was not in his original nine-block plan is a single gong-stroke signalling a point of climax. As in the second act of the opera, the listener is hardly aware that the strings have no role at this stage in the Concerto.

The opening flute and harp motif – a close relative of the instrumental accompaniment to Hermes' aria, 'O divine music', in Act III of *King Priam* – represents the most powerful impulse towards lyricism within the movement. It is also the most tonally secure, leaning mainly towards A major, but accommodating easily excursions away from it. The process is mirrored in the two thematic blocks that succeed it and even more assuredly articulated in the next group of three: but thereafter, there is a sense of tonal flux until the trumpets (from Fig 33 onwards) re-establish the pull towards A major. Thus within the exposition of the ideas, groups A and B are *en repos* whereas group C is overtly *en marche*. It is this control over the tonal emphasis that ensures a logical unfolding for the movement.

Lyricism takes over completely in the central slow movement, with the strings playing for the first time – joined (from the first movement) by harp and piano: and as in the opera, the division of the small body of strings is not the conventional one, using violins divided into firsts and seconds. The mosaic patterns of the first movement are now offset by a long continuous cantilena melody that forms a central thread, to which other motifs are added as accompaniment or decoration. The sound-world overall echoes that of the start of Act III of *King Priam,* not only reflecting Andromache's cello melody but background elements – e.g. a motif for double-basses playing in harmonics that recurs four times to punctuate the succession of musical paragraphs: a motif that functions well in this capacity, as it has a different tonal orientation from that of the main melody for the cellos. The continuation of the melody on the violas (beginning at Fig 84) moves the tonal emphasis sharp-wards towards that originally asserted by the double-basses: this is secured as the violins take over and, soaring to their highest point, remain orientated around A major; it is transformed gradually (from Fig 93 onwards), gravitating towards the B flat tonality hinted at in the solo cello's interpolations.

The finale uses the full orchestra for the first time. It was written rather hurriedly to meet a deadline, after Tippett had been ill, and thus combines rather uncertainly the mosaic methods of the earlier movements with classical rondo form, using more extended thematic ideas, some quoted directly from Act II of *King Priam*. Its effect is rather undisciplined and piecemeal: a martial motif taken from the opera is not as cleverly integrated here as it was in Piano Sonata No. 2 (its tempo 2 idea), while Tippett's control of tonal movement and gauging of contrasts between music *en repos* and *en marche* is less subtle than it was in the preceding movements.

Although the main rondo theme (for trumpet and violins) galvanizes a lot of energy and momentum, and the slow interludes, dominated by a theme for flute and bassoons in canon, are an effective contrast, their relationship is a loose one. In a score replete from start to finish with memorable invention, the bare patches are quite obvious – e.g. the episode starting one bar after Fig 150 and ending at Fig 154 contains more than one rhythmic hiatus; also, some melodic phrases that ring hollow (cf. the one for trumpet and trombone at one bar before Fig 150). What keeps the finale alive are some of its superimpositions of disparate thematic materials – an intriguing portent of things to come in later compositions (cf. the section from Figs 154 to 157). But Tippett's 'non-ending' here is more a refuge than a solution.

Tippett's re-creation of the concerto seemed a logical outcome of his radical reappraisal of the orchestra. Extending many of the same principles to symphonic composition – a domain in which the classic Beethovenian model loomed large and had deeply affected all his early work – caused him much heart-searching. He rationalized his attitude to the symphony thus:

> What is meant by a symphony? First, it implies a *historical archetype* from which we depart and return – for example, the so-called middle-period symphonies of Beethoven. Secondly, there is the *notional archetype*, permitting endless variations to the end of time – for example, the Mahler symphonies, or those of Charles Ives or Lutoslawski ... The older view was that the Mahler symphonies did not conform to our historic archetype of the moment. Alternatively,we might say that Mahler (or Ives or Lutoslawski) gave the symphony new and valid forms; and in so doing, we momentarily abandon the conception of a historical archetype for that of a notional archetype.[7]

Given this terminology, Tippett's first two symphonies are clear instances of the historical archetype: abstract works of a 'neo-classic' character (albeit surmounting such labels with an extraordinary individuality of conception). In his Third and Fourth Symphonies (dating from 1972 and 1977, respectively), Tippett moves very much into the realm of notional archetypes. The Third Symphony is divided into two parts, each pairing two movements; the Fourth Symphony is one continuous movement, with its own individual demarcation of sections. In the background to the Third, however, there lurked an historical archetype that Tippett ultimately was unable to ignore: what he calls the 'famous hybrid work' – Beethoven's Ninth Symphony. Just as Beethoven originally conceived his finale as an instrumental movement (it became the finale of his String Quartet in A minor Op. 132), so also Tippett envisaged writing a series of instrumental blues. In actual fact, he felt encouraged to make them *vocal* blues when it became evident to him that the six songs of Mahler's *Das Lied von der Erde* comprise, in effect, a symphony. The biggest impulse turning both Beethoven and Tippett, in their respective symphonies, towards a vocal finale was the need to communicate an explicit message. So fundamental did Beethoven's example become, in fact, that Tippett also felt he could only cross over into his finale by quoting Beethoven's raucous opening to his own finale. Tippett's subsequent vocal blues and instrumental 'breaks' are also a commentary on Beethoven (and Schiller): a twentieth-century answer to late eighteenth- and early nineteenth-century affirmations of the joy of human brotherhood. The recitative passage for cellos and basses which introduced Beethoven's 'Ode to Joy' variation theme and the theme itself are embedded in the texture of this movement and subject to a kind of dismemberment.

Parallels to Tippett's creative re-consideration of Beethoven can be found in composers as diverse as Charles Ives (cf. his *Concord Sonata*) and Bernd Alois Zimmermann, whose last orchestral work, *Photoptosis*, was composed at roughly the same time as Tippett's symphony (1968). In *Photoptosis*, after an enormously dense climax, Beethoven's presto bars are also quoted, though the outcome is rather different – an attempt to draw order from a collage of further quotations, from *Parsifal*, *The Nutcracker* etc. What Ives and Zimmerman shared with Tippett was a sense of the inescapable moral force within Beethoven's music.

For his own challenge to Beethoven, however, Tippett had to design the right musical context. The notional archetype suggested a ground-plan in which an opening allegro and slow movement were combined and a scherzo preceded the finale. This enabled him to create a vast dramatic canvas into which the Beethoven commentary could be integrated. Moreover, his harmonic language had now expanded greatly.

The heroic, self-imposed disciplines of *King Priam* equipped Tippett sufficiently to accommodate far more chromaticism in his musical language than ever before. This element had already emerged fully-fledged in *The Knot Garden*. In harmonic terms, Tippett was now utilizing chromaticism with the same kind of freedom as Schoenberg used in his pre-twelve-note technique phase: and he was doing so instinctually and without inhibition. Such free chromaticism was always latent in his music (cf. the fugue from his Second String Quartet). But before he could tap its potential he had to acquire and assimilate a whole set of controls. On the one hand, then, he had learnt (from d'Indy) to control and manipulate an expressive flux; and he had concentrated his formal processes in terms of mosaic schemes that entailed great discernment in the choice and combination of sonorities. On the other hand, his empirical exploration of harmony *at the piano* led him to reinvigorate and intensify his earlier diatonically pellucid style. Thus, in his major scores of the late 1960s and 70s, Tippett was able to open a fresh range of pitch-constellations. Such technical exploration, however significant, remained for him a means to an end: and the end was what mattered. In both these dimensions, the Third Symphony opens up vistas.

Tippett has described its genesis thus:

In 1965, attending an Edinburgh Festival concert, I heard some music by Boulez – much of it very slow, almost immobile. I found myself saying that if ever I wanted to use that kind of music, I would have to match it with something extremely sharp, violent and certainly speedy. In retrospect, I realize that I had gone from the sounds coming to my ears from the outside world to the interior world within my own body ... the polarities I had experienced between the outside immobile music I had heard and the fast music I imagined might be set against it, engendered the metaphors for a symphonic conception.[8]

Thus the opening movement is based entirely on two categories of thematic material – what Tippett calls 'Arrest' ('energies of compression') and 'Movement' ('energies of explosion'). In d'Indy's terminology, this would also imply a new version of *en repos* and *en marche*: something borne out also by their contrasted harmonic emphasis, for the six bars of Arrest music are centred upon the tonality of E, but its chords are loaded with extra chromatic notes that eventually explode into the tonal flux of the eight bars of 'Movement' material. Tippett then enlarges upon these polarities, repeating the opposed ideas and extending them – sometimes considerably – five times over, eventually super-imposing them; and as the sound of their cataclysmic confrontation subsides, the slow movement gradually begins to unfold. The two thematic blocks of the opening movement have contrasted scoring: the 'Arrest' music is delivered by insistent brass and percussion; whereas strings, woodwind and piano unleash the energies of the 'Movement' music; this distinction is applied throughout.

Some new thematic material grows out of the extensions to these original thematic 'blocks': the most significant is the dancing theme for violins (at Fig 20) which achieves prominence in the last section of the movement, its rhythmic brightness and initial tonal clarity (centred on A) celebrating an opposite extreme to that of the 'Arrest' music on which it is superimposed. The sharp polarities on which the opening movement is founded return as the basis of the final pages of the symphony and are encapsulated in the sequence of *forte* and *pianissimo* chords with which the work ends (*see* Example 33).

The slow movement in Part I and the scherzo in Part II offer some respite from the overt conflicts prevalent in the rest of the symphony. Indeed, the slow movement comes close to the 'motionlessness' Tippett had originally perceived in Boulez, especially in its use of percussion and of solo wind. Conceived as a kind of 'nature-music', it contrasts high and low textures – the 'windless night sky and the tidal wave below' (in the composer's own words) – using two groups of motifs. The first (which returns later in Part II with its full connotations revealed) has a repeated figure on solo viola and a distant fanfare on two oboes.

The second grows from a shifting web of sonority for lower strings and clarinets (Fig 115), its melodic intervals gradually

Example 33

widening, its dynamic level gradually increasing until it attains an impassioned climax (Fig 120). This is interrupted in much the same way as the final climax of the first movement.

In the context of the movement as a whole, the emergence of a strong thread of some sort might have contradicted the main emphasis within this essentially static movement, which defines its motifs as discrete and separate entities returning, circling round each other but never interacting. Bringing the movement to a close, thus, could also have entailed a contrary thrust towards continuity: but here it is confined simply to a dramatic crescendo on tam-tam and bass-drum, after which the music fades into the distance.

The whole of Part I leaves the listener with a network of unanswered questions. The scherzo, opening Part II, makes these even more overt by continuing explicitly the process previously introduced in the slow movement of Part I, except that there is no pull in an alternative direction. It sets in motion what the composer describes as 'a play of five different musics which are quite long sections that hardly change at all in themselves, but do change in their relationship with each other'. The point is that

these 'musics' are ultimately irreconcilable and their superimposition in a climactic 'jam-session' cannot lead anywhere: it
can only be interrupted dramatically – which is one reason for
Tippett's decision to quote Beethoven's introduction to the vocal
finale of his Ninth Symphony and continue it as a series of
stylistic shifts (cf. Figs 174–192).

The scherzo develops further the concept of orchestral tutti
encountered in the Concerto for Orchestra. Its five 'musics' define
different orchestral strata and tonal orientation. Launching it is an
extended motif for four horns, hovering around E flat tonality most
of the time, before finally giving way to two chromatic motifs – a
rhythmically lurching one for cellos and basses and a flurry of
stratospherically high semiquavers for violins. Horns and violins
combine briefly to introduce a succession of fully-scored woodwind
chords. The games continue until the piano enters, first with theatrical leaps across its entire register, then with arpeggio-flourishes
that introduce a series of phrases, descending stepwise, that could
in principle produce a sense of tonal order, but this never happens:
the five 'musics' continue almost obliviously. Without careful
definition and characterization of the component musical blocks
and their superimposition, the end-result would have been chaos.
For Tippett had set himself a far harder task than, say, Charles Ives,
when interweaving popular tunes in *The Fourth of July* or *The
Housatonic at Stockbridge*. The outcome of Tippett's scherzo was
bound to be as inconclusive as anything in Part I: hence the need
to follow it with something quite unexpected – as it turns out, a
vocal finale.

We have already dealt with Tippett's use of the blues both to
express and to relieve suffering and anguish: but in purely
musical terms, he also needed a means to reconcile the polarities
of the earlier sections of the symphony. If those polarities are
understood as a pull away from secure diatonicism towards an
anarchic chromaticism, then the blues might be one means
whereby the two can coexist: hence, Tippett's blues style intensi-
fies the blues-inflexed notes with his own chromatic distortions,

pushing the voice-lines to the very limits of angularity (*see* Example 34):

Example 34

This mixture of keening and declamation – evident in Denise's first aria in *The Knot Garden* and continuing in the 'Hiroshima mon amour' movement of *The Mask of Time* – reaches an ironic climax when it is superimposed above Beethoven's 'Ode to Joy' theme. Set against the brotherhood of man (evoked in Schiller's poem) are the horrors of the concentration camp. In this context, the recapitulation of the motif for oboes and violas in the slow movement (*see* Example 41), with trumpets substituted for oboes and distant drums rounding off the phrases – distant, subdued war-music – has a searing impact. The confrontational intensity of the opening movement reaches its fullest pitch when the 'Arrest' motif is recalled as a pendant to the singer's line, 'My sibling was the torturer'. The whole of this final scene, indeed, brings together many strands from earlier episodes in the symphony, including the first blues number and its flugelhorn obbligato. Reconciliation is ultimately an aspiration here, not only in terms of Tippett's message, but in the abstract dimension of its tonal language. The risks inherent in Tippett's intuitive exploration of free atonality are never more evident than in the last section of this symphony. The singer's dream of a more compassionate world and the final bleak chordal confrontations for the orchestra do indeed provide for a deeply moving conclusion to the work. But in abstract terms, it sows the seeds of doubt as to whether, technically speaking, here, Tippett's reach exceeded his grasp. A tidier, more fastidious composer would have questioned whether, for instance, in the coda (from Fig 269 onwards) the overlapping instrumental lines that accumulate over repeated pedal notes need better definition, better characterization. The relationship with the voice-line also seems at this point somewhat arbitrary, so that when a solo trumpet (at Fig 288 *et seq.*) echoes what was just sung (at Fig 286 *et seq.*), it is too much of an exception to the rule to register – certainly after about 55 minutes or so of almost continuous music.

To make such criticisms neither denies the overwhelming impact of this extraordinary work – whose effect in the concert-hall is usually devastating – nor diminishes its stature. Nevertheless, only by continuing to compose further major works could Tippett now do justice to both his free-ranging imagination and his ever-widening technical explorations. As if to dumbfound his critics, in fact, Tippett embarked immediately on a Third Piano Sonata (1972–3) which stands as a formidable piece of abstract composition. It has no overt extra-musical connotations, no 'impurities' of style, no quotations from Tippett's own or any other composer's music. It balances the most variegated invention against the tautest organizational principles. Both this sonata and the Fourth – which followed roughly twelve years later – also spring organically from the nature of the instrument and of pianistic performance: and Tippett benefited greatly from the guidance he received from the pianist Paul Crossley (who had commissioned the work) regarding the sonorous potential of the instrument and techniques of performance.

The composer himself relates that 'part of the pleasure of writing for the solo keyboard is the sense of one performer producing all the necessary sounds ... Being only an indifferent piano player myself, I sense this virtuosity through arms and hands rather than fingers, whose skilled movements are beyond me. I am stimulated by the duality of the hands, their possible perceptible independence in one compositional direction and aural unity in another ... So, in this sonata, the independence of the hands is explored mainly in the outer fast movements and their unity in the slow middle one.'

The sonata begins with the hands at the farthest possible distance apart and this physical divergence of the hands to the extreme ends of the keyboard and their return jointly towards the middle became a feature many times repeated: a pianistic equivalent to the extremes of register explored (for instance) in the scherzo of his Third Symphony.

Cast in three movements, the work contains a reconciliation of sonata-style argument and freely inventive fantasy akin to that found in Beethoven's late-period sonatas. The thematic material and its development in the first movement are cunningly fused. First come two starkly opposed musical statements: one consisting of angular two-part highly syncopated dancing counterpoint (*see* Example 35) –

Example 35

the second (beginning after a bar's rest), quiet chords spanning
out across the keyboard (*see* Example 36).

Example 36

Then a smoother version of the opening counterpoint (again
giving prominence to the interval of the minor ninth) turns – after
being interrupted by some jaunty dotted-rhythm counterpoint –
into overt development of the opening idea, absorbing the dotted-
rhythm in the process. An entirely new motif – chords surrounded
by leaping staccato phrases – ushers in all the original material,
now decorated throughout with trills. The last four bars of the
initial idea are raised by a tone and the music continues thereafter
at the higher pitch, until it is interrupted by the last six bars of the
development section now raised by a fifth; at the end of this, the
music is left hanging in the air. Within the movement, tonally,
there is an impetus towards tonal order and security that is hinted

at in the Example 36 motif, but constantly disrupted by the free chromaticism of the rest of the material.

That impetus is only fulfilled by the slow movement. Here a succession of 17 chords or decorative figurations surrounding a chordal core form the basis of a set of four elaborate variations. Each variation raises the pitch by a minor third, so that by Variation 4 they are back at their initial level. Within this format, Tippett explores a comprehensive range of pianistic colour, texture and register. The poetic heart of the work is revealed in the variation that begins at bar 249, where the decorations retreat from the foreground and simply provide punctuation for a long sustained singing line: eventually they return, however, giving rise to a sequence of trilling phrases in contrasting registers of the instrument. Erupting into this tranquil atmosphere, the finale bursts forth as a brilliant toccata in A-B-A form: the B section is an exact mirror image of the first A section, which is shortened when repeated and rounded off with a coda. The movement has the same relentless energy as the finale of the 'Hammerklavier': and maybe Tippett could have set it in relief, emulating Beethoven's finale explicitly by including a short, slow reflective episode (perhaps an echo of his own slow movement) to create a breathing-space within its structure. It comes across anyway as an almost ruthless *tour de force*.

In all the instrumental compositions that followed upon Tippett's opera, *The Ice Break*, right up to his last work, *The Rose Lake*, we can discern a distinct trend towards formal synthesis and an ultimate distillation of invention. This was partly the natural inclination of an artist who, late in life, wanted to make summatory statements. But it also sprang from a desire to explore new, all-embracing formal schemes. Both are evident in *The Mask of Time*: and the three works preceding it – Symphony No. 4, String Quartet No. 4 and the Triple Concerto – may to some extent be considered as preparation for this, Tippett's largest concert-hall composition. Each hints at some of the prime concerns of *The Mask of Time*.

Tippett called the Symphony a 'birth-to-death piece'; he might have said something similar of the Fourth Quartet. The 'birth-image' that opens the symphony is linked in his mind with an early experience back in the 1920s, when he was taken to the Pitt-Rivers anthropological museum in Dorset, and saw there an early film of a foetus growing inside the womb of a rabbit, with the process speeded up so that, at a particular stage, the initial single-cell form shook like a jelly and became two, then later became four, and so on. This image, stored up in his mind for something like fifty years, now generated one of his powerful motifs (*see* Example 37) – a motif so charged with resonances that it is recalled in the first movement of *The Mask of Time* as the chorus, conjuring the ever-present cosmos, sing the word 'space'; and again (in the seventh movement) at the climax of the burial scene for Shelley; and indeed, later still, Tippett was to make it the starting-point of the central movement of his Piano Sonata No. 4.

Tippett: Symphony No. 4, opening

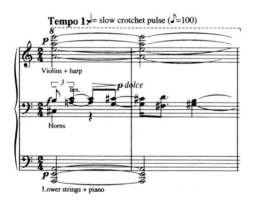

Example 37

The Fourth Quartet shudders into life in a different way, all four instruments hovering around a focal E flat, then gradually burgeoning into rich chord sequences. Both works die away to nothing at the end, the Symphony using actual breathing effects, the Quartet coming to rest with repeated double-stopped chords.

Just as *The Mask of Time* attains its ultimate goal in a final outpouring of wordless singing, so likewise the Fourth Quartet and Triple Concerto make the re-discovery of a lyric impulse their ultimate goal. Just before the end of the Quartet, after a climax of conflict and dissonance has been reached, there is a sudden descent into peaceful rapture as the four instruments – in a highly unusual textural alignment – sing to each other (*see* Example 38): and at the start of the Triple Concerto, after the three soloists have introduced themselves in cadenzas, Tippett re-creates exactly this passage from the Quartet, this time minus the chirrupings of the second violin (*see* Example 39).

The episode in question becomes a main reference-point in the Concerto, recurring later in the opening movement and again near the end of the finale. In both pieces, it seems to signify the ability of the artist to stand apart from worldly turmoil and conjure up an alternative world of lyrical fulfilment. In abstract terms, the symphony, quartet and concerto were also each conceived as a single continuous span of music, whose component sections are nevertheless distinguishable.

Sonata and fantasy are cleverly reconciled in the symphony. On the one hand, it has four main sections – roughly corresponding to a Beethovenian exposition, slow movement, scherzo and recapitulation. Interpolated in amongst these are episodes of free fantasia-style digression and development. The work thus falls into seven sections dovetailed to produce an unbroken flow of ideas and argument. Its notional archetype might be termed the 'symphonic fantasia', as exemplified by Sibelius's Seventh Symphony.

At another level, the work is indebted to the dramatically conceived symphonic poems of Liszt, Strauss and Elgar. The

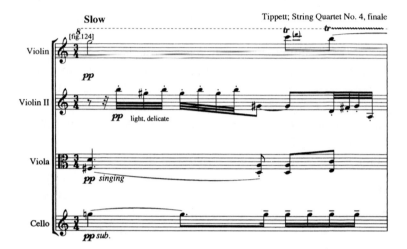

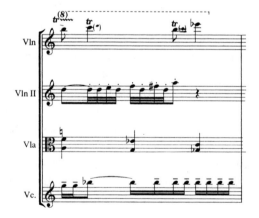

Example 38

Tippett: Triple Concerto, 1st movt

Example 39

orchestration – giving special prominence to brass (six horns, two tubas in addition to the normal complement) and percussion – reflects this provenance, but is not then an excuse for late-romantic opulence, so much as to allow the greatest scope for the creation of a mosaic of distinctively characterized 'thematic blocks'. After the opening introduction – the birth-motif, repeatedly, effortfully moving away from its initial A major/minor orientation – the exposition takes off at a new tempo (Fig 4 *et seq.*) contrasting three main musical ideas of 'power' (brass in the ascendant), 'vigour' (strings) and 'lyric grace' (woodwind). The interplay of these ideas eventually leads to a slow six-bar passage for the six horns, followed by a gently swaying motif for viola and harp: all of this returns twice later – each time raised a tone higher than before – giving the listener opportunities to take stock of all that has happened. The next such opportunity occurs in fact after the development section that now follows – outlined in four easily identifiable stages (starting at Figs 25, 33, 40 and 46) – where it also acts as a link to the section equivalent to a Beethovenian slow movement.

Four well differentiated ideas are now introduced, flowing into each other seamlessly: a flute theme taken up by the bassoon and commented upon by the other instruments; a brass motif which introduces a tender, romantic theme for lower strings (Fig 62); and an oboe theme (Fig 68 *et seq.*), the most extended in the work, to which the cor anglais provides an epilogue (Fig 75). Another development section now bursts forth, a fugal treatment of an insistent, craggy string theme that brings the symphony to its emotional apex, a climax of great violence, from which we are released into the scherzo (Fig 100) – a playful study in virtuosity for woodwind and percussion, their sporting capped by a dancing trio section for the six horns. The most distant digression from the main concerns of the symphony now follows, a paraphrase on 36 bars of a Gibbons three-part fantasia – the one encountered in the first movement of his *Divertimento on Sellinger's Round*. Tippett retains its three-part texture and design, but elaborates and enriches the lines: and so that it does not seem utterly irrelevant, reminiscences of it are incorporated into earlier and later sections of the symphony. After the six horns, viola and harp have once more provided an opportunity for reflection and a change of gear, the various components of the mosaic are now 'collected up' in the manner first deployed in his Piano Sonata No. 2. The opening exposition and its birth-motif are recapitulated and eventually crystallized into two kinds of sharply polarized music: wild, rushing triplets for strings and horns; and a quiet funereal chorale for trumpets, trombones and tubas, wherein the life-blood of the symphony seems to peter out.

In dramatic terms, the piece has sufficient breadth and variety to do justice to its intended life-span of experience: as a kind of latter-day *Ein Heldenleben*, it has its full measure of heroic gestures, ardent passions, bitter-sweet regrets, philosophic reflections and carefree abandonment, but excludes empty Straussian bombast or heavy Teutonic humour. The final recapitulatory episodes, in which scenes from the hero's life, as it were, flash by in quick succession, are particularly effective. More dubious was the inclusion of 'breathing effects', whose scope and exact character were never made clear when the composer originally included them in the score: moreover, they could not be realized satisfactorily until the arrival of digital recording technology. Thus, for years, these breathing effects – so often redolent of obscene telephone-calls – sullied the reputation of the symphony. Now that they are 'performable' on a synthesizer, they can be integrated properly, complementing the orchestral birth-motif, the stormy violence of the central tutti and emerging into the foreground with the gradual expiration of life in the final bars. Nevertheless, such effects remain somewhat too naïvely 'anecdotal' (to use Boulez's jargon) to fit properly in otherwise so consummate a symphonic conception: as such, they constitute an error of artistic judgement. After the Concerto for Orchestra, also, tutti scoring was always going to be a problem. This is evident in the main climactic development section of Symphony No. 4 (particularly from Fig 87), where unisons, octaves and fifths make for a rugged, stark overall texture that has acoustic 'gaps' – and therefore does not cohere well.

Returning, with his Fourth Quartet, to the string medium for the first time in nearly 25 years, Tippett, unusually, almost ignored its contrapuntal capacity and pressed it to its sonorous limits with music of the utmost harmonic density: to such an extent, in fact, that it probably sounds more effective – certainly, at least, more secure – in its string orchestra realization as *Water out of Sunlight* (1986). Moreover, if this work unconsciously emulated Beethoven's *Grosse Fuge* in its sense of strain and technical danger, it has also a deliberate link in that the main theme of the

Examples 40a, 40b

finale is a characterized by an obsessive dotted-rhythm inescapably redolent of that in Beethoven: (*see* Examples 40a, 40b).

The extreme polarities of this work are encountered here. But the emotional apex of the quartet is its slow movement, which starts from a new version of the opening 'birth-motif', centred now around E rather than E flat. This movement sets in train a succession of ardent lyrical ideas: duets for the two violins and the viola and cello, respectively; a cello solo decorated by the two violins and (at its close) the viola; gently murmured exchanges between viola and second violin against a chordal background developing into full-blooded rhetoric; and a lengthy final episode where each instrument wings along its independent course, before being interrupted by the strife of the finale.

Around this slow movement, the other sections group themselves to show what the composer calls 'the general progressions (repeated) ... from a web of sound unwinding into linear clarity, and from intense stillness breaking out through the unwinding into vigour'. This progression is encapsulated in the opening slow movement, whose function is largely introductory, supplying the germ cells for all the later motifs. Conflict then comes clearly to the fore in the second movement. The musical material here – three contrasting themes, with linking ideas and an extended codetta – is heard three times over, transposed and presented in a slightly different order at each repetition. Respite from its intense elaboration of texture and harmonic tension is signalled by a series of extended pizzicati, gradually leading into the calm of the main slow movement.

The finale erupts into this tranquillity with a great discharge of violent, dense music, giving way only to the insistence of the succeeding episode with its Grosse Fuge-inspired theme. At the opposite extreme to this is a chordal motif in crystalline harmonics, whose demeanour is distant, esoteric. Tippett's transition to this – articulated in episodes of fast semiquavers, in unison and octaves – takes a definite path towards clarity. The two thematic extremes remain only until we reach the slow coda at the end, when in the final bars we attain the quietude of a chordal motif present in different forms throughout the work.

Tippett's creative objective at this stage in his career, to rediscover the ardent lyricism that had become secondary in importance in his works since *King Priam*, was triumphantly attained in his Triple Concerto, a work of immense individuality and beauty. Much of its originality stems from the deployment of its three soloists – violin, viola and cello – both in terms of their characterization and their textural alignment. Their opening cadenzas, aimed at distinguishing them as musical personalities, give unexpected pride of place to the viola: and again when they are all heard together, it is the viola's line of double-stopped melody (re-created from String Quartet No. 4, as mentioned above) which is the main focus. Furthermore, the main melody of the rondo-like slow movement, is outlined by the soloists in octaves, but again with the viola at the bottom of the texture, and the cello in the middle (*see* Example 41).

Example 41

The originality and beauty of this melody stem from its fusion of different elements. The connection Tippett always made in his mind between Purcell's 'false relations' and the blues notes heard in jazz is now extended to Indonesian gamelan music. Thus, the cadences of the melody are supported by what Tippett has called a 'blues' gong sound – a reinforcement of the trombone's foreign note, A flat, in the key of F.

These bluesy flattenings of melodic notes are a recurrent, unifying element in Tippett's lyricism here: and the bitter-sweet ending to the movement, with solo viola and horns, clinches the point.

The Triple Concerto deserves the title *Fantasia concertante* even more than Tippett's earlier Corelli-based work bearing that name, for its formal shape is very much dictated by its efflorescence of invention. Out of the elaborate patchwork of sections in the first of its three movements, there emerges an overall binary scheme, in which the five main musical components introduced at the start are realigned, modified or transformed. The opening orchestral motif – if not explicitly a 'birth' motif, certainly one that enables the music immediately to spring to life – introduces each half of the binary scheme, transposed up a tone on its second appearance. The d'Indyesque distinction of music *en repos* and *en marche* is largely evident here as a distinction between the reflective stance of the soloists and the forward propulsion provided by the orchestra: a rationale that gives a sure sense of purpose to an otherwise episodic structure.

Linking the three movements are short orchestral interludes whose function is partly pictorial, or at least signalling a change of 'scene'. The first interlude, thus, with its delicate woodwind and percussion solos and textures, constitutes an evocation of dusk before the nocturnal slow movement. In the second interlude, featuring brass and percussion, nature comes gradually to life again, as a new day dawns at the start of the finale: and indeed, before the finale proper can get going, the soloists extend this interlude to convey a birdsong-like rapture over held pedal-notes, the first violin even choosing to enter with a quotation from the dawn-chorus music for strings in the last scene of *The Midsummer Marriage.*

Certain other features of the concerto, acquired from gamelan music, give it a special character and colouring. One is obviously its prominent use of gongs in the interludes between solo sections in the slow movement: these reinforce the menace that repeatedly threatens to disturb the paradisal mood of the piece – thus making it all the more credible. Another is the use of layered 'colotomic' textures, in which a main central melodic thread is surrounded by decorative versions of the same line and other embellishments: a texture which Tippett had emulated from the transcriptions of gamelan music in Colin McPhee's *Music in Bali*.[9] The most important instance of this is the orchestral 'ritornello' motif that closes each half of the first movement (*see* Example 42). When it returns at the end of the work it is repeated and stage by stage fragmented, until only a single chord is left.

Tippett's orchestral palette in the concerto is also unusual, in that it includes only a single trumpet and trombone, but gives special prominence to solo woodwind instruments, notably bass oboe and alto flute. These last two appear for the first time in the first interlude, and in the slow movement, engage in ruminative dialogue with (respectively) the solo viola and cello.

If the finale is the least satisfactory movement in the concerto, this is partly because not much more remains to be added to the preceding movements. After its dawn-chorus music, it gets under way with an almost Elgarian *nobilmente*-style theme. This is taken up by the orchestra and some development of it begins but is abandoned. There is a change of gear (a few bars that Tippett had to re-write after the première, as they were too insubstantial to register: they still cause a hiatus that is difficult to conceal in performance). Above a new version of the ritornello motif from the first movement, the soloists dance in octaves: at its climax, the opening of the first movement is recapitulated, telescoping the cadenzas into a collective version. But after the succeeding lyrical colloquy has been extended further, the ritornello idea returns in its original format and an ending is contrived from

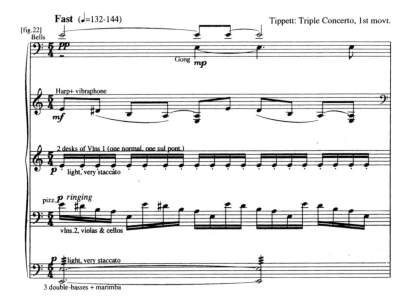

Example 42

antiphonal exchanges between the orchestra and soloists – the music wafting finally into the far distance.

Tippett's remaining major instrumental works are more rounded achievements. His Piano Sonata No. 4 goes, in every respect, way beyond its predecessors for the instrument. It is the most extended of his sonatas, explores the potential of the piano far more idiomatically and consistently than before: and although divided into five movements, it is manifestly conceived as a single sweep of musical thought and experience – almost a pianistic counterpart of Symphony No. 4.

Fascinated with the way Beethoven, in his late sonatas and string quartets, explored different ways of ordering a sequence of five, sometimes six or seven movements, Tippett here makes the central third movement both the emotional apex of the work and a microcosmic version of its structure, for it too has a five-section format, which the composer describes as 'A-B (1/2)-C-B(1/2)-A'. As the basis of the 'A' sections in this movement, Tippett uses a transcription made for him by Paul Crossley of the opening birth-motif from the Fourth Symphony (a pianistic version of Example 37 above). In the opening exposition, the Sonata has 25 bars corresponding to the 21 in the first section of the Symphony – five statements instead of three: yet it contrives to sound more taut, more enclosed within its own territory. This is because the phrases that answer the birth-motif are direct outgrowths, rather than rejoinders, as in the symphony. The trajectory taken by Tippett's musical thinking from the Symphony through to the Triple Concerto, and again within the entire compass of *The Mask of Time*, is an effortful aspiration towards endless, unfettered song. Here, in this movement of Sonata No. 4, Tippett moves directly, without transition, from the tensions of the opening to that lyrical goal: his B section has a three-part texture with a central singing line and outer lines that embellish it. The 'C' section of the movement offers the hard-edged, aggressive contrast that Tippett has always felt to be a necessary context for lyrical outpourings: and the final return to the birth-motif of the Symphony serves to emphasize that such lyricism is a dream easily shattered, constantly needing to be conjured afresh.

The sonata begins with a preludial movement; it continues with a fugue; the fourth movement is a scherzo and the finale a song-like slow movement. All the movements exemplify perfectly Tippett's 'empirical' conception of harmony and tonal movement. In the prelude, for instance, the opening idea is a series of what Crossley has called 'expansions of resonance', acoustic outgrowths of five bass notes – B flat, C, A, C sharp and D. B flat is the tonality in which the work begins and ends. Yet a 'blue' note, F sharp – a distant note in the overtone series emanating from it – is as essential an element in Tippett's understanding of B flat tonality as is F natural (*see* Example 43):

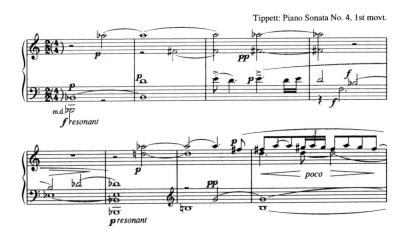

Tippett: Piano Sonata No. 4, 1st movt.

Example 43

In a later lyrical episode in the first movement, based on D tonality, almost every chord has a 'blue' note as part of its acoustic resonance (*see* Example 44):

Example 44

and the poignant opening to the finale likewise subsists on such saturation of tonal harmony with bluesy inflexions.

Indeed, as the scherzo shows, the left-hand/right-hand dialogue in Tippett's piano writing is also an acoustic dialogue, the high-register right-hand chords articulating distant resonances embodied within the left-hand broken harmonies.

The same principle applies even when the texture is reversed (cf. bars 90 *et seq.*) It would be wrong to claim any of this as an innovation specific to Tippett: Chopin's Études are full of comparable effects of harmony and texture; Messiaen made it integral to his own idiosyncratic method. Tippett arrived there by instinct, seeking a liberated form of chromaticism within a language firmly grounded in tonality.

Another work that glances back at Tippett's Symphony No. 4 is the slow movement of his Sonata for solo guitar, entitled *The Blue Guitar*. (The title refers both to Picasso's painting, *The Man with the Blue Guitar* and the poem by Wallace Stevens, 'The Blue Guitar', which the painting inspired.) Tippett uses three 'moods or gestures' – 'Transforming', 'Dreaming' and 'Juggling' as titles for his three movements.

Here, in the slow movement, two contrasting ideas, one lyrical, one recitative-like and rhetorical, are developed at different pitch-levels, before giving way to a transcription of the harp and viola motif (see Figs 23–25) from the Symphony; another harp motif, from the end of Act II of *The Ice Break*, is incorporated into the final section. These self-quotations help crystallize two tonal tendencies within the movement – one towards a dreamy diatonicism, the other towards a disruptive chromaticism. As such, the movement leaves the listener with a characteristic Tippett-ian question mark. The composer indeed intended this as the final movement of the work, but its first interpreter, Julian Bream, opted to end with the scherzo-like fast central movement and his preference was adopted in the published edition of the work; more recent performers, such as Craig Ogden, have restored the slow movement to its rightful place.

Properly considered one of the most substantial works to be conceived for the instrument in recent years, *The Blue Guitar* not only exploits guitar virtuosity and a wide gamut of sonorities (especially in the fast 'Juggling' movement), but, in the preludial 'Transforming' movement, deploys a highly appropriate blues harmony. Equally intrinsic to guitar is its final episode of poignant, self-communing two part counterpoint.

Throughout the major works that Tippett produced in his eighties, there is a tendency towards a similar textural refinement as had evidently come naturally to him in *The Blue Guitar*. This was already evident in *The Mask of Time* and *New Year*. In his String Quartet No. 5 and *The Rose Lake*, it became essential to his strategy of seeking an ultimate distillation of lyricism. Whereas the harmonic density of String Quartet No. 4 threatened to burst the bounds of the medium, Tippett's Fifth Quartet is at the opposite extreme, often allowing the entire weight of the musical expression to be carried by one or two lines.

Beethoven's late synthesis of diverse elements within an extended design once more was his model. Thus the two movements of Tippett's Fifth Quartet are each a mixture of song, dance and quasi-fugal interplay. The first movement, nevertheless, has a sonata-style basis, but retains a potential for unexpected deviation. It falls into two parts, the second longer than the first, both ending with an assertive passage, whose rhythmic chords that testify to the composer's ability constantly to renew quartet textures.

The piece opens with a 'call to attention' – a foreground phrase, consisting of three chords reiterated *forte*, followed by a rhythmically springing, but distant answering phrase, *piano*, which is extended on its third repetition. A fugal-style exposition of ideas unfolds, leading to a more lyrical group and coalescing in a rapturous duet for the violins, to which viola and cello add their voices. A dance-like 'codetta' section follows, continuing until it reaches the rhythmic chords just mentioned. The succeeding development section is not at all routine, however: for suddenly Tippett comes forth with an episode of 'lyrical heterophony' based on a passage from his fifth opera, *New Year.* The main narrative impetus is suspended, giving way to contemplative rapture: and although it resumes, with clear enough goals, this expressive diversion is a harbinger of the kind of music that is dominant in the second movement.

Tippett headed the score of his Fifth Quartet with the following quotation: 'Chante, rossignol, chante, toi, qui as le coeur gai (Sing, nightingale, sing, you with the heart so gay'.)[10] At the start of an early broadcast talk discussing what for him was the essence of being a musician and composer, Tippett mentioned the impact on him of a nightingale singing at night: '... some quality in the night and the sound of the bird-song combine to make a specially intense image. At such time we respond. It's as though another world had spoken by some trick of correspondence between the outside and the inside ...'[11] All this is germane to the second (and longer) of the two movements of the Fifth Quartet, particularly its opening, which certainly has the quality of an 'intense image' of bird-song.

Out of preparatory spread-chords from lower three instruments (barely concealing their origin as improvisations 'till-ready' at the keyboard), the first violin solo takes wing, soaring upwards into its highest register, before skittering down and finally sliding to a point of rest. Such music looks bare enough on paper. But it is so well focused, so daringly concentrated that it suffices to initiate a calm, musical meditation.

But this is not a somnolent, ruminatory pastoral movement after the manner of *The Lark Ascending*. Tippett's explicit model is the central 'Hymn of Thanksgiving' movement in Beethoven's Quartet in A minor, Op. 132. Tippett follows Beethoven in alternating between slow, contemplative music with faster episodes straining effortfully towards affirmation and light. In Tippett's work, when these faster episodes return, they appear first of all transposed down, then next time at their original pitch, but with their lines ornamented to intensify their impact. The cadences rounding off the musical phrases, sentences and paragraphs in this work are more conjured than calculated: the blues notes remain essential to Tippett's harmony, not least in the prolonged final A major chord, where the addition of Stravinskian G sharp and D convey the sense of the strain needed to fix in our minds Tippett's vision of radiance and beauty.

It is not only Beethoven's structure that is emulated here, but his timelessness: and this is even more apparent in *The Rose Lake*. In another essay, 'Towards the Condition of Music', Tippett remarks, '... the time we apprehend in the work of musical art has only a virtual existence by contrast with the time marked by the clock-hands when the work is performed.'[12] *The Rose Lake* exemplifies this to perfection. Its silences, especially towards the end, are as important as the notes themselves in drawing the listener into its own virtual time-continuum.

Tippett has described the work as 'in essence a set of variations': yet it is actually *sui generis*.[13] Rarely has a composer allowed his ideas to flow out so effortlessly discovered the right proportions so organically. Thematically, the corner-stone of the variations is an interval of a major ninth, repeatedly stretching upwards from within the six-horn texture of the first of the five 'lake-songs' (*see* Example 45):

Example 45

This is 'echoed from the sky' in the second song by flute and clarinet in canon. Within the extended third 'full song', it expands triumphantly into a major tenth, propelling the string line (in unisons and octaves) towards climaxes whose intensity comes from the combination of both major ninths and major tenths (*see* Example 46).

Immediately afterwards (Fig 96), the ninths are contracted into major seconds, and inverted. They only blossom again (still in inverted form) as 'The lake song leaves the sky'. Finally, when 'The lake sings itself to sleep', they are once more contracted into major seconds.

Just as important in nurturing the lyric impulse within these songs is an appoggiatura motif (*see* Example 47) which recurs as a wistful, bitter-sweet rejoinder to the passionate outbursts in the second song (Figs 54–56) and even more ardently in the fourth song (Figs 126–130). With its Wagnerian, almost *Tristan*-esque echoes, these episodes summon up a romantic ardour highly appropriate in a score whose essential ambition is to capture those fleeting moments of paradisal oneness between man and nature.

The Rose Lake is also a miraculous set of variations in orchestral sonority. It entails a large orchestra, but this rarely proclaims

Example 46

Example 47

itself with a huge tutti outburst. Instead, Tippett's fascination with mosaic schemes reaches its zenith with an alliance of thematic ingredients and chamber ensemble scorings that seem as apposite as any of those that were dramatically defined in *King Priam* or *The Knot Garden*. Thus the gentle, primordial stirrings of the horn – more likely to evoke the bottom of the Rhine for those who have not yet visited Le Lac Rose – are offset by a series of quick dance-like episodes. Taking turn in the limelight here are hard-edged, hieratic harmonies from woodwind alternating with luminous interweaving two-part counterpoint for harps, reinforced by marimba and vibraphone: and bitingly astringent chord-clusters for trumpets and trombones (assisted by cymbals and tam-tam) alternating with a thrusting dance for roto-toms (whose pitches are reinforced by cellos and violas). Tippett's mosaic schemes are the vehicle for many gradations of harmonic density and rhythmic complexity and as such, they etch themselves quickly into the memory. These components provide the musical structure with episodes of stasis and momentum: and they are instantly identifiable when they return later in the piece.

The climactic song (Fig 79) achieves its intended transformation by replacing this shifting sequence of colours with an extended lyrical line for the strings, trumpets and trombones adding to it a rhythmically and harmonically independent layer of embellishment. This episode of sustained, exultant musical activity attains a climax, to be suddenly replaced by stasis and silence. Even more gradually than at the start of the work, the music burgeons into life again from stillness: rhythmically syncopated repeated notes for roto-toms and harp, joined later by clarinet, alternate with a passage for six horns, and each motif is extended when repeated.

Then comes a kind of fantasia-like interpolation of canonic counterpoint, first for oboes and cor anglais, then for bassoons and contrabassoon: their exchanges are separated by sweeping glissandi that are like cinematic 'dissolves' and eventually lead to the next song-episode. The entire section, apparently a complete digression from the main substance of the work, nevertheless offers some breathing space within its structure.

Two further interpolations – the second quoted from the second scene of *King Priam* – presage the return of the episodes of harmonic and rhythmic contrast from early on in the piece. Likewise, after the six horns have quietly brought the final song to a point of rest, fragments of the 'scene-setting' music from the opening of the work return, but are interrupted by four brittle woodwind chords, the last crescendoing into a fifth, marked 'plop' – a method by which Tippett, as ever, takes the listener out of the world of enchantment into that of reality.

Throughout his compositional *oeuvre*, Tippett highlighted relationships between the pictorial and the abstract – between those sonorities that reside within the actuality of nature, and those contrived artificially, as it were, by instrumental means. Bird-song and human vocalization are rapturously fused in *The Midsummer Marriage*, in the Corelli Fantasia and the Triple Concerto. But Tippett's acoustic universe embraces all the sounds of nature – e.g. in the night music of the slow movement of his Third Symphony, in the second 'dawn' interlude of the Triple Concerto, above all in the montage of choral chants, cries, whispers, screams that (in a tradition that extends from Jannequin's descriptive madrigals to Stravinsky's choral writing in *Les noces*) provide the backcloth to the 'Jungle' movement in *The Mask of Time*.

The Rose Lake offers his most comprehensive and his best integrated sonic-canvas, growing organically from its initial nature-evocation and bird-cries into a sequence of songs that seem to flow seamlessly in and out of their context. In *The Rose Lake*, in short, Tippett displays a consummate mastery of form and fantasy: his controlled manipulation of all the parameters of composition is that which only a mature composer, sure of every note, sure of every step in the progress of the music, could attain. Form and fantasy are here just complementary facets of the same creative impulse, the same defining imagination, the same shaping hand.

8
Time and Eternity

The Vision of St Augustine

Tippett has won both admiration and notoriety as a composer who has constantly stretched himself and his listeners beyond imagined capacities. The notoriety arose partly because of a tendency, prevalent in England until fairly recently, to regard intellectual ideas and tools as irrelevant to musical composition. Tippett's readiness to write, lecture and broadcast about aesthetic issues, especially those that had a bearing on the conception of his works, aroused suspicion. In truth, his intellectual questing is as much part of the excitement of his work as is its more obvious lyric richness and rhythmic buoyancy. There is always an element in Tippett's work of *musica speculativa*: musical conceptions so purely metaphorical, so extraordinary as to defy easy analysis or description – sometimes also appearing to be beyond performable limits. One of the earliest examples of this is the fourth movement of his Third String Quartet. No precedent exists for its formal shape. No expressive model from any past music underlies its progress from complete stillness to a passionate discharge of lyricism, though maybe the slow movement of Beethoven's String Quartet in A minor Op. 132 was lurking at the back of his mind. It is not fanciful, all the same, to see in it a musical metaphor for the act of creation itself.

More than once in his operas, Tippett was in fact impelled to give some intimation of what it is like to be a creative artist effortfully striving towards some exalted transcendental experience. His Messenger-figures represent this side of him well. Madame Sosostris in her great Act III aria in *The Midsummer Marriage* attests to the agony of creation: 'La Pythie', the poem by Paul Valéry which inspired it, was similarly concerned with 'the quest for a poetic language, the evolution of a cry into ordered discourse.'[1] Hermes, in the final interlude of *King Priam*, sings a hymn to the timeless flow of 'divine music'. Tippett brings it to a focus in a Yeats quotation: 'Mirror upon mirror, mirrored is all the show'. The metaphor is taken up again by Priam as he faces death. His final vision is of a 'loop in time': his eyes closed to the external world, he murmurs:

> I see mirrors
> Myriad upon myriad moving
> The dark forms of creation.

From student days Tippett's mind was exercised by concepts of time and their artistic application. In the 1960s, commenting on Edgar Wind's Reith Lectures, 'Art and Anarchy', Tippett asserts that the creative faculty is ultimately independent of both external and internal ferment, entailing a wilful concentration of psychic energy towards specific and extraordinary goals. He confesses himself 'haunted by the feeling that creative time [i.e. the experience of time within an encounter with an art-work] may really be spontaneous and discontinuous'.[2] The comment is not only apposite in relation to the Quartet movement and operatic scenes just mentioned, but germane to his last three decades or so of composition.

Tippett made this the explicit subject-matter of a large-scale musical composition for the first time in *The Vision of St Augustine* (1963–5). While the design of this work is tautly held, its temporal discontinuity and apparent spontaneity of utterance overturn all one's formal expectations.

Augustine (AD 354–430) fascinated Tippett on account of his culture and sensibility (which he derived from Latin literature); because he also battled with the paradox that the Bible – in his view a crude, barbarous, often nonsensical book – was still God's work; but above all, because he introduced a new idea about time into Christian thinking, which is that God is present not only in the cosmos but in man's innermost soul (a perception which Tippett first encountered in an essay by Gilles Quispel).[3] Time,

being a 'working' of God, acquires thus a psychological nuance.
The present is nothing if not an experience in the soul; the past is
a memory image in the soul; and the future exists only as our
psychic expectations. Ordinary time is transient and meaningless.
It disappears when the soul unites with God. 'Divine time' – or
Eternity – is thus separable from measured worldly time. The
soul shifts so speedily from the present (*contuitus*) towards the
future (*expectatio*) or the past (*memoria*) that it is forever
distended (*distentus*) in all directions without a centre. To achieve
a centre, concentration (*internio*) is essential: and Augustine was
amongst those privileged to receive an intimation of such a
centre. In Tippett's composition, the temporal shifts are
articulated as if they are within a single continuum of related
experience: in his subsequent operas, and in *The Mask of Time*,
taking his cue from cinema and television, Tippett deploys them
with even greater freedom to accommodate a wider gamut of
disrelated experiences in time and space.

In the course of his life, Augustine had two visionary
experiences which he describes in his *Confessions*. Tippett, in the
tripartite scheme of his composition, concentrates upon the
second of them, setting the famous sections of Book XI, wherein
Augustine describes the vision of eternity he shared with his
mother, Monica, whilst standing in a window embrasure. But Part
I of the work contains a remembrance also of the first (auditory)
vision – shared with Augustine's dearest friend Alypius – of a
child singing.

In Part I, we encounter straightaway the procedures that are
characteristic of the entire piece: a kind of 'stream of consciousness' technique in the manipulation of the texts, intermingling
extracts from the *Confessions* with a variety of biblical
references. This is allied to a mosaic musical structure,
juxtaposing and superimposing 'thematic blocks' in the manner
he had developed in *King Priam* and further exploited in his
Piano Sonata No. 2 and Concerto for Orchestra. The narrative
entrusted to the solo baritone, setting the scene in the house

where Augustine and his mother were resting before their sea journey back to Africa, is interrupted and illuminated by the chorus, with reminiscences of other experiences, of hymns, prayers and exclamations.

Individual words sung by the baritone bring associative choral interjections into play. *'Tu'* – referring to Monica – prompts a recollection of the Ambrosian hymn, 'Deus Creator Omnium', which the grief-stricken Augustine had repeated to himself at his mother's death, *'ipsa'* sparks off a remembrance of both parents; *'fenestram'* ('window') is echoed in a great choral shout; and *'unde hortus'* ('whence the garden') signposts Augustine's first vision. All these strands are drawn together at the climax of Part I – the vision itself: the point at which worldly time yields to eternity, which is the life of the saints and which is made manifest in the paeans of joy sung by the angels. The chorus now supplements Augustine's half-articulated description with poetic rhapsody from the Book of Job (*'Ubi eras quando ponebam fundamentam terrae?'*) and Psalm 42 (*'Quaemodum desiderat cervus'*): but it is the orchestra which brings the vision fully into focus. The ecstatic, dancing phrases sung by the chorus here are taken over by the orchestra alone and turned into a series of whirling, oscillating patterns whose capacity for further extension is (theoretically) limitless.

In the course of this striving towards ecstatic goals, the actual musical materials undergo dance-like mutations. For instance, the baritone's opening phrases (especially the second) become rhythmically more animated in the chorus part at *'Surge, surge acquile'*, generate an imitative dance for xylophone and piano at *'abscessi ergo'* and another lively version in the baritone line and chorus exchanges beginning *'et praeterita'* (Fig 43). This leads eventually to the leaping motifs that embody the choral allelulias (Fig 61 *et seq.*), giving rise in turn to a lengthy orchestral coda. Likewise, the opening phrases of the chorus acquire new rhythmic interest at *'et inspira'* (Fig 13) and in conjunction with the xylophone/piano duet at *'abcessi ergo'* (Fig 28): and out of this, at *'et praeterita'* (Fig 48), there springs a new accompani-mental motif on violins and violas. Tippett manages thus to ensure both the marriage of an intricate text and a formally cohesive layout.

Tippett's vocal writing articulates a similar progression towards a dance-like expression of ecstasy. Purcell-ian melismas, present in all Tippett's vocal music, from his cantata 'Boyhood's End' right up to *King Priam* (notably in Achilles' war-cry), are now transformed into what the composer calls 'glossolalia', an ancient tradition of exultant wordless vocalization, encountered in many traditions – e.g in the singing of 'Allelulia', in yodelling and in the passionate yelling of a wide range of popular musicians, including those in the worlds of jazz and rock music. Augustine himself called it the *jubilus*: 'for those who sing in the harvest field, or are overcome with joy at the words to the song, being filled with such exultation, the words fail to express their emotion, so leaving the syllables of the words, they drop into vowel sounds – the vowel sounds signifying that the heart is yearning to express what the tongue cannot utter.'[4]

The use of glossolalia in *The Vision of St Augustine* is closely related to the temporal shifts, helping to produce an intensity of utterance, a meditative focus or centre. When the basses sing the 'Deus, Creator Omnium' for the first time in Part I, for instance, the female voices add another layer of ecstatic melismas, while the baritone ululates on the single word *'Tu'* – the total effect being a temporal shift, a memory, a concentration of psychic energy in the chorus part.

Tippett's mosaic-like structure overall is built out of 14 thematic 'blocks', each designated a tempo. Seven of these are introduced in Part I. Moreover, the first four bars of baritone solo, accompanied by lower strings, piano and percussion and followed by 12 bars of choral commentary, with a similar accompaniment but also an important celesta motif as decoration – are the source of many of the other thematic ideas in the piece. Exposition and development overlap throughout: hence the fluidity of cross-reference and the apparent spontaneity that arrest and hold the listener's attention.

In Parts II and III, Tippett introduces another seven blocks of thematic material at different tempi, but these evolve organically from all that has preceded them. In Part II, Tippett deals with the more important of Augustine's two visions. 'We passed through the various levels of bodily things, and the sky itself, whence sun and moon and stars shine upon the earth. And higher still we soared thinking inwardly and speaking and marvelling at your works; so we came to our own souls and went beyond them, so that we might touch that region of unending richness whence you feed Israel for ever with the food of truth ...' The focal image at this point in the work is *light* – the light in the soul, the inner vision. For Tippett supplements Augustine's text first with three other instances of inner illumination, as experienced by the blind Tobias, and by Isaac and Jacob, who both lost their sight in old age. In these three episodes of analogy, the chorus is barely articulate. The musical texture here owes much to the example of the slow movement of Tippett's Concerto for Orchestra, progressing effortfully from low textures to very high. The baritone line itself echoes the viola melody that blossomed in that slow movement:

The lower voices can only utter the inceptive *'O lux'* ('O light') in a stuttering rhythm; the female voices get stuck in the middle of their sentences – and from amongst them, a solo soprano has to carry the burden of the text apprehending the vision. At the climax – where the baritone sings *'et venimus in mentes nostras'* ('and so we came to our own souls') and the chorus joins in with *'intravi in intima mea, et vidi lucem incommutabilem'* ('I went into myself and saw the unchangeable light') – the violins take over the stuttering rhythm of the lower voices, and a trumpet obbligato, clarinet and cymbal rolls surround the voices with a celestial aura. The vision is shared. The chorus, as if outside it all, comments, *'O aeterna veritas et vera caritas et cara aeternitas!'* ('O eternal truth and true love and beloved eternity!') – all sung in octaves and unison.

Augustine's vision promotes an identification with God and specifically His powers of temporal transcendence. Thus, with a blaze of fanfares and choral exclamations the visions of Parts I and II are brought together. The dance-rhythms return, the chorus refers back to the bass solo (*'et praeterita'*) which they accompanied in Part I (cf. Fig 43 and Fig 135), and the 'alleulias' become resplendent, once more prompted by the same quotation from Psalm 42 as appeared in Part I. But Augustine's vision is ultimately a personal one – and Tippett symbolizes this at the close with a new ascending phrase for three horns, embellished by solo flute, clarinet and cello lines which convey something of Augustine's enraptured state in the moment of his vision.

The focal image in Part III is *silence*. We are presented with a large conditional clause: *if* only the world, *if* only heaven, *if* the soul itself, our own breathing, our own voices could fall silent, could be still, then would we too not experience the eternity that is the life of the saints? Life would cease to be the usual sequence of anticipation, followed by fleeting, momentary insights, then a loss of vision and subsequent dependence on mere recollection. Instead of this inadequate situation, the present would in its entirety become revelation, and life itself eternal. At the start of Part III, thus, the chorus constantly echoes the baritone with the word *'sileant'*.

As in Tippett's Second Piano Sonata, the various ingredients in Tippett's musical mosaic are now brought together into a final 'jam session', incorporating recollections of earlier episodes. The dance-rhythms of Part I – at *'et praeterita'* – and *'Deus, Creator Omnium'* – return; the climax of Part II (cf. Figures 43 and 124) is repeated. The alleluias this time culminate in Augustine's final cry, *'Intra in gaudium domini'* ('Enter into the joy of your Lord') – *'gaudium'* producing an exultant melisma accompanied by dancing figurations on the piano, xylophone and woodwind. The chorus caps this cry with a massive outburst, *'Attolite portas'* ('Lift up your heads, O ye gates'), from Psalm 24. The image is apposite. The 'everlasting doors' of the text evoke the window through which earlier

Augustine and his mother had perceived their vision.

But there is now a postscript. A hush descends. The chorus, first singing in Greek, then whispering in the vernacular appropriate to the place of performance, utter words from St Paul's Epistle to the Philippians: 'I count not myself to have apprehended.' Augustine himself has to a considerable extent previously quoted St Paul, especially the half-sentence, 'and forgetting the things that are before' (i.e. the things before time, before the creation of the world).[5] But Augustine omits 'I count not myself to have apprehended'. St Paul humbles himself before the mystic experience. So does Tippett. And so, at the composer's instigation, do we. Since we are not saints, we cannot count upon a future perception of eternity: probably it will be denied to us. Tippett's qualification of Augustine's expression of rapture represents a modern standpoint – a detachment bordering on scepticism. Hermann Broch, in his novel, *The Death of Virgil*, depicted his poet-protagonist in a similar stance. Virgil, on the brink of death, looks back wistfully on the stages of his development as man and poet: he brands the *Aeneid* a failure because it in no way approaches the truth as he now experiences it – a vision of God's eternal love. Aware that when we leave the concert hall, we cannot hold on for ever to the rapture we have known, and maybe we will lose track of it altogether, Tippett questions the very validity of what he has composed – a work that aspires to be the summation point of all musical endeavour – but is it so? The composer's own interpolated comment is a more extreme, more ruthless, version of what the chorus sings at the end of *The Midsummer Marriage*:

> Was it a vision?
> Was it a dream?

The Mask of Time

Tippett has never been a religious artist in the sense of subscribing to any liturgy or any established belief, biblical or otherwise, about how the world came into being. Thus he never had any inclination

to produce a setting of the Catholic Mass, a Requiem, an oratorio
on a biblical subject, or even a combination of religious and
humanistic or anti-religious texts such as we find in Mahler's
Eighth Symphony or Delius's *A Mass of Life*. Nevertheless, at
various stages in his compositional career, he was drawn to make
some comprehensive artistic statement, representative of the
totality of his experience to date. *A Child of Our Time*, the first and
(on the surface) least complicated, was written partly out of the
perceived need to make a political statement, but more profoundly,
out of a desire to step back from the turbulence of the modern
epoch and try to set it in a wider context. *The Vision of St
Augustine*, as we have just seen, is far more focused, an
engagement with those very epiphanies that imbue life with
distinctive, abiding significance. Those sudden moments of
illumination are no less essential to *The Mask of Time*. But now
they are a resource allowed to human individuals struggling to
survive in an often alien cosmic context. Our capacity for
transcendental experience is polarized against an ever-intensifying
destructive tendency and is always fragile and vulnerable.

This, incidentally, is an entirely different stance from that adopted
by, say, Stockhausen, in his seven-part operatic cycle in progress,
Licht (begun 1977), or by Messiaen, in one of his many cosmically
all-embracing compositions, such as *Des canyons aux étoiles*
(1971–4). Neither composer engages with the 'shadow' world in
the way that Tippett does. Both of them instead accommodated evil
within a pre-ordained hieratic structure: and had each of them not
articulated this structure through the medium of a rich, wide-
ranging, exploratory musical language, it might have seemed a
collection of empty stereotypes of the kind found in Disneyland.
Stockhausen and Messiaen are concerned with certainties, with
manifestations of coherence; Tippett addresses issues of
*un*certainty, of scepticism and of the unlikelihood of coherence.
The microcosm for *Licht* is Stockhausen's very own family; the
unity within Messiaen's artistic conceptions is founded upon his
rock-solid Catholicism. Tippett's starting-point is the exact opposite

– a world of fragmentation and multiple polarities: a sense of wholeness is his goal, but its attainment can never be taken for granted.

The grand sweep of *The Mask of Time* makes it initially difficult to assimilate as a whole : to experience it in the concert hall, as opposed to listening to a radio broadcast or a recording, is essential, for it is a curious hybrid, almost a theatre piece, demanding the physical presence of the audience. Its ten movements, lasting a total of about 95 minutes, depict and comment upon a selection of scenes and episodes that stretch from a supposed point at which the world was created and extend right up to Hiroshima and beyond. The first five movements, comprising Part I, proceed chronologically – though with many a leap in time – from the beginnings of the cosmos, through the appearance of animals and humans to the establishment of settled societies, ultimately attaining an imagined paradise, in which man, woman, the animals and the deities are in perfect harmony – except that they are destined to split apart and occupy separate domains, often hostile towards each other.

The second set of five movements, comprising Part II, unfolds in a discontinuous sequence. Its starting-point is Shelley's poetic vision of a tragic 'Triumph of Life', paired with an account of his own actual death by drowning off the coast of Lerici in Italy. Next, in the seventh movement, the rise of man's technological mastery of nature and its elements offers another triumphal sequence, albeit an ambivalent one: for it is finally twisted to expose the perversion of scientific achievements in the development of the atom bomb. Out of its stark violence, there emerges (in the eighth movement, 'Hiroshima mon amour') a climactic threnody (to a text drawn from Akhmatova's 'Requiem' and 'Poem without a Hero') for the innocent victims of brutality and persecution.

The Mask of Time ends neither with nihilism nor with a fabricated optimistic peroration. Instead it focuses on mankind's instinct to survive. The first of the three songs of the Ninth

Movement thus depicts the mythological Orpheus, as understood in Renaissance times and later invoked in Rilke's 'Sonnets to Orpheus'. Returning from hell, having suffered the 'dark side' of the world, Orpheus is well qualified for affirmative song: and even when the Furies tear him apart, his head carries on singing after his death. In a second song, 'The Beleaguered Friends', a group of anti-Nazis in Japanese-occupied Peking in 1944 await the end of the war. Consulting the I-Ching – the oldest book in the world, a book of divination and prophecy – they are given intimations of deliverance. Lastly, a young actor (out of a novel by Mary Renault)[6] visits the temple of Zeus in Olympia, peers at the great statue of the god: as his eye travels up to meet its 'face of power', it proclaims:

> O man, make peace with your mortality
> For this too is God.

The final movement develops gradually out of this into an outpouring of wordless singing, taking its cue (and title) from the final line of Siegfried Sassoon's poem, 'Everybody Sang' – an affirmative signal from the battlefields of Flanders:

> The singing will never be done

– and this final vision of transcendence, of universal harmony, is interrupted as if suddenly a door had shut on the work and its performance.

The variety and scope of Tippett's text – partly written by himself, partly compiled from a great range of sources – would probably make only a confused impression, if Tippett had not evolved a sure method of counterpointing the various ingredients, allowing their inter-relationships to become evident. His method here is essentially cinematic, a further development of the procedures he had cultivated from *The Knot Garden* onwards. The format of *The Mask of Time* is thus entirely different from the standard oratorio. Throughout the work, Tippett's camera zooms back and forth between the mass and the individual: structurally, the 'editing' of the score involves a lot of jump-cutting and cross-cutting in time and place, montage, flashbacks and sudden transformations.

Indeed, while Tippett decided not to make it an actual masque for the theatre, there is every reason to suppose that a filmic treatment of it would be apposite. The outcome could be an enhancement of its contents and integral to its manner of presentation. Germane to all this is Tippett's very description of it as a work 'for voices and instruments' : for although large vocal and orchestral forces are involved, they tend to be deployed as a collection of ensembles and soloists, making up a mosaic scheme overall. (At the back of his mind was the comparable mixture of voices and instruments in Monteverdi's 1610 *Vespers*.) A polarity between the solo singers, representing the individual and the chorus, representing the cosmic backcloth, is evident right at the outset and fundamental throughout.

The fulcrum of the opening movement, entitled 'Presence', is the word 'Sound', whose central vowel is dwelt upon and extended by the chorus against a swirling decorative orchestral background (again, a link with Monteverdi's *Vespers*, specifically its opening movement) (*see* Example 48).

This opening gesture registers a significant symbolic 'presence' near the end of the third movement, 'Jungle', and again in the ninth movement, at the climax of the cry of Orpheus – 'Dare, Divining, *Sound*'. The final movement offers a metamorphosis in which the decorations and sequences of fourths surrounding the original chord on '*Sound*' are lifted into the foreground. As the chorus sing at the start:

> Sound
> where no airs blow

this is the key to the composer's understanding (and probably, for that matter, any composer's understanding) of the universe – for the change from silence (in which there are no air-currents) to sound is in effect a metaphor for creation.

The second movement, 'Creation of the World by Music', following without a break from the choral climax of the first, reinforces this metaphor. Tippett makes reference to ancient traditions in which music is understood as a means to achieve outward or inward order – literally, physically (cf. Orpheus taming the wild beasts with his music; Shiva – the benevolent Hindu god, representing both the destructive principle in life and the power to reproduce and renew – dancing the world into existence) – and order apprehended either through faculties of imagination or intellect.

Phenomena in the material world, which seem to exemplify that order through processes such as reversal or recurrence – an example would be Halley's Comet – might be matched by spiritual ones : indeed, the theme of 'eternal reversal' introduced in the first movement and exemplified in 'The great wild satellite that reverses its course' is as important as any other in this work, a mechanism operative within those situations that suddenly turn bad (cf. the fifth and seventh movements, below) or those that blossom hopefully and positively. For the time being, here, there is a sense of accomplishment and progress as the second

Tippett: The Mask of Time, opening movt.

Example 48

Example 48 (continued)

movement is rounded off with a half-ironic reference to Haydn's *Creation*: 'achieved is the glorious work'.

Throughout, the tenor has pride of place amongst the soloists as the representative of the human individual set against a limitless, ever-present cosmos. In the first movement the tenor – singing from the here and now of the very concert platform – intervenes immediately after the initial entry of the chorus summoning the cosmos into existence. He cries out his personal comment on it all: 'All metaphor,' he sings. *The Mask of Time* is indeed all metaphor. For that very reason, the final song of the ninth movement is allotted to someone concerned with metaphors – the young actor. Tippett is ostensibly echoing Shakespeare's famous lines:

> All the world's a stage
> ... and one man in his time plays many parts.

The tenor at the start sings a line (which Tippett extends) from Yeats's poem 'High Talk': this depicts a whiffler stalking about on stilts in front of a circus parade – a situation analogous to that of the human being trying to remain unswamped amidst the mêlée of experience.

> All metaphor, Malachi, stilts and all
> Malachi, Malachi, all metaphor.

Yeats's assertion: 'I, through the terrible novelty of light stalk on, stalk on ...' stands both for the artist and for the individual human being: both continue to 'stalk on' throughout the work – cf. Orpheus in the ninth movement. The tenor constantly represents the artist and individual. His assertions reach a climax of romantic confrontation when he assumes the role of the poet Shelley in the sixth movement.

In the third movement, 'Jungle', the chorus becomes both predator and prey, supplying a backcloth of animal noises and cries against which the soloists can portray the bizarre and endlessly repeated processes of species generation and destruction in the natural world. Pictorialism akin to that of

Monteverdi, Bach or Haydn is prominent here: and this dimension is encountered in subsequent movements. The fourth movement, 'The Ice Cap moves South-North', depicts tribal wandering, hunting, feasting and ritual. In it, there is a brief interlude of 'descending' music for woodwind and organ, as the scene changes to cave-life ('Clamber downwards to the dark'): this interlude returns in an inverted form, signalling another scene change to the typical place of religious sacrifice, e.g. an ancient pyramid of the kind found in Mexico – hence, 'We clamber up the staircase stone by stone'. In the sixth movement, the mindless triumphal chariot lurches forward over a ground-bass: and in the storm that ultimately overwhelms Shelley, the main brass motif from Symphony No. 4 acquires an explicitly threatening character, as in successive waves it advances the episode to a climax.

As in the final part of Haydn's *Creation*, the soloists in Tippett's fifth movement, 'Dream of the Paradise Garden', become named individuals, though still generalized here as Man, Woman, Ancestor and Dragon. The orchestra too is reduced to groups of soloists. The stuttering rhythm of the two solo violas at the start emulates Monteverdi's *'Ecco mormorar l'onde'* – itself an aptly blissful nature evocation, and an apt reference-point for Tippett's own madrigalian setting of lines from Milton's *Paradise Lost* for six-part chamber choir.

This is the limit of Tippett's depiction of Paradise, for it is soon to disappear. There is no rapturous pre-lapsarian love-duet for the Man and Woman. The initial exchanges between the four characters are very well-mannered, arch, slightly tongue-in-cheek: and their happy concord is summed up in a radiant dance-interlude in sarabande rhythm, for three flutes, harp, three double-basses and percussion. Throughout *The Mask of Time*, Tippett makes play with the idea of *reversal*, an exemplar of the transformation principle at work in nature, especially in his reference to the I-Ching and its predictions based on the sorting of yarrow stalks. Just such a reference is embodied in the choral recitation that now signals the sudden fracturing of that paradisal integrity enjoyed previously by its inhabitants. The four characters break apart from each other: the glorious Dragon is demoted to an ignominious snake; the avuncular Ancestor becomes an 'impotent, celestial ' being, mocked in a hymn-tune parody with organ accompaniment; the Man and Woman are left poignantly alone, as the semi-chorus return, their evocation of paradise now a wistfully remembered dream, fading out at the close with the horn calls echoing nostalgically into the distance.

The traditional paradise imagined here is indeed as much an illusion as the psychedelic one in *The Ice Break*. Transcendence is not something that can be won easily, let alone taken for granted: and the second part of *The Mask of Time* asserts the exact opposite – that individuals are more than likely to be sacrificed in the ruthless, inexorable onward movement of the universe. On the other hand, there are redemptive factors all the way through, manifest in the occasional ecstatic outbursts of affirmative song.

In the 'Jungle' movement, the soloists are unable to find an explanation for the everlasting struggles of prey and predator – of the water-bug that literally sucks away the life from a frog, or of the lacewing that lays eggs, eats them up and lays them again – least of all an explanation from the Lord God on high. For the time being, a sudden illumination, echoing that experienced by Annie Dillard in *Pilgrim at Tinker Creek* (on which much of the text here is based),[7] has to suffice: and it is conjured musically in a purple passage for the soprano and mezzo-soprano, pouring out Monteverd-ian roulades. (Tippett was to use the same music at the climax of the love-duet for Pelegrin and Jo-Ann in Act III of *New Year*).

The sixth movement, opening Part II of *The Mask of Time*, casts the tenor as poet-protagonist and romantic idealist. He has spent the night on a hill meditating on the world: this matches his pose at the start of the work, in which he represented Yeats brooding on the world, high up in his tower – hence the recurrence of the motif for flutes, trombones and percussion that

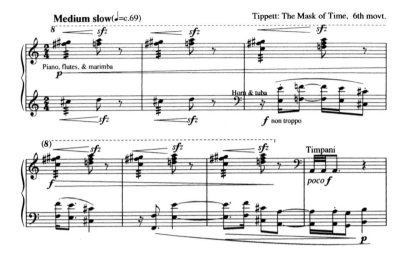

Example 49

initially introduced the tenor's quotation from Yeats's *High Talk*. (*see* Example 49).

The generalized mêlée of experience in an unstoppably evolving world, evoked at the start of the first movement, become now something more specific: the image, in Shelley's late poem, *The Triumph of Life*, of the triumphal Chariot of Life, rolling ruthlessly onwards, throwing off bodies in all directions. As the chariot disappears into the distance, the poet's question – 'Then what is life?' – is left unanswered. The scene changes now to midday and Shelley himself goes off to sea in a boat, tries in vain to defy the storm which blows up and perishes. Once more there is a scene-change: it is night, the poet's body has been recovered and (for legal reasons) is being burnt. But the heart (according to legend) refused to burn: hence Tippett's lyrical conflagration for the soloists here. Clinching the links between this movement and the opening one is the recurrence at this point of the musical image of a 'resounding' universe.

The short choral episodes of the eighth movement, 'Mirror of

Whitening Light', are introduced by three extended instrumental preludes on the Latin hymn *'Veni, creator spiritus'*. Assertive strings, piano and drums set the scene for Pythagoras' discovery of the laws of number and the 'graphics of measurement'; the woodwind then invoke a mysterious, magical context for the alchemists' attempts at the mutation of elements; and brass and percussion unleash a tumbling profusion of rhythmically competing fanfares, exultantly proclaiming the modern scientific advances that culminated in the splitting of the atom. These preludes, each one stylistically differentiated and brilliantly crafted, are the dominant element in the movement.

The jubilation suddenly switches round, becomes a violent fulguration. Shiva, who (in the second movement) danced the world into being, now dances its destruction, with violent rhythmic outbursts on brake-drums set against an explosive percussive background: this is Hiroshima. The tumult subsides: there follows the threnody, 'Hiroshima mon amour'. The voice of the soprano is heard keening against a hymn-like accompaniment hummed by the male singers in the chorus. The orchestra is silent throughout this: and when it re-enters, it is only to provide reminders of the violence of war – quoting the trumpet fanfares from Act II of *King Priam*, but answering them now with repeated chordal sequences for the strings (distant echoes of those inspired by Beethoven's Fourth Piano Concerto in the last song of *The Heart's Assurance*).

Tippett's filmic methods are at their subtlest (and riskiest) in the Three Songs that follow. The opening scene-setting trio (soprano, mezzo-soprano and tenor) refers back to the first movement – Orpheus 'turning, returning' from hell (echoed by the chorus) and 'stalking on' into the daylight. The solo baritone appears initially as the Renaissance Orpheus, quoting Dowland's 'I saw my lady weep'; but then merges this with a great declamation from Rilke –

> Who alone already lifted
> the lyre among the dead

> dare, divining, sound
> the infinite praise

– the chorus emphasizing 'sound' by recalling their very opening chord sung on that word. At this point, we reach the absolute kernel of Tippett's message in *The Mask of Time*: that affirmation is most authentic when it comes from those who have suffered[8] – a new metamorphosis of 'I would know my shadow and my light'.

The next song, 'The Beleaguered Friends', for mezzo-soprano and chorus, is more transitional: some of its thematic ideas – such as the repeated gong-notes intended to signal a change of scene to China – are jejune. The setting (some of it spoken) of a text drawn from the I-Ching and the musical components are loosely, sketchily put together. Out of this grows a more assured and convincing evocation of spring, over an undulating, repeating bass-line, and the free-wheeling tenor solo surges inexorably towards the choral entry (set against a background of fanfares for trumpets and trombones), which proclaims Zeus' admonition towards acceptance of both the limitations and the glorious potential of human mortality.

Leading without a break into the tenth movement, a rich texture of overlapping vocal lines over a repeated ground-bass now begins to accumulate. In this final wordless movement, the chorus (representing the cosmos) and the soloists (individual human beings) are finally reconciled, uniting in a transcendental vision which, though it is interrupted and left suspended in mid-flight, cannot fail to be retained by listeners in their minds as they leave the concert hall. If the full impact of that tidal wave of musical invention which Tippett unleashes in *The Mask of Time* only registers fully in live performance, this is above all true of the silence at the end.

9
Portrait of the Artist

The Quest

During the greater part of his career, Tippett implicitly accepted
the Frazer-derived notion of a primal, worldwide religion of
mankind, characterized by certain archetypal events and
expressed in tribal societies through vegetation magic (e.g. the
personification of the change from winter to spring). His
acceptance of Frazer was reinforced by his reading of Francis
Cornford's theories[1] – also Frazer-derived – about the origins of
tragedy and comedy in ancient Greece. Hence the format for *The
Midsummer Marriage*, at whose dramaturgical core is the
traditional *agon*, or combat between the seasons, along with the
death of the year-king or year-god and the perpetuation of
fertility. Out of all this came the continuing general emphasis in
Tippett's work upon human reconciliation and renewal – even
when it is clear that conflict will be resumed at some future date,
to be resolved all over again. 'The moving waters renew the
earth,' sing the soloists and chorus in the final General Ensemble
of *A Child of Our Time*. Decades later, in the penultimate scene
of *The Ice Break*, the chorus, when Yuri's operation proves
successful, again signal a fresh beginning, quoting the evocation
of spring from the masque scene of *The Tempest*.

By this time in Tippett's life – his early seventies – the
prospects for hope and forgiveness in the world at large still
seemed precarious. The Cold War continued, the nuclear threat
remained, as did widespread oppression of races or minorities.
The ironic sensibility which he felt had become widespread and
endemic after the First World War[2] made the dream of the
Peaceable Kingdom much harder to envisage, let alone sustain:
hence the self-debunking stance of Astron in *The Ice Break*.
Astron's Jungian advice concurs with that of Zeus in the ninth

movement of *The Mask of Time*: the answers lie within ourselves and our own world, not in solutions from the gods above.

Reinforcing this, in his Third Symphony, Tippett asserts that he and other mortals are more capable of compassion than any god:

> We fractured men
> Surmise a deeper mercy;
> That no god has shown.

The conclusion of this work lays bare the conflict between Tippett's desperate desire for a compassionate world and his ironic awareness of the brutality of the age. Although he can say with Luther King, 'I have a dream', he knows that the promise will be broken over and over again. Thus, in the music for this declaration of faith in humanity, we find no sense of 'the spontaneous and discontinuous', no attempt to leave behind the actualities of time and place. The polarities that rent the music asunder at the start are still there at the finish.

These psychological divisions are multiplied in Tippett's depiction of the artistic and spiritual development of Dov, the musician in *The Knot Garden*, acknowledged by the composer in the early 1970s as the closest he had come to supplying a self-portrait. Dov sings not only for himself, but for all his generation. As a musician he is torn between the desire to unburden his own personal situation and to make utterances of wider relevance. In the opera, this psychological duality is reinforced by Dov's sexual ambivalence: but at the end, he summons up the courage to set aside these personal problems and go off in search of his true vocation as an artist. His spiritual journeys unfold in *Songs for Dov*, which adds two further songs to the one Dov sang in Act II of the opera.

Dov travels round the world as both loner and musician. In Tippett's words, he searches 'for that southern land where we hope never to grow old, but which, proving an illusion, drives us ever on towards another beckoning country; ... [he] sings of the *Wanderjahre*, those years of illusion and disillusion, innocence and experience which we all pass through to reach what maturity we may; and then journeying "full circle west", [he comes] back to the "big town" and the "home without a garden" across the tundra of Siberia. Dov, as the grown man, the fully-fledged mature creative artist, struggles with the intractable problems of "poets in a barren age"...'[3] The nub of the issue now is the tension between the pastoral and the urban, between the eternal values of nature and the ephemera of the town. This tension runs quite deep within Tippett's own thinking. His concept of an alien, disintegrative 'town culture' has links with the poetic depiction of the modern urban wilderness, begun in Eliot's 'Love Song of J. Alfred Prufrock', canonized by *The Waste Land* and echoed in many other writers. There is no myth of return or renewal that can compete with its desolation and fragmentation. Greater self-knowledge, sudden unexpected epiphanies are the only credible gateways to relief.

At this point in his song-cycle Tippett, through Dov, joins Pasternak (whose mouthpiece was Zhivago) in suggesting that the lyric poets of the present day could try and sustain the pastoral metaphor against the changing fashions of the town. Whereas 'the living language of our time is urban', there are however, no poems which exemplify it: Pasternak can only react with rhetorical questions:

> Then why does the horizon weep in mist
> And the dung smell bitter?
> Surely it is my calling
> To see that the distances should not lose heart
> And that beyond the limits of the town
> The earth should not feel lonely?

Dov's comment on this is simply a piece of dismissive colloquial irony, 'Sure, baby.'

Communicating the essence of this through music, Tippett allows the stylistic order and cohesiveness maintained in Dov's first song, with its pulsating electric guitar rhythms and bluesy melodic inflexions, to be destroyed in the second and third songs of the cycle. Cinematic jump-cutting and collage are used to encapsulate the choices faced by Dov (in the successive strophes of the No. 2) – retreat into past traditions and cultures, escape into self-indulgence and commercialism, outmoded ritual – from all of which he turns away. The second song, already touched upon in Chapter 5, leads straight into the third by way of the 'dissolve music' that Tippett used for scene-changes throughout *The Knot Garden*. What follows it is the same music as came after it in the opera – a romantic motif for three horns and shimmering high strings. There it signalled the appearance of Thea; here it gives rise to a plangent oboe solo, whose intimacy signals a possible change of emphasis in Dov's quest.

The third song, while through-composed, remains stylistically fragmented, as Dov faces a crucial set of creative choices: to be a rhetorical commentator on the problems of mankind – or to be the lyricist singing from the heart. This division has affected many artists. Returning across the Siberian tundra, Dov looks in on Zhivago and Lara in 'the forest hut where they had shacked up together'. They are not there; they have left only a fragment of a love poem, for the two lovers have

> gone away
> Back to the town ...
> Each, alone, into the swarming city.

For the Siberian journey, Tippett develops mainly the two Thea motifs introduced at the opening of the song, but at the point where Zhivago is 'scribbling in his attic', he incorporates a brief quotation (on the viola) from the scene for the scribe Pimen in Mussorgsky's opera, *Boris Godunov*. The tenderness between Zhivago and Lara is also encapsulated in another quotation, this time from Act II of *The Knot Garden*, when Dov cradles Flora in her distress. In fact, the whole song proceeds by stylistic leaps and bounds. 'The living language of our time' sparks off two episodes of Tippett-ian boogie-woogie. In the final section setting Pasternak's lines, stark wind chords and a wailing trumpet melody are answered antiphonally by declamatory string phrases in octaves. There is no resolution, harmonic or otherwise: the final ironic comment – 'Sure, baby' – is left exposed and unaccompanied save for a tap on the claves separating the two words.

Critics of Tippett's cinematic methods in this score and others of the same period have been most concerned about his ability to integrate diverse materials. What they missed was the relevance of such techniques to his theme – the stratification of experience into discreet, unreconcilable entities. Nevertheless, for reasons of both content and style, Tippett was impelled to go beyond *Songs for Dov*: for as a paradigm of Tippett's own artistic development it was inadequate and inconclusive.

Visions of Paradise

Faced with the hell of the modern city – actual as much as metaphorical; faced with related artistic chaos and stylistic disintegration – other creative figures this century have looked towards alternative, utopian solutions. Ezra Pound, in his *Cantos*, took refuge in paradisal landscapes of light and clean white cities and buildings, viewing them as psalmodic objects. A parallel to this might be Le Corbusier's clean, glassy visions of architectural order and *virtù*. Likewise, Boulez envisaged a new musical order emanating from the investigations that were undertaken at his specially built musical research centre, IRCAM. All shared in a cool detachment from the physicality of things: which is not far short of saying a detachment from – even an indifference towards – the human condition.

Devoted to the theatre as a powerhouse for both change and social integration, Tippett continued his search for solutions that come from within – solutions imagined, conjured into existence, believed in and defended by flesh-and-blood human beings. After *The Ice Break*, he began to widen his concept of the artist's role and function. Lyricism – and all that it could suggest, metaphorically – once more began to occupy the forefront of his music: but not simply as a mellowing of the strident, abrasive language so prominent in his works of the 1960s and 70s; nor as a nostalgic return to old compositional habits; least of all as a turning away from the issues of the present: none of that belonged in Tippett's temperament. Rather, it became the key ingredient in a a new integrative, pyschologically healing role.

Both in the slow movement of the Triple Concerto and in the fifth movement of *The Mask of Time*, lyricism is deployed to conjure a paradisal rapture: though in each case, the dream is subject to threats and is ultimately broken. In *New Year*, Jo-Ann's conquest of her fears and her discovery of the strength to go out into the Terror Town are celebrated in her dance in the Paradise Garden. Tippett implies that for everyone, such intimations of paradisal states are necessary in order that we may survive the rigours and difficulties of modern life. Thus, late on, his concept of the artist laid more emphasis on its most primal role – that of shaman, or medicine man.

New Year is, in fact, remarkable as a conflation of two kinds of theatre: a classic ritual of renewal and regeneration; and the ancient shamanistic activities that make such renewal possible, facilitating the change of the solstice and all that it might imply. The message of *A Child of Our Time* – 'I would know my shadow and my light' – a message of self-awareness and reconciliation, is still relevant. But now Tippett stresses *artistic* efforts to rise about the shadow world. They are essentially moments of illumination. In *The Knot Garden*, they are only possible, 'If for a timid moment/ We submit to love.' More sustained is the final visionary movement of *The Mask of Time*, 'The singing will never be done', signalling a rebirth from cataclysm. In *New Year*, after Jo-Ann and Pelegrin have shared their transcendental love and she has danced in the Paradise Garden, he and the other inhabitants from Nowhere Tomorrow vanish, but she goes out into the Terror Town strengthened and sustained by what she has experienced.

After completing this opera, Tippett spent his remaining creative years, from one point of view, fashioning artefacts that exemplified the artist's participation in a self-perpetuating process of metaphor-creation; at the same time he assumed the role of compositional shaman, striving to hold more permanently a vision of paradisal unity – becoming in effect a religious artist in the etymological sense of the term, binding things together.

Tippett deliberately described *Byzantium*, as 'an artefact: an artistic object in which all the emotion of the artist had disappeared inside'. Much the same applies to his Fifth String Quartet and to *The Rose Lake*. A climactic passage in Joyce's *Portrait of the Artist as a Young Man* encapsulates the creative position Tippett had now reached: 'The personality of the artist ... refines itself out of existence, impersonalizes itself, so to speak ... The artist, like the God of creation, remains within or behind or beyond or above his handiwork, invisible, refined out of existence, indifferent, paring his fingernails.'[4]

Setting to music Yeats's 'Byzantium', Tippett still asserts his presence as an artist, conspiring with the poet in the image-making process:

> Those images that yet
> Fresh images beget
> That dolphin-torn, that gong-tormented sea.

But in the two works with which Tippett completed his *oeuvre*, his own personality no longer obtrudes. He is simply the shamanistic messenger and healer, communicating something greater than the occasional transient vision. He aspires now to an untrammelled lyric utterance that embodies a full and absolute identification between man and nature: the 'songs' (literal and metaphorical) of the nightingale, the lake, the sky, in these pieces amount to Tippett's most all-encompassing musical metaphor.

Music of the Mind and Body

Tippett has lived long enough to have his achievements lauded worldwide and himself (often to his embarrassment and distaste) put on a pedestal. For many people – in and out of the world of professional music – he has become a 'living legend'. But he has also witnessed the beginnings of a backlash. Thus, his ninetieth birthday brought forth not only the usual panoply of tributes from colleagues and admirers, but a sneering, patronizing dismissal in the *Daily Telegraph*[5] and a more serious, though somewhat muddled attempt at critical dismemberment in *Musical Times*.[6] The final bar of the world première of *The Rose Lake*, was followed by a yell of protest from a so-called 'heckler' – one of a group of self-appointed arbiters of musical taste whose own compositional efforts entail replacing modernism and atonality with nice tunes. The only consequence, however, here, was a doubly vociferous ovation for the veteran tunesmith.

Certain leitmotifs recur in critical commentaries on Tippett and his work. Ignoring the composer's soundly formulated reasons for producing his own texts and opera libretti – reasons based on advice from no less a writer than Eliot – a confederacy of dunces repeatedly level the charge that his libretti are confused, clumsy, full of clichés and tasteless colloquialisms. (No mention, of course, of the fact that the words are to be *sung*, not read: in fact, the 'singability' of certain words and how well they come across within different voice-ranges has always been one of Tippett's prime concerns.) The favourite term of abuse for *The Knot Garden* is 'psycho-babble'. A regular knee-jerk reaction to Tippett's stylistic pluralism, from the mid-1970s onwards, denigrates his 'trendiness', his violation of technical proprieties being compounded by the wearing of snazzy T-shirts and multi-coloured sneakers. Even amongst academic critics, one can discern two main categories of response: those who find Tippett's early music approachable, even admirable, but who feel that, particularly from *The Knot Garden* onwards, he went off the rails; and those who feel that up to *King Priam* he was essentially an English traditionalist, unexpectedly thereafter joining the company of continental modernists. In fact, there are strong threads running through his work from start to finish – a few have been examined in the course of this book – and any attempt to ring-fence particular groups of pieces is futile. Tippett's music is an artistic entity that defies partial assessment.

A lot, of course, has depended on how well his music was performed. Paul Crossley once opined that an alternative history of twentieth-century music might focus on the many inadequate, sometimes downright disastrous first performances of major compositions – and their consequences. For without doubt, composers from Mahler, Stravinsky, Schoenberg and Elgar onwards have had to endure assessments of their work based on poor execution or completely misconceived interpretations.

In Tippett's case, the technical demands he made on performers – right from his first published work, String Quartet No. 1 – inevitably slowed the pace at which he was appreciated and accepted. In fact, a sequence of pieces selected from any phase in Tippett's career constantly brings new stylistic and technical traits into prominence, implying new modes of execution. These traits arise not just from a wilful desire for novelty, but are a product of Tippett's absorption with the actual physicality of musical performance – the contrasts between various kinds of voices and the inherent properties of instruments. Furthermore, the ideas behind each piece are usually so urgent, so provocative, even, that to elide the technical risks results only in a kind of sanitization at variance with the composer's intentions. Fortunately, within the UK, America and Australia, Tippett has had the luck not merely to find performers ready to grapple with the new demands made upon them, but prepared also to pass their expertise and acquired wisdom on to the next generation: the latter are not then obliged to start in an interpretative vacuum. Small wonder the composer is so delighted now by the realizations of his music by young, upcoming performers.

Meanwhile, Tippett has remained an easy target for those who judge his operas according to the character and accomplishment of the stage productions they have attended – whether the staging was done with expertise and insight, or alternatively, was misguided, perverse, inconsistent, over-literal, over-symbolic, intermittently inspired, occasionally adroit, or a mixture of any of these and other attributes.

The bedrock of Tippett's entire career has been a tradition-based concept of the role of the composer in society, something he has held to unswervingly. In postwar Britain and Europe, state funding for the arts blossomed and commissions for works became a regular ingredient in artists' lives and expectations; more recently, an entire realm of commercial exploitation has opened up, through recording and the mass media. Composers now have much higher material expectations than before.

Coming to maturity before all this, without commissions or other forms of sponsorship, without opportunities for disseminating his music widely, and without a substantial private income, Tippett went on writing simply because he had to. From today's standpoint, this might seem absurdly idealistic, even anachronistic. But it was in his bones. During his late sixties, he put it thus:

> I know that my true function within a society which embraces all of us is to continue an age-old tradition, fundamental to civilization, which goes back into pre-history and will go forward into the unknown future. This tradition is to create images from the depths of the imagination and to give them form whether visual, intellectual or musical. For it is only through images that the inner world communicates at all. Images of the past, shapes of the future. Images of vigour for a decadent period, images of calm for one too violent. Images of reconciliation for worlds torn by division. And in an age of mediocrity and shattered dreams, images of abounding, generous, exuberant beauty.'[7]

This creative integrity informs all Tippett's efforts as an artist. Moreover, Tippett was always clear that he would only be properly appreciated when he had completed a large enough corpus of work which could then be assessed as a whole. His *oeuvre*, now complete and embracing all the important genres, exhibits an amazingly wide spectrum of compositional tendencies – from the most conservative to the most innovative and subversive. From his First Piano Sonata to *The Mask of Time* and *New Year*, one is aware too of a euphoric recklessness of the imagination, a sense of delight and liberation that often run counter to the so-called spirit of the times.

At one end of this spectrum, Tippett always cherished the tradition of folk-song and dance in his native country, but refused to be bound by it. His own early musical invention was nourished by vernacular music of all kinds and it remained a vital element in his make-up. But at no stage did he take refuge in bland pastoralism or narrow nationalism. 'Boyhood's End', for instance, was at the opposite pole to the many pre-war settings of, say, A. E. Housman. Hudson's recollections of his pristine experiences of nature in early life, so vividly brought to life in Tippett's cantata, belong in the Southern Hemisphere: 'to lie in the long hot grass in *January*' is something quite remote from English experience! At the same time, Tippett's dramatic treatment of Hudson's text adopted a fresh, Purcellian approach to English word-setting.

The Concerto for Double String Orchestra, too, has occasionally been held up as an example of what Constant Lambert memorably dubbed the 'cowpat' school of English music. Not only, however, is a Beethoven quartet movement the main structural reference-point in the piece, but the vernacular element in this Concerto is undoubtedly at variance with such labelling. It entails complex rhythmic structures and bluesy harmony that suggest a wider orientation: intriguingly, Aaron Copland, when he accidently heard a broadcast of the work, thought it must be by an American composer. Again, far from following the dictates of nationalism and making folk-music the basis of his style, Tippett dispensed with the vernacular altogether when it was irrelevant to his purpose (e.g. in *King Priam* or *The Vision of St Augustine*).

If Tippett relates to any English tradition it is to the pluralism of Shakespeare and to the strained imagery of the seventeenth-century Metaphysical poets. With the latter there is a comparable sense of worlds and temperaments in sharp collision. Poets like John Donne, Andrew Marvell or Abraham Cowley brought together the definitions and distinctions of medieval scholasticism, the new ideas in emergent science and in systematic materialist thinking, together with a fresh curiosity about the psychology of love and religion – fusing them all into fantastic verbal conceits. Likewise, Tippett, throughout his career, and especially in his compositions from the mid-1960s onwards, opened up his work to ideas and experiences from all the arts and sciences, from the I-Ching to biogenetics. The techniques of cross-cutting, flashback, collage and montage, which he used increasingly facilitated an interaction of metaphors far removed from each other. Tippett observed it in Eliot's poetry: he observed its extension within American culture. If, therefore, he himself were to opt for a specific identity, it would be Anglo-American rather than English.

At the same time, Tippett shared with Elgar, Holst, and Britten a closeness to European culture that gave their music a broad and substantial basis. While Elgar and Britten owed more to Germanic models, Tippett (like Holst) tended to cast his net wider: in particular, from his early days, he was drawn to the music of Debussy and much of his idiosyncratic empiricism has its roots in a Francophile sensitivity to sounds as individually perceived 'moments' – chords, sonorities, textures, 'discovered' at the piano.

The counterbalance to this was Tippett's allegiance to Beethovenian formal methods. This constituted neither a sterile academicism, nor a neo-classic, puritanical reaction against the anarchic, subjective freedom of late romanticism. For him it was a vehicle for serious, trenchant discourse, a means to assert the intellectual side of his nature. Craftsmanship remained of fundamental importance to his music, long after he found alternatives to the Beethovenian sonata-allegro, and no matter what direction his music took, or how diverse its ingredients. The pacing and proportions of *The Ice Break* are no less carefully calculated than those of his early string quartets or *A Child of Our Time*. All the traditional virtues are indeed so completely subsumed within his mature handling of a variety of musical genres that they tend to be taken for granted. Even Tippett's use of diatonic tonality acquired in the mid-1940s acquired a distinctive slant. His fondness for building tonal schemes around chords in fourths enabled him to add a dimension of ambiguity, a blurring of key definitions (e.g. in Symphony No. 1 and *The Midsummer Marriage*) that became one of his main fingerprints. Early critics attributed some of this to the influence of Hindemith, but it was more a product of his Francophile leanings, isolating sonorities in a *pointilliste* manner, eliding key-differentiation for allusive effect.

There are flaws in a number of Tippett's works – and quite a few have been pointed out in the course of this study. Haste was always an enemy. Impatience to move on to the next compositional challenge could leave the existing one, in some respects, only partially realized. Self-confidence sometimes led to quirkiness – though more in his texts than in his music. The imaginative strains within a piece could give rise to unnecessary stress for the performers: the string writing in Symphony No. 3 is a case in point. The bulk of the time, though, Tippett's skills have been well-directed: and there was never the slightest chance that he would contribute to the repertoire of so-called 'experimental music', or 'work-in-progress', to be continually revised or re-composed altogether.

Tippett's personal self-discovery through Jungian analysis reinforced also his creative tendency to search for meanings below the surface, to uncover collectively applicable messages: hence the theatrical synthesis he was to attain in *A Child of Our Time* and *The Midsummer Marriage*: hence also his desire to relate to the archetypes underlying classic musical forms, rather than just their surface procedures. The expansions of his musical language – rhythmic and melodic early on, harmonic and textural later – are always thus a means to an end; and for the most part, his objectives are extremely well calculated.

The vigour of Tippett's intellect, as encountered in his writings and broadcasts, tends to stimulate by scattering ideas in all directions. In his compositions, on the other hand, despite a comparable profusion of notes, Tippett holds more resolutely to a specific purpose: this is no less true of an all-ecompassing work like *The Mask of Time* than it is with Symphony No. 2 or *The Vision of St Augustine*. And the intellect matters in Tippett's work. Early on, he distanced himself from coteries and cults, shrewdly determining his own artistic goals. In his maturity, it is possible to discern a kind of dialectic between the compositions themselves and what they might have become – a consequence of the self-critical, self-questioning appraisal of genres, content and styles that was essential to his pre-compositional thinking. The sub-text to all his music is a debate about how and why creative choices are made.

Tippett's music also uninhibitedly celebrates the human body. Dance is as important to him as song, its physicality the threshold of that eroticism which courses deeply through his music – overwhelmingly so in *The Midsummer Marriage* and the *Corelli Fantasia*, returning again with almost equal intensity in *New Year*. (Nothing like this exists in Vaughan Williams or Britten; and Walton's attempt in *Troilus and Cressida* to create a *Tristan* for the 1950s proved a damp squib.) Born into a society that veiled all physical intimacies in increasingly seductive euphemisms, that still imagined moderate masturbation produced blindness and mental illness, and which set certain forms of sexual behaviour off limits, Tippett aligned himself with contemporary playwrights and novelists – from Wedekind to Pinter, Proust to Kundera – in an unfettered, unstereotyped exploration of human sexuality: its extremes of tension and ecstasy, violence and tenderness became a major concern within his work.

Tippett's eroticism has little to do with the clichéd super-sensuality of a great deal of commercial popular music, let alone the Puccinian epigones evident in the hit-tunes of recent musical theatre. Neither is it simply a sublimation of repressed desire. There is no gay sub-text to Tippett's work, as there is throughout Britten's. It has sometimes been observed that the succession of words (actually taken from *Roget's Thesaurus*!) sung by the exultant chorus at the close of Act I of *The Midsummer Marriage* ends emphatically on the word 'gay'. Likewise, the Yeats quotation at the end of the same opera also finishes with the same word:

> All things fall and are built again
> And those that build them again are gay.

In the former instance, 'gay' is being used in its older sense of 'cheerful'; in the latter, Yeats intended it to signify 'heroic' or 'brave':[8] only more recently has 'gay' superseded 'queer' as a synonym for homosexuality. In the three Ritual Dances in Act II of the opera, female predators attempt to kill male victims: this might be regarded as an unconscious projection of a homosexual's fear of women – but in the context of *The Midsummer Marriage*, it has far wider ramifications. In the psychology of the sex-chase, a switching of roles is constant and unpredictable: and Tippett pinpoints that even more precisely in *The Knot Garden* – the opera in which, as we have seen, he chose to bring sexuality absolutely into the limelight.

On the other hand, in *King Priam*, neither the passionate heterosexual urges that drew Paris to Helen, nor the intense homosexual love between Achilles and Patroclus, is allowed to burgeon into florid celebration. Both are unmistakably present, but only because they represent alternatives to the violence and destructiveness of the war between Greece and Troy. The same theme, which Tippett first explored in *The Heart's Assurance*, returns in the blues songs of his Third Symphony: the wild intensity of sexual arousal is evoked in its second blues – whose extreme language regularly causes a flutter amongst the prim and straitlaced:

> ... O, I'll go prancing with my toe-tips
> flying and my knee-bones
> jerking and my thighs,
> with what between there lies,
> My thighs aflame.

– but in the third blues, love becomes a means of escape from suffering, even an antidote to it:

> As I lay down beside my mate,
> Body to body,
> We did not heed the sorrow.

Eroticism is so important an element in Tippett's works that its absence is sometimes conspicuous. Certain of Tippett's later operatic characters – like Olympion and Yuri in *The Ice Break* or Donny in *New Year* – might conceivably have benefited from far greater development of the sexual dimension to their personalities, though to do so would perhaps have undermined the concentration of Tippett's drama in each case.

Erotic exploration and compositional innovation can be considered two very important, complementary facets of Tippett's creative personality. To draw such a parallel may seem specious and glib: another of those short-circuit methods that brush aside nuance and subtlety of reference, linking works of art to sociological or political ideas in the crudest possible way. (The theories and judgements of the musicologist Theodor W. Adorno are a classic instance of this.) But it is a matter of sheer fact that these two elements within Tippett's personality flowered together – as the composer himself acknowledged – at the time he wrote his First String Quartet. And right into Tippett's late eighties, his sexual and compositional drives remained unusually strong. Both then suddenly declined and stopped altogether. Such a connection should not be overlooked or ignored.

The issue might be considered in wider, historical context. Towards the end of the nineteenth century, Wagner and his followers, in their quest for the ultimate in musical representations of sensuality, pushed chromatic harmony and tonality to a point of apparent disintegration: and when Schoenberg allowed himself the same freedoms, he became so disturbed that eventually he had to formulate a rationale, a set of didactic procedures matching those freedoms with appropriate controls.

In Tippett's case, as the expressive spectrum of his music (and particularly its explicitly erotic component) broadened during the late 1960s, his own harmonic and tonal language also suddenly took off into free atonality. But unlike Schoenberg, he felt no need for any systemization. For concurrently he had investigated other technical parameters and with these his new-found atonal freedoms fitted well: fresh concepts of instrumental sonority and texture; radical alternatives to classical musical logic, that replaced its carefully planned transitions between scenes and equally well signposted episodes of development and recapitulation with cinematic jump-cutting, flash-backs and fast-forward temporal displacements. To an unusual and unpredictable extent, Tippett's innovations all cohered into a comprehensive and distinctive idiom.

Sometimes, in consequence, Tippett broke through from art into activism. Now if subversion has always been part of his temperament, he was never by nature an agit-prop artist or a propagandist. Nor does one find in Tippett's *oeuvre* those journalistic – not to say opportunistic – pieces that are often rushed out in commemoration of those lost in whatever disaster, or mourn the death of the composer's friends from illnesses and epidemics. For Tippett such immediate problems had to be fitted into a larger scheme of things, seen in a wider perspective: hence the abiding strength and universality of application – and the appeal – of *A Child of Our Time* and *The Heart's Assurance*. When Tippett does, however, point an accusatory finger, as in his Third Symphony, or when he stands up to demand 'One humanity/One justice', at the end of *New Year*, the effect is electrifyingly well-timed and justified.

More often than not, artistic values take precedent, indeed remain paramount. The strongest thread running through all Tippett's work – at its simplest, at its most complex – is an abiding faith in art as 'apprehensions of the inner world of feelings'. While accepting much in modern technological society, Tippett quotes a warning given by Darwin: 'The loss of these tastes (for one or more of the arts according to our predilections) is a loss of happiness and may possibly be injurious to the intellect and more probably to the moral character, by enfeebling the emotional part of our nature.'[9]

Tippett's music has thus to be judged not only by its engagement with external issues – with matters of life and death, of joy and suffering – but by its advancement of all manner of musical techniques in order to tap those inner resources of feeling and understanding. For many younger composers now he is a kind of model or 'peer figure'. Unlike Schoenberg, Hindemith, Messiaen and others, however, he became such a figure simply by virtue of what he is, and what he has done, rather than by teaching, surrounding himself with disciples, or codifying his own technical principles.

Emulating Tippett's own musical idiom is probably inadvisable: his formal, rhythmic, harmonic, textural, even textual fingerprints are so idiosyncratic as to limit rather than liberate the originality of some other creator.

Emulating, on the other hand, Tippett's multi-facetedness, his integrity, his sense that art remains – both through its dialogue with technology and its independent ontology – alive and ever capable of unlocking new and resplendent vistas of experience: that is the real challenge. Asked about the possibility of 'another Tippett in the next millennium', the composer's eventual response was to say that what would matter more would be 'metamorphoses, fresh reincarnations galore'.[10]

Appendix
Arrangements, Transcriptions
and Paraphrases

In general, Tippett has been disinclined to allow works of his to be transcribed for other musical combinations: he is, in this respect, the polar opposite of Percy Grainger. Working amongst amateurs early on, he had made his own versions of works like *The Village Opera* and *The Beggar's Opera*, tailoring them to the forces available. But when it came to his own mature compositions, he was ill at ease with well-intentioned efforts to promote them in formats other than the original. In the 1940s, Walter Goehr, for instance, made a version of the slow movement of Tippett's String Quartet No. 1, adding a double-bass to the cello line. The composer was unhappy with this. Where the task of arranging a work was more akin to composition, and involved transforming a piece into something new, uncovering latent dimensions and even giving it an entirely new title, and where he himself could participate in the process, Tippett felt more positive. This happened rarely, however, as he tended to regard it as a distraction from his real task of producing fresh works. In 1958, he himself prepared the version for unaccompanied mixed chorus of the five Negro spirituals from *A Child of Our Time* – and these are now performed just as often as the oratorio itself, probably more. Also, in 1964, he made a transcription for flute, oboe and piano (or harpsichord) of Hermes's aria, 'O divine music' from his opera, *King Priam*. With the composer's agreement, a Salvation Army trumpeter who worked at Schott, Brian Bowen (no relation of the present writer) arranged Tippett's Suite in D for brass band. 'Boyhood's End' has also been published in a transposed version for baritone and piano: but the composer feels that this and his *Songs for Achilles* are not intended for sopranos ...!

The bulk of the published arrangements – or new versions – of specific compositions by Tippett have been the product of my own association with the composer in recent decades. The first of them was the reduced scoring of *The Knot Garden*, undertaken in 1984 at the request of Opera Factory/London Sinfonietta.

None of Tippett's five operas requires a vast orchestra. *The Midsummer Marriage* and *King Priam* have both been successfully toured around small British theatres for several years. In the former case, the orchestration is essentially that of a Beethoven orchestra, with, in addition, harp, celesta and a small amount of percussion. The key factor in *King Priam* is the strength of the string body: as has been observed, Tippett's re-thinking of the orchestra here involved doing away with the conventional division of violins into firsts and seconds, and the minimum number of players (6 violins, 4 violas, 4 cellos, 2 basses) is largely determined by those episodes where there is already extensive dividing up of the whole string body – e.g. in Act I scene 2 (Fig 92 *et seq.*).

The soloistic tendencies within Tippett's orchestration are even more pronounced in *The Knot Garden* and it was that which reduced its cohort of around 70 players to a minimum of 22. As it happened, only about a third of each act required instrumental redeployment (rather than re-orchestration), many pages of the score entailed no adjustments whatsoever, or only minor ones, and not a note of Tippett's music was changed. In the rest, a certain amount of doctoring facilitated the 'faking' of sonorities such as those of two piccolos or two double-basses. For balance purposes, I omitted the xylophone and occasionally reinforced tutti passages.

In rationalizing the percussion parts so that only two players were needed, I sometimes requested other players in the ensemble to perform on percussion when they were unused for several pages on end. The chamber version requires versatility but no more virtuosity than was demanded by the original. For the most part, the string textures could be undertaken by soloists (three violins, the third of them doubling as second viola; viola; cello and double-bass). In one or two episodes, the lack of a rich string sonority may be evident (e.g. in the duet for Denise and Mel in Act II), but I have compensated as best I could and generally the strings balance with the rest of the ensemble quite well in this context. The other advantage is that the chamber-sized orchestra is rarely in danger of overwhelming the voices: which is one of the reasons the opera has since been undertaken by a number of student groups.

A reduced version of *The Ice Break* is feasible for many of the same reasons, but there are as yet no firm plans for one to be made. For the Houston première of *New Year*, I prepared a slightly reduced version of the score, as the theatre pit was not large enough to accommodate Tippet's full requirement (about 53 players). But the composer's original is preferable.

All the other arrangements and transcriptions in which I have collaborated with the composer have entailed some degree of elaboration of the original or even re-composition of a kind.

Water out of Sunlight (1988)

This is the title chosen by the composer for the string orchestra arrangement of his String Quartet No. 4 which I undertook at his request for the Academy of St Martin-in-the-Fields. While Tippett would never sanction an 'enlargement' of his first three and his fifth string quartets, whose style is so linear, the harmonically dense, sonorously adventurous idiom of String Quartet No. 4 sets it apart from the others and lent itself well to transcription.

In a programme-note Tippett explained his title thus:

> When I asked T. S. Eliot once why he had called his late poems *Four Quartets*, he told me the title arose from his passionate love and admiration for Beethoven's late quartets. I shared his passion; and certainly my own Quartet 4 relates to that world of intimate and intense musical sound.

The most enduring image out of the poems for me has been the drained pool in the rose-garden, which comes at the start of 'Burnt Norton'. The relevant lines are:

> Dry the pool, dry concrete, brown edged,
> And the pool was filled with water out of sunlight,
> And the lotus rose, quietly, quietly,
> The surface glittered out of heart of light,
> And they were behind us, reflected in the pool.
> Then a cloud passed, and the pool was empty.

... In the poem, the movement from 'drained pool' to 'water out of sunlight' comes more than once, as it does also in the quartet. The transcription from four solo strings to string orchestra should make the 'sunlight' brighter. Yet the journey from inchoate murmurs to resplendent sound and back remain in essence the same.

The transcription of the Quartet still uses solo strings as a reference-point, featured, however, amongst a multiplicity of possible string textures. Some of these simply allot double-stoppings in the original to divided groups of players, or sharing out the passages in harmonics in the last movement. Some are used to build up a crescendo by adding players gradually, or their numbers are reduced gradually for a diminuendo. The implied echo effects of the final bars are realized within a 17-part string texture (hence the minimum number of players for the piece is 17). The episode in the slow movement between Figures. 61 and 66 is also illumined by harmonics on chordal points of rest.

The Heart's Assurance (1990)

Studying the piano-writing in this song-cycle (about whose difficulties of execution Britten was only the first of many executants to complain!), many connections can be observed between its sonorities and those to be found in other Tippett scores of the late 1940s, most notably *The Midsummer Marriage*.

These connections are to some extent brought out in this orchestrated version, which uses flute, oboe, clarinet, bassoon, four horns, trumpet, harp and percussion (military drum, snare-drum, triangle) and strings.

Four horns may seem excessive in this chamber orchestra context. But as has been observed earlier, romantic horn-calls are fundamental to Tippett's orchestral idiom. Other pictorial ingredients of the kind found in *The Midsummer Marriage* suggest themselves – e.g. the opening of the Ritual Dances is echoed in the very first bars of the opening song; again, the third song is like a sketch for the third Ritual Dance. In the culminating fifth song, where the singer calls out across the battlefield, Tippett's allusion to the Last Post is now made explicitly, in the echoing call of the trumpet off-stage.

Prelude: Autumn, for oboe and piano (1991)
This version of one of the instrumental interludes from Tippett's cantata, 'Crown of the Year', was one of a collection of tributes to the oboist Janet Craxton, performed in 1991 at a BBC Radio 3 concert by Nicholas Daniel and Julius Drake. In the slow outer sections the original oboe part is unchanged and is set against a keyboard version of string quartet accompaniment. In the faster central section, the oboe takes over some of the first violin part, while the original piano part is elaborated to accommodate string parts and bell sonorities, some of its textures modelled on those of Tippett's Piano Concerto.

The Shires Suite (1995)
For a variety of reasons, this was not published until 1995. Written over a period of five years, with individual movements given their first performances independently of the final entity, the score went through several different editors' hands at Schott and was full of anomalies, inconsistencies and errors. When it was eventually prepared by the present writer for publication, Tippett was keen that there should be some alternative versions

of the three movements involving chorus, so as to facilitate wider performance by schools and youth orchestras.

My transcription of the choral parts took its cue from the general emphasis in the Suite on canonic imitation, so that they were now to be performed by three spatially separated antiphonal groups, set apart from the orchestra. Groups A and B consist of flutes and clarinets (with a minimum of 2 players on each line); Group C consists of a horn and trumpet. The placing of the groups obviously varies according to the hall where the Suite is performed, but the aim is to obtain the maximum degree of excitement in the imitative exchanges between groups. At the end the horn and trumpet are as far in the distance as is practical, to obtain the effect of a magical echo. Some of the choral parts in the central cantata are meanwhile transcribed for on-stage orchestral brass and strings. The overall intention is to have the maximum number of players taking part, the maximum diversity and theatricality in its sonorous impact.

New Year Suite.(1990)

The *New Year* Suite was prepared concurrently with the opera from which it is taken. Tippett was nevertheless concerned that it should be an independent piece that could stand up in its own right and not be merely a collection of excerpts. The outcome is thus a continuous composition, lasting about 25 minutes, in thirteen episodes that offer musical portraits of two of the main characters – Donny and Jo-Ann. They are set in the context of the New Year celebrations of Act II. Additionally, Tippett wanted the worlds of fantasy and dreams within the opera re-created for the concert hall. Thus, as in the opera, the orchestra includes electro-acoustic elements on tape. In some episodes, the voice-parts in the original are transferred to appropriate instruments and there is some extra linking music and occasional enrichment of the original texture.

The Suite opens with taped music for the landing of the spaceship, to be followed by the prelude to Act II, introducing the New Year rituals: the Shaman's Dance and the Hunt for the Scapegoat. In the opera, Donny was picked upon as the scapegoat, so here he is presented in two numbers, his Skarade (Act I) and his Dreamsong (Act III). At the halfway point in the Suite, there is a dream interlude (distant voices on tape), to be followed by Jo-Ann's Dreamsong (Act I), her love scene with Pelegrin and dance in the Paradise Garden (Act III). In the last three episodes, the New Year rituals resume with the Beating out of the Scapegoat (the Bad Old Year) and the Ringing in of New Year, with 'Auld Lang Syne'; as the celebration dies down, the taped music takes over, signalling the take-off once more of the spaceship.

Festal Brass with Blues (1983)

Tippett has composed numerous small pieces for brass – four original fanfares, and a fifth arranged by the present writer from the seventh movement of *The Mask of Time*. In his Praeludium for brass, bells and percussion (1962), he developed the fanfare into a much larger scale prelude, using the mosaic technique of his recently completed *King Priam* to create sharp contrasts between the different components in the ensemble – six horns and two tubas offset against three trumpets and three trombones in turn, all of them complemented by the bells and percussion. The thematic ingredients are stated, re-stated, varied, condensed and overlapped in the most subtle way.

In *Festal Brass with Blues*, Tippett's sole excursion into brass band composition, he embarked on something even more ambitious, a one-movement fantasy largely based on themes from his Third Symphony – hence its title. In the opening part of the work, a gradual accumulation of ideas (some derived from the Symphony) and a mixture of counterpoint and antiphonal contrasts, produces a festive mood, of sorts. As in the transition from the purely orchestral part of the symphony to its vocal blues, so here, at the climax, Tippett quotes the opening of the finale of Beethoven's Ninth Symphony, continuing with a transcription of the slow blues that follows (plus the quiet linking music that precedes it), with the flugelhorn taking the main solos (as in the Symphony). As this is all developed, the texture thins considerably, and though the earlier music returns, the polarity established between festal outbursts and reflective, ironic blues remains right up to the quiet, mysterious end to the work.

'Triumph': a paraphrase on The Mask of Time (1992)

'Triumph' was commissioned by a consortium of American university wind bands: and it should be noted that their instrumental line-up is quite different from that of brass bands. Here, Tippett adds even more explicitly to the paraphrase genre, by means of which Liszt and others in the nineteenth century enabled operatic and orchestral music to reach wider audiences, and which has always been absolutely germane to jazz and commercial popular music (even though probably no one has ever made use of the term in those contexts). A 'paraphrase' is much closer to an original composition than a transcription: and this one, on music from *The Mask of Time*, might be compared with the nineteenth-century operatic overture, in that it incorporates some of the most important motifs and episodes, at the same time remaining an independent work in its own right.

The core of 'Triumph' is drawn from the sixth movement of *The Mask of Time*, which, as has already been observed, is a triptych centred on the poet Shelley. The work begins with the scene-setting introduction to this movement, but this is cut short: instead, the cosmic metaphor of 'Sound' that opens *The Mask of Time* – the recurrent *Ur*-motif of the entire work – is invoked (actually transposed up a semitone) before the music for the triumphal chariot begins, with its ever-present ground-bass. This continues, as in the original, with the episode in which Shelley drowns at sea: and the 'Sound' motif returns after the bells and woodwind have tolled for the burning of the poet's body.

The Mask of Time ends with a triumphal assertion of human survival in a destructive world. 'Triumph' ends with a similar final gesture of triumph of its own: as in Beethoven's 'Egmont Overture', the music suddenly changes direction and fanfares blaze out in a climax of virtuosity. This section is (like Fanfare No. 5) a new version of the third of the instrumental interludes based on 'Veni, creator spiritus' in the seventh movement of *The Mask of Time*. The embellishments to the hymn are further elaborated here: and the hymn itself is made more prominent. But the last few bars – continuing from a transcription of the chorus's lines 'Fire and Arithmetic' – are new.

The mosaic character of Tippett's scoring – 'for voices and instruments', as he himself put it – made it possible to replace the 'blocks' of sonority for solo singers and choral groups with wind sonorities fresh to the work – four saxophones, cornets and tenor tubas (or baritones) – though they are deployed freely, not just as exact equivalents. And while Tippett, in the drowning-at-sea episode, built his original music around a brass motif from his Fourth Symphony, but using only one bass tuba, here the two bass tubas are reinstated.

Suite, The Tempest (1995)

Tippett's incidental music for *The Tempest* was first heard in a production at the Old Vic Theatre, London, in April 1962. Apart from the three Songs for Ariel which were subsequently published, he produced dances, mood-music and a more extended piece for the masque scene of Act IV. The musical director at the theatre, John Lambert, also used some of the music for a ballet score for the London Dance Group in 1964. Meanwhile, *The Tempest* became the main reference-point for Tippett's third opera, *The Knot Garden*: he incorporated quotations from some of his Ariel songs both in the opera and in the song-cycle, *Songs for Dov,* which followed.

Little was heard of the rest of his *Tempest* music until 1985, when Andrew Parrott and Ian Cotterell produced for BBC radio, *A Vision of the Island*, intermingling Tippett's music with a lot of Shakespeare's own dialogue. A concert version of this, *To the*

Elements be Free!, devised by Parrott and Roger Savage, was presented by the Nash Ensemble at the Barbican's ninetieth birthday celebrations for the composer in February 1995.

But Tippett was never particularly happy with the music as it stood. So, when invited by the BBC to contribute something to their celebrations (also in 1995) of the tercentenary of Purcell's death, he agreed to a two-fold plan: the composition of a new 'Caliban's Song' – which was premièred separately in a Westminster Abbey concert given on 21 November, the actual date of Purcell's death – and a reorganization, refurbishment and enlargement of the rest of the incidental music to make a proper concert suite, using a larger mixed ensemble (14 players in all) than that of the original theatre band. This final Suite was first performed on 14 December the same year. It comprises eleven numbers, intermingling songs and dances as follows:

1 Prelude
2 Song for Ariel I: 'Come unto these yellow sands'
3 Dance
4 Song for Ariel II: 'Full fathom five'
5 Solemn Dance
6 Trumpet Tune with Boogie
7 Caliban's Song
8 Interlude: Dreaming
9 Masque
10 Song for Ariel III: 'Where the bee sucks'
11 Exit Dance

The original instrumental pieces are here extended and enriched to make them sound less like 'incidental music'. Music adapted from Act I of *The Knot Garden* – a trumpet tune and boogie-woogie – leads at its climax straight into Caliban's song, the fast ground-bass of the boogie giving way to the slow ground-bass of the new song, a setting of the text, 'Be not afeard, the isle is full of noises'. This song ends, 'I cried to dream again', and leads without a break into 'Dreaming', a transcription for harp and viola of the slow movement of Tippett's *The Blue Guitar* (which itself had incorporated harp and viola motifs from his Fourth Symphony and fourth opera, *The Ice Break*) .

Tippett's original 'Masque' movement has been pruned slightly and re-scored so that it now comprises a duet for tenor and baritone, followed by a baritone solo: both are settings of lyric poems roughly contemporary with *The Tempest*. The final Exit Dance is based on a sarabande-like dance piece which Tippett had first composed for the Paradise Garden scene in *The Mask of Time* and re-used in Act III of *New Year*: this leads finally into a reprise of part of the Solemn Dance.

Notes

The following abbreviations have been adopted in the references below:

MAQ *Moving into Aquarius*, Michael Tippett (Paladin, 1974)

MAG *Music of the Angels: Essays and Sketchbooks of Michael Tippett*, ed. Meirion Bowen (Eulenberg, 1980)

TOM *Tippett on Music*, ed. Meirion Bowen (Oxford University Press, 1995)

TTB *Those Twentieth Century Blues*, Michael Tippett (Pimlico, 1994)

1 Innocence and Experience

1   Charles Stanford: *Musical Composition: A Short Treatise for Students* (London, 1911), ch. 2, p.10

2   In the rest of the programme, Tippett conducted Parry's *The Pied Piper of Hamelin*, Mozart's A major Piano Concerto (with Smith as soloist), Stanford's *Songs of the Fleet* and Bach's *Coffee* Cantata.

3   *The Times*, 7 April 1930, p.12

4   *Daily Telegraph*, 7 April 1930

5   TTB, p.52

6   *See* TTB, pp.145–56

7   Francesca Allinson, *A Childhood* (London, 1937)

8   'Tributes and Reminiscences' in Ian Kemp (ed.), *Michael Tippett: A Symposium on his Sixtieth Birthday* (London, 1965), p.67

9   Ibid. p. 67

10 TTB, p. 58

11 'Poets in a Barren Age' in MAQ, p. 152

12 See Malcolm Chase and Mark Whyman: *Heartbreak Hill* (Cleveland County Council & Langbaurgh-on-Tees Borough Council, 1991)

13 *See* TTB, pp. 47–9

14 London, 1938

15 A selection of the dreams and Tippett's commentaries are published in TTB, ch. 6, pp.63–112

16 *Picture Post*, vol. 1, no. 9, 26 November 1938, p.13

17 TTB, p.112

18 Odon von Horvath: *Ein Kind unserer Zeit*, trans. R. Wills Thomas as *A Child of Our Time* (London, 1938)

19 *See* TTB, pp. 260–1

20 'The Younger English Composers: IX. Michael Tippett' in *Monthly Musical Record*: 69 (March/April 1939), pp.73–6

21 'Music of our Time' in *Hinrichsen's Year Book 1944*, ed. Ralph Hill and Max Hinrichsen (London, 1944), p.16

22 Recorded by Decca for Rimington Van Wyck Ltd

23 'Tippettan Discovery' in *Scrutiny*, 10 (January 1942), pp. 309–12

24 'Gramophone Notes' in *New Statesman and Nation* 22 (1 November 1941), pp. 397–8

25 *Observer*, 25 April 1943, p. 2

26 *See* Charles Stuart: 'Morley College Music' in *Musical Times*, vol. 92, September 1951, pp. 393–8; also Denis Richards, 'Ruin – and Recovery' in *The Offspring of the Vic: A History of Morley College* (London, 1958), pp. 248–71

27 'Music at Morley College' in *Hinrichsen's Year Book 1944*, ed. Ralph Hill and Max Hinrichsen (London, 1944), pp.147–9

28 Saygun (1907–71) and Tippett continued on friendly terms for some years afterwards and corresponded frequently. (Eighteen letters from Tippett to Saygun are in the latter's archives at Bilkent University in Ankara.) Both composers had written a major oratorio at almost the same time in their careers and Saygun had conducted his, *Yunus Emre*, in Paris, just prior to his visit to London. Tippett tried (unsuccessfully) to interest Schott in publishing Saygun's work: he also agreed to give the London première; likewise

Saygun promised to arrange a performance of *A Child of Our Time* in Turkey, but none of these projects came to fruition.

29 HMV DA 1921–2 (two 10″ discs, 78 rpm), 1948
30 Official typewritten application form dated 25th November 1940, sent to the Ministry of Labour and National Service.
31 The original is now held at the British Library
32 Fred May's son, Steve May, later wrote a play for radio, *Fair Hearing* (1995), relating his father's and his own experiences as conscientious objectors. It featured a thinly disguised portrayal of Tippett using his imprisonment as a means to attract publicity as a composer.
33 They are published in TTB, pp.145–56
34 *Observer*, 24 March 1944, p. 2
35 Oskar Kokoschka, *Letters 1905–76* [translated from the German by Mary Whittall] (London, Thames & Hudson, 1992), p.183
36 *See* TTB pp. 213–15

2 Trials and Tribulations

1 'The Birth of an Opera', Parts 1–5, in the *Observer*, 2, 9, 16, 30 November, 7 December 1952, p.10 each issue. Reprinted (and re-edited) in TOM, pp.185–208
2 Paul Sacher (b. 1906), founder-conductor of the Basle Chamber Orchestra and of the Schola Cantorum Basiliensis. His name is celebrated for the remarkable list of compositions he commissioned from major composers (such as Bartók and Stravinsky) and for the help he gave to musicians in distress in the pre-war and wartime periods.
3 '"This Opera Baffles Us Too", Say Singers', in *News Chronicle*, 26 January 1955, p.3
4 '*The Midsummer Marriage*' in *Sunday Times*, 30 January 1955, p.11
5 'Mr Tippett's Opera' in *Sunday Times*, 6 February 1955, p.11

6 'Marriage of Mumbo and Jumbo' in *Daily Telegraph and Morning Post*, 29 January 1955, p.8

7 *Daily Express*, 28 January 1955

8 '*The Midsummer Marriage*' in *Musical America* 75 (March 1955), pp.7 and 47

9 '*The Midsummer Marriage*' in the *Observer*, 30 January 1955, p.11

10 '*The Midsummer Marriage*' in *The Score*, No. 11 (March 1955), pp.60–1

11 Dent was correct. *See* Chapter 6, n.10

12 The *Guardian*, 18 January 1996

13 '...In music, practicability of text may not be the concern of the critics: to orchestral players in the mass, it may mean the difference between confidence and doubt. The comprehensive technique of the BBC Symphony Orchestra is equal to all reasonable demands.' R. J. F. Howgill, BBC Controller of Music, in *The Times*, 21 February 1958.

14 cf. Gertrude Rachel Levy, *The Gate of Horn* (London, 1948)

3 Brave New Worlds

1 Kemp, *Michael Tippett: A Symposium*

2 *See* Paul Binding, *Lorca: The Gay Imagination* (London, 1985)

3 *See* Eric Pinkett, *Time to Remember* (Northampton, 1969), esp. pp. 21–6

4 *See* Humphrey Carpenter, *The Envy of the World – Fifty Years of the BBC Third Programme and Radio 3* (London, 1996)

5 Op. cit.

6 TOM, pp. 107–8

7 Robin Holloway, 'Splendid but silly: Michael Tippett's self-wonderment and slow-maturing glory' (*Times Literary Supplement*, 27 September 1991, p. 20)

8 The *Observer*, September 1991

4 Songlines

1   TTB, p. 249

2   '... Du musst steigen oder sinken
                Du musst herrschen und gewinnen
                Oder dienen und verlieren
                Leiden oder triumphieren,
                Amhoss oder Hammer sein.
                ('... You must climb or fall
                dominate and win, or serve and lose
                suffer or triumph,
                be anvil or hammer.')
I am indebted to Ian Kemp for recently identifying this link.

3   Anonymous nineteenth-century American ballad

4   *See* TOM, pp. 57–65

5   *See* TTB, Chapter 7, esp. pp.163–87

6   Peter Pears, 'Songs and Text' in *Michael Tippett: A Symposium on his Sixtieth Birthday* (London, 1965), pp. 47–9

7   TOM, p.106

8   Ibid. p.107

9   Ibid. p.108

5 Protests and Polemics

1   TOM pp.117–77

2   *See* Chapter 1, n.18

3   Warner Bros. (1936)

4   TOM, p.182

5   Ibid. p.182

6   MAG pp.121–3

7   TTB, pp.260–1

8   TOM p.179

9   Ibid. p.170

10 Ibid. p.113

6 Illusion and Actuality

1   MAQ, p.50
2   *See* TTB pp.166–7
3   Cambridge, 1914
4   TOM, p.200
5   Ibid. p.200
6   Ibid. p.202
7   Ibid. p.200
8   Ibid. p.201
9   Ibid. p.199
10 *See* Chapter 2, note 12; cf. Tippett's letter to Eric Walter White (14 September 1949): 'In a biography of St Joan I read yesterday the historical material for the couplet "Joan heard the voice first/In father's garden at high noon".' Quoted in Eric Walter White, *Tippett and his Operas* (Barrie & Jenkins, 1979, p.58). The biography to which Tippett refers is Frances Wimwar's *The Saint and the Devil: A Biographical Study of Joan of Arc and Gilles de Rai* (Hamish Hamilton, 1948)
11 cf. Tippett's letter (White, op. cit. p.58): 'I've come across some fascinating allied stuff in a Yeats biography (Norman Jeffares). Yeats equates the four elements to four (historical) ages. (I'll show you his notes to the poem.)

>   He with body waged a fight
>   Body won and walks upright. (Earth)
>
>   Then he struggled with the heart;
>   Innocence and peace depart. (Water)
>
>   Then he struggled with the mind;
>   His proud heart he left behind. (Air)
>
>   Now his wars with God begin;
>   At stroke of midnight God shall win. (Fire).

It's the last couplet that's interesting – and Yeats's (similar) order.'

12 Robert Graves, *The White Goddess* (London, 1948), pp.23–4

13 'Lapis Lazuli'

14 *The Hidden God*, translation by Philip Thody of Lucien Goldmann: *Le Dieu Caché* (Routledge, 1964), p.333

15 'At Work on King Priam', in *The Score*, No. 28, January 1961, p.59

16 *See* TOM, pp.208–9

17 TOM, p.204

18 *Stravinsky in Conversation with Robert Craft* (Penguin Books, 1961), p.164

19 Galina von Meck, *As I Remember Them* (London, 1973), p.322

20 See TOM, p.226

21 Quoted from the typescript for an unidentified talk/article entitled *Son et Lumière*

22 This is a transformation of the scene in Shaw's *Back to Methuselah*, in which the egg with a girl inside appears on stage; she asks to be let out, the egg is cracked open and she goes straight for the first handsome man she sees. The original image is preserved in Lev's reference to the 'naked human chick'; cf. Michael Tippett, 'Back to Methuselah' and 'The Ice Break' in the *Shaw Review*, vol. XXI, no. 2, May 1978, pp.100–3

23 Cf. John Garrard (ed.), *The Russian Novel from Pushkin to Pasternak* (Yale University Press, New Haven & London, 1983)

24 *See* TTB, pp. 265–8

25 *See* 'The Scapegoat', Part VI of J. G. Frazer, *The Golden Bough* (London, 3rd edition, 1925)

26 Adapted from a children's rhyme supplied to the composer by the critic Paul Driver. The cry 'Co-co-ri-co' comes from T.S. Eliot's *The Waste Land* and is recalled in Tippett's *Byzantium*, as a way of articulating the song of the nightingale

27 Tippett had been very moved by the film, *Birdy* (1984)

28 Tippett's own description. *See* Peter Brook, *The Empty Space* (London, 1968), Chapters 2 and 3

29 TOM, p. 227

30 Tippett heard these words spoken by Mark Knopfler of Dire Straits at the seventieth-birthday concert for Nelson Mandela in London, in 1988. *See* TTB, p. 268

7 Form and Fantasy

1 This was in 1951, when Tippett had been conducting *A Child of Our Time* in Monte Ceresio

2 *Poétique musicale: sons forme de six leçons.* The Charles Eliot Norton Lectures for 1939–40 (Cambridge, Mass. 1942). Trans. Arthur Knodel and Ingolf Dahl as *Poetics of Music* (Cambridge, Mass. and London, 1947)

3 MAQ, p.101

4 *See* Chapter 1 note 25

5 Vincent d'Indy: *Cours de Composition Musicale* (Paris, 3 vols, 1903–50); *see also* MAG, pp. 31–2; also Ian Kemp, *Tippett: the Composer and his Music* (OUP, 1986), pp. 89–90, 136, 146–7, 169

6 TOM, p.93

7 Ibid. p.89

8 Ibid. p.96

9 Colin McPhee, *Music in Bali: A Study in Form and Instrumental Organization in Balinese Orchestral Music* (Yale University Press, New Haven and London, 1966); *see*, for instance, McPhee's example 320

10 Quoted from a French-Canadian folksong, 'A la claire fontaine': a disappointed lover sings it as she goes to a well to bathe

11 TOM, p.4

12 Ibid. p.10

13 Ibid. p.108

8 Time and Eternity

1 Paul Valéry: *Poems* in *Collected Works* (London, Routledge, 1971, trans. David Paul), note on p.459
2 See TOM, pp.16–21
3 'Time and History in Patristic Christianity' in *Man and Time: papers from the Eranos Yearbooks* ed. Joseph Campbell (London, Routledge, 1958), vol. 3, pp.85–107
4 TOM, p. 231
5 Ibid, p. 236
6 Mary Renault, *The Mask of Apollo* (London, 1966)
7 Annie Dillard, *Pilgrim at Tinker Creek* (New York, 1974)
8 *See* Walter A. Strauss, *Descent and Return: The Orphic Theme in Modern Literature* (Harvard, 1971)

9 Portrait of the Artist

1 *See* Francis M. Cornford, *The Origins of Attic Comedy* (Cambridge, 1914)
2 *See* Paul Fussell, *The First World War and Modern Memory* (Oxford University Press, 1975), p.35: '...There seems to be one dominating form of modern understanding: that it is essentially ironic; and that it originates largely in the application of mind and memory to the events of the Great War.'
3 *See* MAQ, pp.146–56
4 James Joyce, *A Portrait of the Artist as a Young Man* (Penguin edition, 1960), p.24
5 Norman Lebrecht in the *Daily Telegraph*, 2 January 1995
6 Deryck Puffett, 'Tippett at 90' in *Musical Times*, vol. 136, No. 1823, January 1995, pp.6–14
7 MAQ, pp.155–56
8 *See* Ian Kemp, *The Composer and his Music* (Oxford University Press, 1987), 2nd edn, p. 493 n. 101
9 TOM, p.15
10 Ibid. p. 309

Select Bibliography

In the first edition of this book, I acknowledged the latest available up-to-date bibliography, listing all Tippett's compositions, recordings of them, the composer's prose and verse writings and all published writings about him, which had been compiled by Paul D. Andrews and published by Bedfordshire County Library (with addenda) in 1980. Nine years later this was superseded by *Michael Tippett: A Bio-Bibliography*, compiled by George Theil (Greenwood Press, New York/Westport, Conn./London, 1989). The following selection is mainly indebted to Theil, but is naturally supplemented with a lot of extra material that has appeared since the publication of his book. From Tippett's numerous appearances on television, in interviews and documentaries about his life and work, and in programmes centred upon specific compositions, I have compiled a selection that seems to me representative of the best and most useful that has been achieved within this particular genre.

Writings by Michael Tippett

The main body of Tippett's prose and verse writings appeared first in the following two volumes (which have been out of print for some years):

Michael Tippett, *Moving into Aquarius* (Routledge & Kegan Paul, 1959): 2nd edn. containing extra material (Paladin 1974)

Meirion Bowen (ed.), *Music of the Angels: Essays and Sketchbooks of Michael Tippett* (Eulenberg, 1980)

The bulk of the contents of these volumes, revised and re-edited, along with extra material, is now available in:

Meirion Bowen (ed.), *Tippett on Music* (Oxford University Press, 1995); German edition, translated Meinhard Saremba (Schott, Mainz, 1998)

Writings about Tippett

Books

Clarke, David, *Form and Structure in the Music of Michael Tippett* (2 vols, Garland Publishing Inc, New York & London, 1989)

Hurd, Michael: *Tippett* (London, Novello, 1978)

John, Nicholas (ed.), *The Operas of Michael Tippett* (London, John Calder; New York, Riverrun Press, 1985)

Kemp, Ian (ed.) *Michael Tippett – A Symposium on his Sixtieth Birthday* (London, Faber, 1965)

—*Tippett: The Composer and his Work* (Eulenberg/Da Capo, 1984; 2nd edition, OUP, 1987)

Lewis, Geriant (ed.), *Michael Tippett OM: A Celebration* (Tunbridge Wells, Kent: The Baton Press, 1985)

Matthews, David: *Michael Tippett – An Introductory Study* (Faber, 1980)

Michael Tippett: A Man of Our Time (Catalogue of the Tippett Exhibition) (London, Schott, 1977)

White, Eric Walter: *Tippett and His Operas* (London, Barrie & Jenkins, 1979; New York, Da Capo, 1981 with a new introduction by Andrew Porter)

Whittall, Arnold: *Britten and Tippett: Studies in Themes and Techniques* (CUP, 1982; 2nd edn 1991)

Articles

Aechternacht, Stephen M., 'Tippett in America/America in Tippett' (*Composer* no. 70, summer 1980, pp.28–33)

Allenby, David, 'Tippett's New Year' (*Tempo*, no. 175, December 1990, pp.35–6)

Amis, John, 'A Child of Our Time' (*The Listener*, vol. 45, March 1951, p.436)

—'New Choral Work by Michael Tippett: *A Child of Our Time*' (*Musical Times*, vol. 85, February 1944, pp.41–2)

—'Seven Years' Hard Labour' (*Music and Musicians*, vol. 3, February 1955, p.11)

Amraci, Emre, 'Saygun and Tippett' (article, in Turkish, in *Orkestra Dergisi*, September 1996, pp.15–20)

Anderson, Julian, 'Tippett's 90th year' (Royal College of Music *Annual Review*/RCM Magazine, 1995, pp. 23–6)

Ardoin, John, 'Tippett in America' (*Opera Quarterly*, vol. 4, winter 1986/87: pp.1–20)

Atkinson, Neville T., 'A Child of Our Time' (*Musical Opinion*, vol. 86, June 1963, pp. 527, 529)

—'Michael Tippett's Debt to the Past' (*Music Review*, vol. 23, no. 3, 1962, pp.195–204)

—'Tippett for Schools Music' (*Music in Education*, vol. 29, 1 January 1965, pp.19–20)

Ball, Andrew, 'Tippett's Piano Sonatas: A Pianist's Reactions' (*Music and Musicians*, January 1985, p.6)

Bergmann, Walter, 'Der Englische Komponist Michael Tippett' (*Melos* 15, March 1948, pp.74–5)

—'SRP News: Michael Tippett at 70' (*Recorder and Music Magazine*, vol. 5, no. 1, 1975, p. 34)

—'Tippett, Michael' in *Die Musik in Geschichte und Gegenwart*, vol. 13, cols. 427–9 (Kassel, Bareneiter, 1966)

Bowen, Meirion, 'An Introduction to Tippett's *The Knot Garden*' (*Music and Musicians International*, vol. 36, no. 8, April 1988, pp. 24–5)

—'Britten und Tippett: die Erneuerung der englischen Musik' (*Osterreichische Musikzeitschrift* 41, March/April 1986, pp.155–64)

—'Michael Tippett's *New Year*: A Modern Masque' (*The Opera Journal*, vol. XXII, no. 3, 1969, pp. 3–8)

—'*New Year*: A Lifetime of Ideas and Images' (*Opera Cues*, vol. 30, No. 1, 1989, pp.14–20)

—'Michael Tippett at 90: Still A Child of Our Time' (*BBC Music Magazine*, February 1995, pp. 22–5)

—'Travels with my Art' (*Guardian*, 2 January 1985, p.7

—'Tippett's Byzantium' (*Musical Times*, vol. 132, no. 1783, September 1991, pp. 438–440)

Cairns, David, *'The Midsummer Marriage'* in *Responses: Musical Essays and Reviews*, pp. 33–45 (London, Secker & Warburg, 1973)

—'Sir Michael Tippett: A 70th Birthday Tribute' (*Gramophone*, vol. 52, January 1975, pp.1313–14)

—'The Tippett Question' (*Spectator*, 3 May 1963, pp. 568–9)

Carnegy, Patrick, 'The Composer as Librettist' (*Times Literary Supplement*, 8 July 1977, pp. 834–5)

Chase, Malcolm & Whyman, Mark, 'The Operas: Sir Michael Tippett' in *Heartbreak Hill: A Response to Unemployment in East Cleveland in the 1930s*, pp. 21–6 (Cleveland County Council & Langbaurgh-on-Tees Borough Council, 1991)

Clarke, David, *'New Year'* (*Music and Letters*, vol. 71, 1990, pp. 468–72)

—'The Significance of the Concept 'Image' in Tippett's Musical Thought: A Perspective from Jung' (*Journal of the Royal Musical Association*, vol. 121, part 1, 1996), pp. 82–104

—'Tippett in and out of "Those Twentieth-Century Blues": the context and significance of an Autobiography' (*Music and Letters*, vol. 74, August 93, pp. 399–411)

—'Visionary Images' (*Musical Times*, vol. 136, no. 1823, January 1995, pp.16–21)

Clements, Andrew, *'The Ice Break'* (*Music and Musicians*, vol. 26, no. 1, September 1977, pp. 42–4

—'Senior Citizen' (*New Statesman 99*, 18 January 1980, pp. 98–9)

—'Tippett's Fourth' (Symphony) (*Music and Musicians*, vol. 27, no. 1 September 1978, pp. 20–2)

—'Tippett's Fourth Quartet' (*Music and Musicians*, vol. 27, May 1979, pp. 28–30)

—'Tippett at 80' (*Opera*, vol. 41, 1990, pp. 672–6)

Crossley, Paul, 'Tippett's New Sonata' (Piano Sonata No. 3) (*Listener*, vol. 89, no. 2304, 24 May 1973, p.697; reprinted in *Tippett's Piano Sonatas*, Schott, 1975)

—'Tippett's Third Piano Sonata' (*Composer*, no. 70, Summer

1980, pp.15–16)

Dennison, Peter, 'Reminiscence and Recomposition in Tippett' (*Musical Times*, vol. 126, January 1985, pp.13, 15–18)

Dickinson, A. E. F., 'Round About the Midsummer Marriage' (*Music & Letters*, vol. 37, no. 1, January 1956, pp. 50–60)

—'The Garden Labyrinth' (*The Music Review*, vol. 25, no. 11, July 1971, pp.176–80)

Docherty, Barbara, 'Sentence into cadence: the word-setting of Tippett and Britten' (*Tempo*, September 1988, pp. 2–11

Driver, Paul, 'Byzantium in Chicago' (*Tempo*, no. 177, June 1991, p. 46)

—'The Mask of Time' (*Tempo*, no. 149, June 1984, pp. 39–44)

—'Tippett's Triple Concerto' (*Tempo*, no. 135, December 1980, pp. 49–51)

East, Leslie, 'Tippett Enters his Seventies' (*Music and Musicians*, vol. 23, January 1975, pp. 26–8)

Edberg, Ulla-Britt, 'Michael Tippett' (*Nutida Musik*, 22, no. 1, 1978/79, pp.7–15)

Edelman, Maurice, 'A Composer Listens to his Own Oratorio' (*Picture Post*, 3 March 1945, pp.19–21)

Evans, Peter, 'Tippett at 75' (*Musical Times*, vol. 121, November 1980, pp.701–2)

Ewans, Michael, '*King Priam*' in S. Steven Lane (ed.), *International Dictionary of Opera* (St James Press, Detroit/London/Washington DC, 1990) vol. 1, pp. 683–4

– '*The Midsummer Marriage*' (ibid., vol. 2, pp. 871–2)

Fingleton, David, '*The Ice Break*' (*Music and Musicians*, vol. 25, no. 11, July 1977, pp. 28–30)

—'*The Knot Garden* and *Owen Wingrave*: Operatic Development or Experiment' (*Contemporary Review*, 219, November 1971, pp. 246–51)

Ford, Andrew, *Michael Tippett* in *Composer to Composer: Conversations about Contemporary Music* (St Leonards, New South Wales, 1993), pp. 237–41

Gilbert, Anthony, 'Musical Space: A Composer's View' (*Critical*

Inquiry 7, Spring 1981, pp.605–11)

Glock, William, 'The Midsummer Marriage' (*Score*, no. 11, March 1955, pp. 60–1)

—'Music' (*Observer*, 26 April 1943, p.2)

Goddard, Scott, 'Michael Tippett and the Symphony' (*Listener*, vol. 43, 12 January 1950, p. 84)

—'Michael Tippett's Operas' (*Listener*, vol. 69, 10 January 1963, p.101)

—'Tippett, Michael Kemp' in *Grove 5* (Macmillan, London, 1954, vol. 8, pp. 482–4)

—'Tippett's Ritual Dances' (*Listener*, vol. 49, 12 February 1953, p. 281)

—'Tippett's Second Symphony' (*Listener*, vol. 59, 30 January 1958, p. 217)

Goehr, Alexander, 'Tippett at Sixty' (*Musical Times*, vol. 106, January 1965, pp.22–4)

Goodwin, Noel, 'Michael Tippett: A New Orchestral Experience' (*Listener*, vol. 71, 9 January 1964, p. 93)

—'Tippett the Explorer' (*Music and Musicians*, vol. 13, February 1965, pp. 20–3, 57)

—'Tippett's Concerto for Orchestra' (*Tempo*, No. 66/67, Autumn/Winter 1963, pp. 47–51)

Harbison, John, 'Six Tanglewood Talks (4,5,6): IV. Technique' (*Perspectives of New Music*, vol. 24, Fall-Winter 1986, pp. 46–51)

Harewood, Earl of, 'Michael Tippett (b. 1905)' in *Kobbé's Complete Opera Book*, (rev. edn, London, Bodley Head 1987), pp.1,136–1,156

Halbreich, Harry, 'Tippett Arrive' (*Le Monde de la Musique*, No. 68, June 1984, pp.22–8, 30)

Harries, Meirion and Susie, 'Choosing A Subject' (*Opera Today*, New York, St Martin's Press, 1986)

Hayes, Malcolm, 'The Ice Break' (*Tempo*, No. 181, June 1992, pp. 32–3)

Hill, Peter, 'Tippett's Fifth String Quartet' (*Tempo*, No. 182,

September 1992, p. 28)

Hill, Ralph & Max Hinrichsen, *Hinrichsen's Year Book 1944: Music of Our Time* (Hinrichsen Editions Ltd, London, 1944)

Holloway, Robin, 'Splendid but silly: Michael Tippett's self-wonderment and slow-maturing glory' (*Times Literary Supplement*, 27 September 1991, p.20)

Hopkins, Antony, '*The Magic Flute* and *The Midsummer Marriage*' (*About the House*, vol. 5, no. 11, 1980, pp. 20–3)

Humphreys, Ivor, 'Sir Michael Tippett talks about the Genesis of *The Mask of Time*' (*Gramophone*, 65, May 1987, pp.1525–6)

Hurd, Michael, *Tippett* (Novello, London, 1978)

Jacobson, Bernard, 'Composer Michael Tippett: An Appreciation' (*Stereo Review*, 32, March 1974, pp. 60–5)

—Essay in *Tippett in America* (Schott, 1975)

Johnson, Stephen, 'Four in One: Stephen Johnson talks to Paul Crossley' (about Piano Sonata 4) (*Gramophone*, 63, October 1985, p. 455)

Jones, Allan Clive, 'An Introduction to the Life and Work of Michael Tippett' (*Classical Guitar*, 2, January/February 1984, pp. 29–30)

Kemp, Ian, (ed.), 'The Dream Works of Tippett' (*Times Literary Supplement*, 27 October 1972, pp.1275–6)

—'Rhythm in Tippett's Early Music' (*Proceedings of the Royal Musical Association* 105, 1978/79, pp.142–53

—'Tippett, Michael' in *The New Grove*, vol. 19, pp.1–11, Macmillan, London, New York, 1981)

Kenyon, Nicholas, 'Tippett's Act of Creation' (*Sunday Times*, 1 April 1984, p. 37)

Klein, John W., 'Some Reflections on *King Priam*' (*Musical Opinion* 86, February 1963, p. 273)

Laaff, Ernst, 'Gesprach mit Michael Tippett' (*Musikleben* 2, July/August 1949, pp.190–1)

Labie, Jean-François, 'Connaissez-vous Michael Tippett' (*Diapason*, no. 266, November 1981, pp. 30–1)

Lange, Art, 'Tippett's Fourth Symphony' (*Tempo*, no. 123,

December 1977, pp. 53–4)

Lewis, Geraint (ed), 'Behind Tippett's Mask' (*Musical Times*, vol. 129, no. 1741 February 1988, pp.74–7)

—'Contemporary Composer Series: Sir Michael Tippett' (*Music Teacher* 65, October 1986, pp. 23–6)

—*The Ice Break*; *King Priam*; *The Knot Garden*; *The Midsummer Marriage*; and *New Year* in *New Grove Dictionary of Opera*, vol. 2, p.780, pp. 994–6; pp.1011–2; vol. 3, pp. 377–9, 585)

—'*New Year* in the New World' (*Musical Times*, vol. 130, no. 1761, November 1989, pp. 665–9)

—'New Year is Here' (*Musical Times*, vol. 131, no. 1769, July 1990, pp.355–7)

—'Tippett' in *New Grove Dictionary of Opera*, vol. 4, pp. 724–44

—'Tippett: The Breath of Life: An Approach to Formal Structure' (*Musical Times*, 126, January 1985, pp.18–20)

Manning, R. J., 'A Child of Our Time' (*Monthly Musical Record*, 75, October 1945, pp.176–82)

Mason, Colin, 'Michael Tippett' (*Musical Times*, vol. 87, no. 1239, May 1946, pp.137–41)

—'Tippett and his Oratorio' (*Listener*, vol. 38, no. 972, 11 September, 1947, p. 452)

—'Michael Tippett's Opera' (*Listener*, vol. 53, no. 1439, 20 January 1955, p.129)

—'Tippett's Piano Concerto' (*The Score*, no. 16, June 1956, pp. 63–8)

—'Michael Tippett's Piano Concerto' (*Listener*, vol. 56, no. 1439, 25 October 1956, p. 681)

—'Chamber Music in Britain since 1929' in *Cobbett's Cyclopaedic Survey of Chamber Music*, vol. 3 (OUP, 2nd edition, 1963, pp. 99–103)

Mellers, Wilfrid, 'Tippett and his Piano Concerto' (*Listener*, vol. 61, no. 1554, 8 January, 1959, p. 80)

—'Michael Tippett and the String Quartet' (*Listener*, vol. 66, no. 1694, 14 September 1961, p. 405)

—'Michael Tippett in 1957' (*Listener*, vol. 57, 28 March 1957, p. 533)

—'New Trends in Britain: A Note on Rubbra and Tippett' (*Modern Music* 21 No. 4, 1944, pp. 212–16

—'Recent Trends in British Music' (*Musical Quarterly* 38, April 1952, pp.185–201)

Milner, Anthony, 'An Introductory Note to Tippett's *Midsummer Marriage*' (*Musical Times*, 96, January 1955, pp.19–20)

—'Rhythmic Techniques in the Music of Michael Tippett' (*Musical Times*, vol. 95, no. 1339, September 1954, pp.468–70)

—'The Music of Michael Tippett' (*Musical Quarterly*, vol. 50, no. 4, October 1964, pp. 432–8)

Newman, Ernest, 'Verbal & Musical Rhythm' (*Sunday Times*, 6 January 1946, p. 2; 13 January 1946, p.2)

Northcott, Bayan, 'Bayan Northcott Writes about Tippett's Early Work' (*Listener*, 86, 11 November 1971, p. 666)

—'Composers of the Sixties: Michael Tippett' (*Music & Musicians*, 18, January 1970, pp. 32–6, 40)

—'Opening Up: British Concert Music Since the War' (*Musical Newsletter* 5, no. 3, 1975, pp. 3–9)

—'Since Grimes: A Concise Survey of the British Musical Stage' (*Musical Newsletter* No. 4, Spring, 1974, pp. 7–11, 21–2

—'Tippett Today' (*Music and Musicians*, vol. 19, no. 3, November 1970, pp. 34–5, 38, 40, 42–5)

—'Tippett's Third Symphony' (*Music and Musicians*, vol. 20, no. 10, June 1972)

Oliver, Michael, 'Tippett at 80: Images of Reconciliation' (*Gramophone* 62, February 1985, pp. 965–6)

—'Tippett's *King Priam*' (*Gramophone* 59, November 1981, p. 669)

Ottaway, Hugh, 'Michael Tippett: The Composer's World and its Development Through to *The Knot Garden* and Third Symphony' (*HiFi News and Record Review*, 19, April 1974, pp.91–2

Payne, Anthony, 'Tippett's *The Vision of St Augustine*' (*Tempo*, no. 76, Spring 1966, pp.19–21)

Pettitt, Stephen, 'New Worlds in "New Year"' (*Opera*, vol. 61, 1990, pp. 672–6)

Pirie, Peter J., *The English Musical Renaissance* (Gollancz, London, 1979)

—'Michael Tippett: A Child of Our Time' (*Musical Opinion* 182, January 1959, pp.235–6)

—'Tippett at Sixty' (*Listener*, I72, 31 December 1964, p.1069)

Pople, Anthony, 'Tippett, Sir Michael (Kemp)' in Brian Morton and Pamela Collins (eds), *Contemporary Composers* (St James Press, Chicago and London, 1992, pp. 923–6)

Porter, Andrew, '*The Midsummer Marriage*' (*Opera*, 6, February 1955, pp.77–82)

—'*The Ice Break*' (*New Yorker*, 19 September 1977; reprinted in *About the House*, vol. 5, no. 4, Christmas 1977, pp. 48–50)

Puffett, Derrick, 'The Fugue from Tippett's Second String Quartet' (*Music Analysis* 5, July/October 1986, pp. 233–64)

—'Tippett at 90' (*Musical Times*, vol. 136, no. 1823, January 1995, pp.6–14)

Rees, David, 'Slightly dotty, rather Messianic: Michael Tippett' in *Words and Music* (Millivres Books, Brighton, 1993), pp.143–54

Richards, Denis, 'Ruin – and Recovery' in *Offspring of the Vic: A History of Morley College*, pp. 248–71 (Hodder & Stoughton, London; Taplinger, New York; 1968)

Rodda, Richard Earl, 'Genesis of a Symphony: Tippett's Symphony No. 3' (*Music Review* 39, May 1978, pp.110–16)

Rosenthal, Harold, 'Midsummer Reflections on *The Knot Garden*: Peter Hall talks to Harold Rosenthal' (*Opera* 21, December 1970, pp.1090–3)

—'Tippett on Opera: Sir Michael Tippett talks to the Editor' (*Opera* 23, December 1972, pp.1055–9)

Rubbra, Edmund, '*The Vision of St Augustine*' (*Listener*, vol. 75, no. 1920, 13 January 1966, p.74)

Saremba, Meinhard, 'Schöne neue Welten – Michael Tippett (geb. 1905)' in *Elgar, Britten & Co: Eine Geschichte der britischen Musik in zwolf Portraits* (M & T Verlag AG, Zurich/St Gallen, 1994).

Schafer, Murray, *British Composers in Interview*, pp. 92–102 (Faber, 1963)

Scheppach, Margaret, 'Michael Tippett' in C. Steven Lane (ed.), *International Dictionary of Opera* (St James Press, Detroit, London, Washington DC, 1990), vol. 2, pp.1344–6

– *'The Ice Break'*, *'The Knot Garden'*, *'New Year'* (ibid. vol. 1, p. 627; pp. 691–2; vol. 2, pp. 929–30)

Sillars, Stuart, *'A Child of Our Time'* in *British Romantic Art and the Second World War* (Macmillan, London, 1991), ch. 6, pp.124–41

Souster, Tim, 'Michael Tippett's Vision' (*Musical Times*, vol. 107, no. 1475, January 1966, pp. 20–2)

Spence, Keith, *'Midsummer Marriage* and its Critics – A Topical Retrospect'* (*Musical Times*, vol. 112, no. 1535, January 1971, p. 28)

Sternfeld, Frederick, 'Midwinter Birthday' (*Records and Recording* 18, January 1975, pp.14–16)

—and David Harvey, 'Musical Magpie: Words and Music in Michael Tippett's Operas' (*Parnassus: Poetry in Review* 10, Fall/Winter, 1982, pp.188–98)

Stuart, Charles, 'Morley College Music' (*Musical Times*, vol. 92, September 1951, pp.393–8)

Sutcliffe, Tom, 'Tippett and *The Knot Garden*' (*Music and Musicians*, vol. 19, no. 4, December 1970, pp. 52–4)

Tear, Robert, *Tear Here*, pp.111–19 (André Deutsch, London, 1990)

Thomas, Philip, 'Tippett's Piano Sonatas' (*Tempo* no. 195, January 1996)

Thorne, Michael, 'Michael Tippett' (*Hi Fi News and Record Review* 20, January 1975, pp.115, 117)

Trilling, Ossia, 'Gesprach mit dem Komponisten Sir Michael

Tippett' (*Opernwelt*, 18, no. 9, 1977, p. 45)

Truding, Lorna, 'Ein Kind unserer Zeit' (*Neue Zeitschrift für Musik*, 118, November 1957, p. 667)

—*König Priamos*, Michael Tippett's neue Oper: Uraufführung in Coventry (*Das Goetheanum* 41, 1962), pp. 340–2

Walker, Jane, 'Parables for Our Time' (*Classic CD*, Issue 4, August 1990, pp. 34–7)

Wanamaker, Sam, 'Preparing for *The Ice Break*' (*Opera*, 28, July 1977, pp. 629–32)

Warrack, John, '*The Ice Break*' (*Musical Times*, vol. 118, no. 1613, July 1977, pp. 553–6)

—'*The Knot Garden*' (*Musical Times*, 111, November 1970, pp.1092–3, 95)

—'Tippett and his new opera' (*Opera*, 26, January 1975, pp.12–16)

—'Tippett's Concerto for Three' (*Classical Music*, 16 August 1980, p.7)

—'*The Vision of St Augustine*' (*Musical Times*, vol. 107, no. 1477, March, 1966, pp. 228–9)

Whittall, Arnold 'Lately celebrated' (*Musical Times*, vol. 136, no. 1827, May 1995, pp.238–40)

—'Resisting Tonality: Tippett, Beethoven and the sarabande' (*Musical Analysis*, 9: 1990, pp. 267–86

—'Three Individualists' in *Music since the First World War* (OUP, 1977, pp. 212–34)

—'A War and a Wedding: Two Modern British Operas' (*Music and Letters* 55, no. 3, 1974, pp. 299–306)

Tippett on Television and Video

(Commercial video recordings of complete performances of Tippett compositions are included in the Worklist and Discography on pp.284–305)

Programmes marked * below are commercially available

Poets in a Barren Age Documentary directed by Mischa Scorer (BBC, 1971)

Sir Michael Tippett: A Musical Biography Interview with Melvyn Bragg, interspersed with lengthy extracts from Tippett compositions played by the London Sinfonietta conducted by David Atherton. Directed by Alan Benson (London Weekend Television: *The South Bank Show*, 1979)*

Composer and Audience: Tippett and Sondheim Interview with Trevor Herbert centred on a section of *The Mask of Time*. Directed by Tony Coe (BBC Open University, 1984)

Tippett and his Fourth Piano Sonata Interview, also featuring Paul Crossley. Directed by Ken Price (Harlech Television, 1985)

A Full Life Interview with Jill Cochrane. Directed by John Miller (TV South; now Meridian Television, 1985)

Tippett at Malvern Programme centred on Malvern Festival's celebrations of Tippett's eightieth birthday. Directed by Keith Cheetham (BBC, 1985)

Wege sur neuen Musik: Tippett Interview with Gerd Albrecht plus rehearsal and performance of Triple Concerto (Berlin Radio Orchestra). Directed by Barrie Gavin (Senders Frei, Berlin 1988)

Sinfonietta 2: Singing the Uncertainties Interview with Paul Crossley and performance of *Songs for Dov* with Nigel Robson (tenor)/London Sinfonietta conducted by the composer. Directed by Derek Bailey (London Weekend Television, 1989)

Songs of Experience: Tippett at 85 Documentary directed by Mischa Scorer, including introduction to *New Year*, with excerpts from Houston Opera rehearsals and world première (Antelope West/BBC 1991)

Tippett's New Quartet Rehearsal of Tippett's Fifth String Quartet by Lindsay Quartet at the composer's home; followed by the world première performance at Octagon Theatre, Sheffield, May 1992. Directed by Tony Scull (Yorkshire Television)

List of Works and Select Discography

The following is a chronological list of Tippett's compositions. Details of scoring and other requirements of the published works are contained in the complete catalogue available from the composer's exclusive publishers, Schott & Co. Ltd, 48 Great Marlborough Street, London W1V 2BN. A twice-yearly newsletter, *Tippett in Focus*, containing up-to-date information on the composer and forthcoming performances of his music can also be obtained free of charge from Schott & Co Ltd. A complete Chronological Discography, compiled by Alan Woolgar, can likewise be obtained from Schott. My own Select Discography eschews nostalgia in favour of realism: thus nothing pre-vinyl or for wind-up gramophones is included; also, bearing in mind the volatile state of the recording industry, I have given details only of the latest reissues of older recordings. Lastly, I should mention that information about Tippett is now available on the Internet: **http://www.schott.music.com**

Most of Tippett's compositions exist in two manuscript versions: a preliminary pencil score and a 'final' copy in ink. The composer abandoned this procedure only during the composition of *The Mask of Time*, when easy access to photocopiers made the labour of producing a neat hand-copied version in ink unnecessary. Apart from a few items acquired for other collections, or missing, the manuscripts of Tippett's published works, either complete or incomplete, are all at the British Library.

Early Works

(Some of these are incomplete; the manuscripts of some are also lost.)

c.1926/27 'Bolsters – a ballet'; 'The House that Jack Built': 'Cheerly Men': 'Yang-Tsi-Kiang'; 'Three Jovial Huntsmen' (all arrangements for piano trio)

c.1927 'The Undying Fire' (H.G. Wells), for baritone, Chorus and Orchestra

1927/29 *The Village Opera* (ballad opera in 3 acts with text and music by composer)

c.1928 String Quartet in F minor

1928/30 Concerto in D for flutes, oboe, horn and strings

1928 String Quartet No. 2 in F major (revised 1930)
Songs for voice and piano, on texts by Charlotte Mary Mew ('Sea Love'; 'Afternoon Tea'; 'Arracombe Wood')
Sonata in C minor

1929 Variations for Dudley (Parvin), for piano
Ten Variations on a Swiss folksong as harmonized by Beethoven
Three Songs (Charlotte Mew) for voice and piano ('Sea Love'; 'Afternoon Tea'; 'Arracombe Fair')

1930 'Jockey to the Fair': Variations for piano
'Psalm in C – The Gateway', for chorus and small orchestra (text by Christopher Fry)
Incidental music to James Elroy Flecker's *Don Juan*
Sonata in E minor, for violin and piano

c.1930/1 Symphonic Movement for full orchestra

1932 String Trio in B flat

1933/34 Symphony No. 1 in B flat (revised in 1934)

1934 *Robin Hood* (ballad opera, dialogue by David Ayerst, lyrics by Ruth Pennyman)

c.1935 'Miners', for chorus and piano (text by Judy Wogan)

1937 'A Song of Liberty', for chorus and orchestra (text from Wiilliam Blake's *The Marriage of Heaven and Hell*)

1938 *Robert of Sicily* (opera for children, text by Christopher Fry, adapted from Robert Downing, music arranged by the composer for children's choirs, trumpet, clarinet, cello, piano and bell)

1939 *Seven at One Stroke* (play for children, text by Christopher Fry, music arranged by the composer for flute, clarinet, trumpet, violin, cello, piano)

Published works

1934/35 **String Quartet No. 1** (revised 1943)

First performance by the Brosa Quartet, London, Mercury Theatre
9 December 1935; revised version by the Zorian Quartet, Wigmore
Hall, London, 26 February 1944   20 mins

Edinburgh Quartet
(latest reissue EMI CMS 7 635222)
Fidelio Quartet
(latest reissue PRT GSGC 7057; cassette PRT ZCGC 7057)
Lindsay Quartet
(latest reissue ASV CDDCS 231)
Britten Quartet
(latest reissue Collins Classics 70222)
Kreutzer Quartet
(Chandos CHAN 9560)

1936/37 **Sonata No. 1** (for Piano); revised 1942 and 1954 (originally titled
'Fantasy Sonata')
First performed by Phyllis Sellick, Queen Mary Hall, London,
November 11, 1938)   21 mins

Margaret Kitchin
(Lyrita RCS 5)
John Ogdon
(latest reissue EMI CMS 7 635222)
Paul Crossley
(Philips 6580 06)
Stephen Savage
(Queensland Conservatorium Muscon TAM 0639)
Paul Crossley (2nd recording)
(latest reissue CRD CRD 3430/1)
Ananda Sukarlan
(Erasmus Muziek Producties WVH 139)
Nicholas Unwin
(Chandos CHAN 9468)

1938/39 **Concerto for Double String Orchestra**
First performed by South London Orchestra, conducted by the
composer, Morley College, London, 21 April 1940   23 mins

Philharmonia Orchestra, conducted by Walter Goehr
(latest reissue Music for Pleasure MFP 2069)
Bath Festival Orchestra/Moscow Chamber Orchestra, conducted by
Rudolf Barshai
(latest reissue HMV Classics HMV 5 687832)
Academy of St Martin-in-the-Fields, conducted by Neville Marriner
(latest reissue Decca 421 389 4)

London Philharmonic Orchestra, conducted by Vernon Handley
(latest reissue Classics for Pleasure CFPSD 4754)
Bournemouth Symphony Orchestra, conducted by Rudolf Barshai
(EMI EL 27 0273 1/ Cassette EL 0273 4/ CD CDC 747 3302)
Scottish Chamber Orchestra conducted by the composer
(latest reissue Virgin Ultra Violet CUV 5 61326 2)
English String Orchestra, conducted by William Boughton
(latest reissue Nimbus NI 7026)
Academy of St Martin-in-the-Fields, conducted by Sir Neville Marriner
(EMI CDC 555 452-2)
City of London Sinfonia, conducted by Richard Hickox
(Chandos CHAN 9409)
BBC Symphony Orchestra, conducted by Andrew Davis
(Teldec 4509 945 2)
English Sinfonia conducted by John Farrer
(Carlton Classics 30366 00542)

1939/41 *Fantasia on a Theme of Handel.* for piano and orchestra
First performed by Phyllis Sellick with the Walter Goehr Orchestra conducted by Walter Goehr, Wigmore Hall, London, 7 March 1942
16 mins

Margaret Kitchin/London Symphony Orchestra, conducted by the composer
(latest reissue BMG 75605 513042
Howard Shelley/Bournemouth Symphony Orchestra conducted by Richard Hickox
(Chandos CHAN 9233)

A Child of Our Time (oratorio for SATB soloists, chorus and orchestra, with text by the composer)   66 mins

Elsie Morrison, Pamela Bowden, Richard Lewis, Richard Standen/Royal Liverpool Philharmonic Orchestra and Chorus, conducted by John Pritchard
(latest reissue: CD Belart 461 1232 cassette Belart 461 1234)
Jessye Norman, Janet Baker, Richard Cassilly,
John Shirley-Quirk/BBC Singers/BBC Choral Society/ BBC Symphony Orchestra, conducted by Colin Davis
(latest reissue Philips 446331-2)
Sheila Armstrong, Felicity Palmer, Philip Langridge, John Shirley-Quirk/Brighton Festival Chorus/Royal Philharmonic Orchestra, conducted by André Previn
(latest reissue IMP Classics 30367 02052)

Faye Robinson, Sarah Walker, Jonn Garrison, John Cheek/City of Birmingham Symphony Orchestra and Chorus, conducted by the composer
(Collins Classics 13392)
Cynthia Haymon, Cynthia Clarey, Damon Evans, Willard White/London Symphony Orchestra and Chorus, conducted by Richard Hickox
(Chandos CHAN 9123)
Jill Gomez, Helen Watts, Kenneth Woollamm, John Shirley-Quirk/BBC Symphony Chorus/BBC Symphony Orchestra, conducted by Gennadi Rozhdestvensky
Carlton Classics BBCRD 9130

'Five Negro Spirituals' (from *A Child of Our Time*) (unaccompanied version)

Canterbury Cathedral Choir, conducted by Allan Wicks
(Grosvenor GRO 1034)
Leeds Parish Church Choir, conducted by Donald Hunt
(Abbey LPB 754)
Schola Cantorum of Oxford, conducted by Nicholas Cleobury)
(L'Oiseau Lyre DSLO 25)
Cambridge University Chamber Choir, conducted by Richard Marlow
(latest reissue Gamut GAM CD502)
Christ Church Cathedral Choir, Oxford, conducted by Stephen Darlington
(Latest reissue: Nimbus NI 7026)
Hull Choral Union, conducted by Alan Spedding
(Hull Choral Union [no catalogue no.])
Choir of Canterbury Cathedral, conducted by David Flood
(York CD 116)
Cora da Cultura Inglesa, São Paolo, conducted by Celso Antunes
(H & B Fonographica 616007)
Vancouver Bach Choir, conducted by Bruce Pullan
(CBC SMCD 5121)
Finzi Singers, conducted by Paul Spicer
(Chandos CHAN 9265)
The Sixteen, conducted by Harry Christophers
(Collins Classics 14462)

1941/42   **String Quartet No. 2 in F sharp**
First performed by the Zorian Quartet, Wigmore Hall, 27 March 1943   21 mins

Amadeus Quartet
(latest reissue Argo DA 34)
Fidelio Quartet
(latest reissue PRT GSGC 2064)
Lindsay Quartet
(latest reissue SASV CDD CS 231)
Britten Quartet
(latest reissue Collins Classics 70222)
Carl Pini Quartet
(Australian HMV SQXLP 7552)
Kreutzer Quartet
(Chandos CHAN 9560)

1942 **Two Madrigals** for unaccompanied chorus SATB
'The Windhover' (poem by Gerard Manley Hopkins)   2 mins
'The Source' (poem by Edward Thomas)   3 mins
First performed by Morley College Choir, conducted by Walter
Bergmann, Morley College, London, 17 July 1943

Schola Cantorum of Oxford, conducted by Nicholas Cleobury
(L'Oiseau Lyre DSLO 25)
Finzi Singers, conducted by Paul Spicer
(Chandos CHAN 9384)

1943 '**Boyhood's End**' (cantata on a text by W. H. Hudson, for tenor and
piano)   12 mins
Manuscript (ink): Britten/Pears Library, Aldeburgh, UK
First performed by Peter Pears and Benjamin Britten, Morley
College, 5 June 1943

Peter Pears/Noel Mewton-Wood
(latest reissue ARGO DA 34)
Philip Langridge/John Constable
(L'Oiseau Lyre DSLO 14)
Martyn Hill/Andrew Ball
(Hyperion CDA 66749)
Stanford Olsen/Craig Rutenberg
(Musical Heritage Society 513383F)

Fanfare No. 1, for 4 horns, 3 trumpets and 3 trombones
First performed by the Band of the Northamptonshire Regiment,
conducted by C. Marriott, St Matthew's Church, Northampton, 21
September 1943   3 mins

Locke Brass Consort, conducted by James Stobart

(latest reissue: Chandos CHAN 6573)
Philip Jones Brass Ensemble, conducted by Howard Snell
(latest reissue: London 430 369 2)

'Plebs angelica', motet for double chorus
First performed by the Fleet Street Choir, conducted by T. B.
Lawrence, Canterbury Cathedral, on 16 September 1944   4 mins

Canterbury Cathedral Choir, conducted by Allan Wicks
(Grosvenor GRS 1030)
Royal College of Music Anniversary Service, Westminster Abbey
(EMI ESD 7172)
Christ Church Cathedral Choir, Oxford, conducted by Stephen
Darlington
(Nimbus NI 5266)
The Finzi Singers, conducted by Paul Spicer
(Chandos CHAN 9384)
St Paul's Cathedral Choir, conducted by John Scott
(Hyperion CDA 66826)

1944   **'The Weeping Babe'**, for soprano solo and unaccompanied chorus
SATB (poem by Edith Sitwell)   3 mins
First performed by BBC Singers, conducted by Leslie Woodgate,
BBC Home Service, 24 December, 1944

John Alldis Choir, conducted by John Alldis
(latest reissue Decca 425 1582)
Schola Cantorum of Oxford, conducted by Nicholas Cleobury
(L'Oiseau Lyre DSLO 25)
Christ Church Cathedral Choir, Oxford, conducted by Stephen
Darlington
(Nimbus NI 5266)
The Finzi Singers, conducted by Paul Spicer
(Chandos CHAN 9265)

1944/45   **Symphony No. 1**
First performed by the Liverpool Philharmonic Orchestra, conducted
by Malcolm Sargent, Philharmonic Hall, Liverpool, on 10 November
1945   35 mins

London Symphony Orchestra, conducted by Colin Davis
(latest reissue Decca 425 646 2)
Bournemouth Symphony Orchestra, conducted by Richard Hickox
(Chandos CHAN 9333)

1945/46   **String Quartet No. 3**
First performed by the Zorian Quartet, Wigmore Hall, 19 October

1946   31 mins

Fidelio Quartet
(latest reissue PRT GSCG 7057)
Lindsay Quartet
(latest reissue ASV CDDCS 231)
Duke Quartet
(Factory FACD 246)
Britten Quartet
(latest reissue Collins Classics 70222)
Kreutzer Quartet
(Chandos CHAN 9512)

1946   **Preludio al Vespro di Monteverdi**, for organ
First performed by Geraint Jones, Central Hall, Westminster, 5 July
1946 (prior to a performance of Monteverdi's *Vespers* (1610))

                                                            4 mins

Paul Morgan (Exeter Cathedral organ)
(EXON EAS 18)
Simon Preston (organ of Colston Hall, Bristol)
(latest reissue Decca 414 647 1)

'Little Music', for string orchestra
First performed by the Jacques Orchestra, conducted by Reginald
Jacques, Wigmore Hall, 9 November 1946   10 mins

Academy of St Martin-in-the-Fields, conducted by Neville Marriner
(latest reissue Decca 421 389 4)
Orchestra of St John's, Smith Square, conducted by John Lubbock
(OYE TPLS 13069)
Soloists of Australia, conducted by Ronald Thomas
(Latest reissue Chandos CHAN 6576)
Guildhall String Ensemble, conducted by Robert Salter
(RCA RD 87846)
English Sinfonia, conducted by John Farrer
(Pickwick IMP Masters MCD 60)
CBC Vancouver Chamber Orchestra, conducted by John Avison
(CBC SM 124)
English String Orchestra, conducted by William Boughton
(Nimbus NI 7026)
Academy of St Martin-in-the-Fields
(EMI CDC 555 452-2)

1946/52   *The Midsummer Marriage*, opera in 3 acts with text by the
composer

First performed by the Royal Opera, Covent Garden, London, conducted by John Pritchard, produced by Christopher West, scenery and costumes by Barbara Hepworth and choreography by John Cranko, Royal Opera House, Covent Garden, 27 January 1955

180 mins

Soloists, Chorus and Orchestra of the Royal Opera House, Covent Garden, conducted by Colin Davis
(Lyrita SRCD 2217)

Ritual Dances (from *The Midsummer Marriage*)   29 mins
for (optional) soloists/chorus and orchestra
First performed by the Basel Kammerorchester, conducted by Paul Sacher, Basel, 13 February 1953
Royal Liverpool Orchestra and Choir, conducted by John Pritchard
(latest reissue ARGO DPA 571/2)
Excerpt from complete recording of the opera (above) (not the concert version): Soloists/Royal Opera House Chorus and Orchestra, conducted by Colin Davis
(Latest reissue: Philips 7311 112)
Bournemouth Symphony Orchestra, conducted by Rudolf Barshai
(EMI EL 27 0273/1/Cassette EL 0273 4/CD CDC 747 22 3302)
Soloists, Chorus & Orchestra of Opera North/English Northern Sinfonia, conducted by the composer
(Nimbus NI 5217)
BBC Symphony Chorus and Orchestra, conducted by Andrew Davis
(Teldec 4509 945 2)

Sosostris's aria (from *The Midsummer Marriage*)

Alfreda Hodgson (mezzo soprano)
Orchestra of Opera North, conducted by the composer
(Nimbus NI 5217)

1948   **Suite in D (*Suite for the Birthday of Prince Charles*)**, for orchestra
First performed by the BBC Symphony Orchestra, conducted by Adrian Boult, BBC Third Programme, 15 November 1948

16 mins

Leicestershire Schools Symphony Orchestra, conducted by the composer
(PYE GSGC 14103)
London Symphony Orchestra, conducted by Colin Davis
(Philips 412 378 1/cassette 412 378 4)
Chicago Symphony Orchestra, conducted by Georg Solti

(latest reissue Decca 425 646 2)
Orchestra of Opera North, conducted by the composer
(Nimbus NI 5217)

1950/51   **The Heart's Assurance**, song-cycle for high voice and piano (poems by Sidney Keyes and Alun Lewis)
First performed by Peter Pears and Benjamin Britten, Wigmore Hall, 5 May 1971   17 mins
Manuscripts: Britten/Pears Library, Aldeburgh, UK

Peter Pears/Noel Mewton-Wood
(latest reissue: Argo DA34)
Philip Langridge/John Constable
(L'Oiseau Lyre DSLO 14)
Martyn Hill/Andrew Ball
(Hyperion CDA 66749)
Margaret Field/Andrew Ball
(Redcliffe Recordings RR009)

Version with chamber orchestra accompaniment (arranged Meirion Bowen)
John Mark-Ainsley, City of London Sinfonia, conducted by Richard Hickox
(Chandos CHAN 9409)

1952   **Dance, Clarion Air**, madrigal for five voices SATB, with text by Christopher Fry
First performed by the Golden Age Singers and the Cambridge University Madrigal Society, conducted by Boris Ord, Royal Festival Hall, London, 1 June 1953   5 mins

Golden Age Singers, Cambridge University Madrigal Society,, conducted by Boris Ord

(Columbia 33CX 1063)
Canterbury Cathedral Choir, conducted by Allan Wicks
(Grosvenor GRS 1030)
Schola Cantorum of Oxford, conducted by Nicholas Cleobury
(L'Oiseau Lyre DSLO 25)
St Cecilia Singers, conducted by Andrew Millington
(Abbey Alpha ACA 514)
Christ Church Cathedral Choir, Oxford, conducted by Stephen Darlington
(Nimbus NI 5266)
Cambridge University Chamber Choir, Director: Timothy Brown
(Gamut GAM CD 529)

Bristol Bach Choir, conducted by Glyn Jenkins
(Priory PRCD 352)
Finzi Singers, conducted by Paul Spicer
(Chandos CHAN 9265)

1953   ***Fantasia Concertante on a Theme of Corelli***, for string orchestra
First performed by the BBC Symphony Orchestra, conducted by the
composer, Usher Hall, Edinburgh, 29 August 1953

16 mins

Manuscripts: Fitzwilliam Museum, Cambridge (pencil); British
Library (ink, with some pencil sketches), 1st section only
Bath Festival Orchestra, conducted by the composer
(latest reissue: HMV Classics HMV 5 687832)
Academy of St Martin-in-the-Fields, conducted by Neville Marriner
(latest reissue Decca 421 389 4)
Orchestra of St John's, Smith Square, conducted by John Lubbock
(PYE TPLS 13069)
Academy of St Martin-in-the-Fields, conducted by Neville Marriner
(latest reissue Decca 421 389 4)
Scottish Chamber Orchestra, conducted by the composer
(latest reissue Virgin Ultra Violet CUV 5 61326 2)
Royal Philharmonic Orchestra, conducted by Sir Charles Groves
(latest reissue Carlton Home Entertainment 3036700682)
Academy of St Martin-in-the-Fields, directed by Kenneth Sillito
(Collins Classics 12292)
English String Orchestra, conducted by William Boughton
(latest reissue Nimbus NI 7026)
Bournemouth Symphony Orchestra, conducted by Richard Hickox
(Chandos CHAN 9233)
St Paul Chamber Orchestra, conducted by Christopher Hogwood
(Decca 440 376 2)
National Arts Centre Orchestra, conducted by Mario Bernardi
(CBC SM 287)
Norwegian Chamber Orchestra, directed by Iona Brown
(NAIM Audio NAIM CD 009)
BBC Symphony Orchestra, conducted by Andrew Davis
(Teldec 4509 945 2)
BBC Symphony Orchestra, conductedby Raymond Leppard
(BBC Radio Classics BBC RD 9140)

Fanfare No. 2, for 4 trumpets*   2 mins

*Tippett was asked to write this for the 1953 St Ives Festival. It proved too difficult for the
amateur players there, so he wrote a simpler one, Fanfare No. 3, which they were able to
perform. The details of the eventual first performance of Fanfare No. 2 are undocumented.

The Wallace Collection
(Collins Classics 12294 CD 12342)

Fanfare No. 3, for 3 trumpets
First performed by trumpeters from RAF St Mawgan, Cornwall,
6 June 1953   1 min

1953/54   ***Divertimento on Sellinger's Round***, for chamber orchestra
First performed by the Collegium Musicum Zurich, conducted by
Paul Sacher, 5 November 1954   16 mins
Manuscripts: British Library (pencil) – movements 3, 4, 5. with
pencil score of 'Four Inventions for Recorders': movements 1 and 2
(pencil) and 3, 4, 5 (ink) Paul Sacher Stiftung, Basel

English Chamber Orchestra, conducted by Norman Del Mar
(Lyrita SCRS 111)
Academy of St Martin-in-the-Fields, conducted by Neville Marriner
(EMI CDC 555 452-2)
City of London Sinfonia, conducted by Richard Hickox
(Chandos CHAN 9409)
National Arts Centre Orchestra, Vancouver, conducted by Mario
Bernardi
(CBC SM 287)

1953/55   **Concerto for Piano and Orchestra**
First performed by Louis Kentner and the City of Birmingham
Symphony Orchestra, conducted by Rudolf Schwarz, Town Hall,
Birmingham, 30 October 1950   30 mins
Manuscript: The Barber Institute, University of Birmingham

John Ogdon/Philharmonia Orchestra, conducted by Colin Davis
(latest reissue: HMV ClassicsHMV 5 687832)
Martino Tirimo/BBC Philharmonic Orchestra, conducted by the
composer
(Nimbus NI 5301)
Howard Shelley/Bournemouth Symphony Orchestra, conducted by
Richard Hickox
(Chandos CHAN 9233)

1954   **Four Inventions**, for one descant and one treble recorder
First performed by Freda Dinn and Walter Bergmann at the Froebel
Institute, Roehampton, 1 August 1954 at Froebel Institute
                                                        9 mins

1955   **Sonata for four horns**

First performed by the Dennis Brain Wind Ensemble, Wigmore Hall,
London, 20 December 1955   20 mins

Barry Tuckwell Horn Quartet
(Argo ZRG 535)
The Wallace Collection
(Collins Classics 12292)
Michael Thompson Horn Quartet
(EMI CDC 555 452-2)

1956   **Bonny at Morn** (Northumbrian folksong, set for unison voices,
2 descant recorders and 1 treble recorder)
First performed at the International Pestalozzi Children's Village
10th anniversary, Trogen, Switzerland, April 1956   3 mins

Schola Cantorum of Oxford, conducted by Nicholas Cleobury
(L'Oiseau Lyre DSLO 25)
Christ Church Cathedral Choir, Oxford, and instrumental ensemble,
conducted by Stephen Darlington
(Nimbus NI 5266)

Four songs from the British Isles, unaccompanied chorus SATB
(1. England: 'Early One Morning'; 2. Ireland: 'Lilliburlero';
3. Scotland: 'Poortith cauld'; 4. Wales: 'Gwenllian')
First performed by the London Bach Group, conductor, John
Minchinton, in the Abbaye de Royaumont, Seine-et-Oise, France,
6 July 1956   14 mins

Schola Cantorum of Oxford, conducted by Nicholas Cleobury
(L'Oiseau Lyre DSLO 25)
National Youth Choir, conducted by Michael Brewer
(Pickwick PCD 10077)
Finzi Singers, conducted by Pual Spicer
(Chandos CHAN 9265)

1956/57 **Symphony No. 2**
First performed by the BBC Symphony Orchestra, conducted by Sir
Adrian Boult, Royal Festival Hall, London, 5 February 1958
32 mins

London Symphony Orchestra, conducted by Colin Davis
(latest reissue Decca 425 646 2)
Bournemouth Symphony Orchestra, conducted by Richard Hickox
(Chandos CHAN 9299)
BBC Symphony Orchestra, conducted by the composer
(*BBC Music Magazine* vol. III No. 6)

1958   **Crown of the Year**, cantata with text by Christopher Fry for chorus (SSA), descant and treble recorders (or flutes), oboe, clarinet, trumpet (or cornet), percussion, (drum, Indian bells, handbells, xylophone) and piano   28 mins
First peformed by Badminton School Choir and Ensemble, Badminton School, Bristol, conducted by the composer, 25 July 1958
Christ Church Cathedral Choir, Oxford, and instrumental ensemble, conducted by Stephen Darlington
(Nimbus NI 5266)

Prelude: Autumn, for oboe and piano (arr. by Meirion Bowen from section 6 of 'Crown of the Year')   4 mins

'Wadhurst', hymn tune ('Unto the hills around do I lift up my longing eyes') Written for the Salvation Army and published in the *Musical Salvationist* (July/August 1958)

1958/61   **King Priam**, opera in 3 acts with text by the composer
First performed by the Royal Opera, Covent Garden, conducted by John Pritchard, produced by Sam Wanamaker and with scenery and costumes by Sean Kenny, Coventry Theatre, Coventry, 29 May 1962.
Manuscripts: Library of Congress (pencil)
British Library (ink)   116 mins
Soloists, London Sinfonietta Chorus, London Sinfonietta, conducted by David Atherton

(latest reissue Chandos CHAN 9406/7)

Kent Opera/Channel 4 TV production (originally directed by Nicholas Hytner), conducted by Roger Norrington, directed for television by Robin Lowe and designed by David Fielding
(Video issued by RM Arts/Polygram 079-248-3)

Prelude, Recitative and Aria: arrangement (1963) of third interlude from Act III of *King Priam*, for flute, oboe and piano (or harpsichord)   5 mins
First performed by Oriana Trio, BBC Radio, February, 1964

1960   **'Music'**, unison song, for voices, strings and piano, or voices and piano (poem by Shelley)
First performed by the combined choirs of the East Sussex and West Kent Choral Festival, conducted by Trevor Harvey, Assembly Hall, Tunbridge Wells, Kent, 26 April 1980   4 mins

Christ Church Cathedral Choir, Oxford, and instrumental ensemble,
conducted by Stephen Darlington
(Nimbus NI 5266)

'**Words for Music Perhaps**', incidental music for speaking voice(s),
bass clarinet, trumpet, gong, xylophone, violin, cello and piano, to a
sequence of poems by W. B. Yeats
First performed BBC Third Programme, Bee Duffell, Sheila
Manahan, Allan McCelland with ensemble, conducted by the
composer; 8 June 1960. First concert performance, Michael Hordern,
English Chamber Orchestra, conducted by Norman Del Mar, Queen
Elizabeth Hall, London, 9 January 1980   14 mins

'**Lullaby**', for six voices, or alto (or countertenor) solo and small
choir (SSTTB), poem by W. B. Yeats
First performed by the Deller Consort, Victoria & Albert Museum,
31 January 1960   6 mins

Schola Cantorum of Oxford, conducted by Nicholas Cleobury
(L'Oiseau Lyre DSLO 25)
Finzi Singers, conducted by Paul Spicer
(Chandos CHAN 9265)

1961   *Songs for Achilles*, for tenor and guitar, texts by the composer (the
first song appears in Act II of *King Priam*)   14 mins
First performed by Peter Pears and Julian Bream at Great Glenham
House, Aldeburgh Festival, 7 July 1961
Manuscripts: British Library (pencil), nos. 2 & 3;
private collection (ink), nos. 2 & 3

Philip Langridge/Timothy Walker
(L'Oiseau Lyre DSLO 14)
Martyn Hill/Craig Ogden
(Hyperion CDA 66749)

Magnificat and Nunc Dimittis, for chorus (SATB) and organ
                                                          7 mins
First performed by the Choir of St John's College, Cambridge,
conducted by George Guest, St John's College Chapel, Cambridge,
13 March 1962
Manuscript: St John's College, Cambridge

Schola Cantorum of Oxford, conducted by Nicholas Cleobury
(L'Oiseau Lyre DSLO 25)
Choir of St John's College, Cambridge, Alexander Martin (organ),
Director, George Guest
(Nimbus NI 7026)

Finzi Singers/Andrew Lumsden (organ), conducted by Paul Spicer
(Chandos CHAN 9265)
Rochester Cathedral Choir/William Whitehead (organ)
(Priory PRCD 529)

1962 **Sonata no. 2**, for piano   14 mins
First performed by Margaret Kitchin, Freemason's Hall, Edinburgh,
3 September 1962

John Ogdon
(latest reissue EMI CMS 7 63522 2)
Peter Cooper
(latest reissue PRT GSGC 2064)
Paul Crossley
(Philips 6580 093)
Thalia Myers
(Phoenix DGS 1013)
Paul Crossley (2nd recording)
(CRD CRD 3430/1)
Steven Neugarten
(Metier Sound & Vision MSV 92009)
Nicholas Unwin
(Chandos CHAN 9468)

Incidental Music for Shakespeare's *The Tempest* for flute/piccolo,
clarinet/bass clarinet, horn, trumpet, trombone, percussion, harp,
harpsichord, tenor and baritones.Written and first performed in a
production of the play at the Old Vic Theatre, London, 1964
Adapted for radio by Andrew Parrott and Ian Cotterell as *A Vision of
the Island*, for speakers, four men's voices and chamber ensemble,
and first performed on BBC Radio 3 by Robert Eddison, Stephen
Boxer, members of the Taverner Consort and Nash Ensemble,
conducted by Andrew Parrott
First published edition:
Suite: *The Tempest* (arranged by Meirion Bowen)   25 mins
includes additional movements, composed/arranged 1995 notably:
'Caliban's Song', for 2 flutes/piccolo, clarinet/bass-clarinet/claves,
horn, trumpet, trombone, percussion, piano/celesta/percussion, harp,
string quintet
First performed by Martyn Hill (tenor), Stephen Barrell (baritone),
Nash Ensemble, conducted by Andrew Parrott, Purcell Room,
London, 17 December 1995
'Songs for Ariel', for voice and harpsichord (excerpt from incidental
music for *The Tempest*; also arranged in 1964 with an instrumental

accompaniment of flute/piccolo, clarinet, horn, percussion ad lib (bells, bass drum) and piano/harpsichord   5 mins
First performed by Grayston Burgess (counter-tenor), Virginia Pleasants (harpsichord), Fenton House, Hampstead, London, 21 September 1963

Peter Pears/Benjamin Britten
(Argo ZK28/9)
Philip Langridge/John Constable
(L'Oiseau Lyre DSLO 140
Anthony Rolfe-Johnson/Graham Johnson
(Hyperion CDA 66480)
Martyn Hill/Andrew Ball
(Hyperion CDA 66749)

'Trumpet Tune & Boogie'; 'Caliban's Song'
(excerpts from *Suite*, *The Tempest*)
First performed by David Wilson-Johnson (baritone), Nash Ensemble, conducted by Andrew Davis, Westminster Abbey, London, 17 November 1995

Praeludium for brass, bells and percussion
First performed by the BBC Symphony Orchestra, conducted by Antal Dorati, Royal Festival Hall, London, 14 November 1962
                                                                                6 mins

English Northern Philharmonia, conducted by the composer
(Nimbus NI 5217)
London Brass
(Teldec 2292 46442 2)
Bournemouth Symphony Orchestra, conducted by Richard Hickox
(Chandos CHAN 9276)

1962/63   **Concerto for Orchestra**
First performed by the London Symphony Orchestra, conducted by Colin Davis, Usher Hall, Edinburgh, 28 August 1963   31 mins

London Symphony Orchestra, conducted by Colin Davis
(latest reissue: Philips 420 075 2)
Bournemouth Symphony Orchestra, conducted by Richard Hickox
(Chandos CHAN 9384)

1963/65   ***The Vision of St Augustine***, for baritone, chorus and orchestra
                                                                                35 mins
First performed by Dietrich Fischer-Dieskau/BBC Symphony Orchestra and Chorus, conducted by the composer, Royal Festival

Hall, London, 19 January 1966
John Shirley Quirk/London Symphony Chorus/London Symphony
Orchestra, conducted by the composer
(latest reissue: BMG BMG 75605 513042)

John Shirley-Quirk/London Sinfonietta Chorus and Orchestra,
conducted by David Atherton
(BBC Radio Classics 15656 91902)

1966/70   ***The Shires Suite,*** for chorus and orchestra
First (complete) performance by the Schola Cantorum of Oxford and
Leicestershire Schools Symphony Orchestra, conducted the
composer, Town Hall, Cheltenham, 8 July 1970   18 mins
Version using orchestral transcriptions of choral movements (arr.
Meirion Bowen)
First performed by the Northern Junior Philharmonic Orchestra,
conducted by Nicholas Cleobury, City Hall, Newcastle-upon-Tyne,
31 July 1995

1966   **Severn Bridge Variations: no. 6, 'Braint'** (part of a composite
work with Malcolm Arnold, Alun Hoddinott, Nicholas Maw, Daniel
Jones, Grace Williams and Tippett)   10 mins
Manuscript: BBC
First performed by the BBC Training Orchestra, conducted by
Adrian Boult, Brangwyn Hall, Swansea, 11 January 1967

1965/70   ***The Knot Garden***, opera in 3 acts with text by the composer

First performed by Royal Opera, Covent Garden, conducted by
Colin Davis, produced by Peter Hall, designed by Timothy O' Brien
and with costumes by Tazeena Firth, Royal Opera House, Covent
Garden, 2 December 1970   87 mins

Soloists, Orchestra of Royal Opera House, Covent Garden,
conducted by Colin Davis
(latest reissue Philips 446331-2)

1970   ***Songs for Dov***, for tenor and small orchestra, with text by the
composer (first song appears in Act II of *The Knot Garden*)
First performed by Gerald English, London Sinfonietta, conducted
by the composer, University College, Cardiff, 12 October 1970)
          26 mins

Robert Tear/London Sinfonietta, conducted by David Atherton
(Argo ZRG 703)
Nigel Robson/Scottish Chamber Orchestra, conducted by the
composer
(Virgin Ultra Violet CUV 5 61326 2)

1970/72 **Symphony No. 3**, for soprano and orchestra, with texts by the composer   55 mins
First performed by Heather Harper and the London Symphony Orchestra, conducted by Colin Davis, Royal Festival Hall, London, 22 June 1972)

Heather Harper/London Symphony Orchestra, conducted by Colin Davis
(latest reissue Decca 425 646 2)
Faye Robinson/Bournemouth Symphony Orchestra, conducted by Richard Hickox
(Chandos CHAN 9276)
Josephine Barstow/BBC Symphony Orchestra, conducted by Raymond Leppard
(BBC Radio Classics BBC RD 9140)

1971 ***In Memoriam Magistri***, for flute, clarinet and string quartet (written in memory of Stravinsky)   3 mins
First performed by the London Sinfonietta, conducted by Elgar Howarth, St John's, Smith Square, London, 17 June 1972
Manuscript: lost (published in *Tempo* no. 97, 1971, pp.24–5)

1972/73 **Sonata No. 3 for piano**   22 mins
First performed by Paul Crossley, Assembly Rooms, Bath, 26 May 1973

Paul Crossley
(Philips 6700 063)
Stephen Savage
(Queensland Conservatorium Muiscon TAM 0639)
Paul Crossley (2nd recording)
(CRD CRDC 4130/1)
Graham Caskie
(Metier Sound & Vision MSV CD 92004)
Nicholas Unwin
(Chandos CHAN 9468)

1975/76 ***The Ice Break***, opera in 3 acts with text by the composer
First performed by Royal Opera, Covent Garden, conducted by Colin Davis, produced by Sam Wanamaker, scenery and costumes by Ralph Koltai, Royal Opera House, Covent Garden, 7 July 1977
                                                                     75 mins

Soloists, London Sinfonietta Chorus, London Sinfonietta, conducted by David Atherton
(latest reissue Virgin 0777 7590 482 6)

1976/77 **Symphony No. 4**
First performed by the Chicago Symphony Orchestra, conducted by
Georg Solti, Orchestra Hall, Chicago, 6 October 1977

32 mins

Chicago Symphony Orchestra, conducted by Georg Solti
(latest reissue Decca 433 668 2)
Bournemouth Symphony Orchestra, conducted by Richard Hickox
(Chandos CHAN 9233)
BBC Symphony Orchestra, conducted by the composer
(BBC *Music Magazine* vol. III, no. 6)

1977/78 **String Quartet No. 4**
First performed by the Lindsay Quartet at the Assembly Rooms,
Bath, 20 May 1979   23 mins

Lindsay Quartet
(latest reissue ASV CDDCS 2331)
Britten Quartet
(latest reissue Collins Classics 70222)
Kreutzer Quartet
(Chandos CHAN 9560)

Water out of Sunlight (string orchestra version of String Quartet No.
4 by Meirion Bowen)
First performed by the Academy of St Martin-in-the-Fields,
conducted by Neville Marriner, Royal Festival Hall, London, 15
June 1988

1978/79 **Triple Concerto**, for violin, viola, cello and orchestra
First performed by Gyorgy Pauk, Nobuko Imai and Ralph
Kirshbaum, with the London Symphony Orchestra, conducted by
Colin Davis, Royal Albert Hall (Proms concert), 22 August 1980

31 mins

Gyorgy Pauk/Nobuko Imai/Ralph Kirshbaum/London Symphony
Orchestra, conducted by Colin Davis
(latest reissue Philips 420 075 2)
Ernst Kovacic/Gerard Caussé/Alexander Baillie/BBC Philharmonic
Orchestra, conducted by the composer
(Nimbus NI 5301)
Levon Chiligirian/Simon Rowland-Jones/Philip de Groote/
Bournemouth Symphony Orchestra, conducted by Richard Hickox
(Chandos CHAN 9384)
Ernst Kovacic/Rivka Golani/Karine Georgian/London Sinfonietta,
conducted by David Atherton

(BBC Radio Classics 15656 91902)

1980 **Fanfare No. 4:** (The Wolftrap Fanfare)   2 mins
First performed by Washington National Symphony Orchestra, conducted by Hugh Wolff, Wolftrap Farm for the Performing Arts, Vienna, Virginia, 29 June 1980

1980/82 *The Mask of Time*, for voices and instruments (soprano, mezzo-soprano, tenor, bass, chorus and orchestra), text written and compiled by the composer   95 mins
First performed by Faye Robinson, Yvonne Minton, Robert Tear, John Cheek, Tanglewood Festival Chorus, Boston Symphony Orchestra, conducted by Colin Davis, Symphony Hall, Boston, 5 April 1984

Faye Robinson/Sarah Walker/Robert Tear/John Cheek/
BBC Singers/BBC Symphony Chorus/BBC Symphony
Orchestra, conducted by Andrew Davis
(EMI CMS 7 647112)

Fanfare No. 5, for brass (1986), arranged by Meirion Bowen from the seventh movement of *The Mask of Time*   2 mins
First performed by the Philip Jones Brass Ensemble, Queen Elizabeth Hall, London, 8 June 1986

'**Triumph**': A paraphrase on music from *The Mask of Time*, for symphonic wind band (1992)   15 mins
First performed by Ohio State Band & University of Michigan State Band, 24 February 1993 at the College Band Directors National Association Conference, Ohio State University

1982/83 *The Blue Guitar*: sonata for solo guitar   15 mins
First performed by Julian Bream, Ambassador Auditorium, Pasadena, California, 9 November 1983

Eleftheria Kotzias
(Pearl SHE CD 9609)
Norbert Kraft
(Chandos CHAN 8784)
David Tannenbaum
(New Albion Records NA 032 CD)
Craig Ogden
(Nimbus NI 5390)

1983 *Festal Brass with Blues* for brass band
First performed by Fairey Engineering Works Band, conducted by

Howard Williams, Hong Kong Arts Festival, 6 February 1984

11 mins

London Collegiate Brass, conducted by James Stobart
(CRD CRDC 4144)
The Wallace Collection
(Collins Classics 12292)

1983/4   **Sonata No. 4**, for piano   40 mins
First performed by Paul Crossley, Japan America Theatre, Los
Angeles, 14 January 1985

Paul Crossley
(CRD CRD1130/1)
Nicholas Unwin
(Metier Sound & Vision MSV CD92009)

1985/88   *New Year*, opera in 3 acts, text by the composer   102 mins
First performed by Houston Grand Opera, October 1989, conducted
by John De Main, directed by Peter Hall, with choreography by Bill
T. Jones, designs and costumes by Alison Chitty

1988/90   *Byzantium,* for soprano and orchestra   25 mins
poem by W. B. Yeats
First performed by Faye Robinson and the Chicago Symphony
Orchestra, conducted by Georg Solti, Orchestra Hall, Chicago,
March 1991

Faye Robinson/Chicago Symphony Orchestra, conducted by Georg
Solti
(Decca 453 668 2)

1990/91   **String Quartet No. 5**   25 mins
First performed by the Lindsay Quartet at the Crucible Theatre,
Sheffield, 9 May 1992

Lindsay Quartet
(latest reissue ASV CDDCS 231)
Kreutzer Quartet
(Chandos CHAN 9512)

1991/93   *The Rose Lake*: A Song without Words for orchestra   25 mins
First performed by the London Symphony Orchestra, conducted by
Colin Davis, Barbican Arts Centre, London, 17 February 1995

London Symphony Orchestra, conducted by Colin Davis
(BMG 75605 513042)

Index of Works by Tippett mentioned in the text

General Index